TEIGNMOUTH PIER

A PICTORIAL HISTORY

Viv Wilson

Written and Published by Viv Wilson

First published November 2003

Email : viv_wilson@lineone.net

Designed and Printed by Exeprint, Exeter
Email : sales@exeprint.co.uk

Initial Reader : Jim Stowers
Final Proof Reader : Dick Petherick

Acknowledgments

I am grateful to Anthony Brenner for suggesting the compilation and for funding the printing of this book. Particular thanks are due to everyone for contributing information and memories. It was pleasing to be able to include Iris Volkner, daughter of long-term Pier Manager Joe Angliss. Teignmouth & Shaldon Museum's growing archives were trawled in the search for interesting material. Ted Collins loaned several photographs. A pictorial history owes everything to the photographers who recorded the pier down through the decades. George Denney, Fred Groves, J.J. Payne and Herbert J. Wilson captured images during the pier's first 80 years. Post-war photographers include those who had a promenade pitch at the pier entrance and also Ivy Hindley, Elizabeth and Reginald Lewis, B.J. Wareham and Gordon Walker. Photographs from 1970 to the present day are credited to Anthony Brenner, John Burgess, Eileen Gray, Fred Rees, John Silverman, Fred Walters and Viv Wilson.

Author's Prelude

Sometime in 1998, Anthony Brenner casually mentioned he would like me to compile a book about Teignmouth Pier at some point. The Millennium would have been an obvious date to aim for but I was side-tracked into writing Teignmouth at War Books 1 and 2. It was not until Christmas morning 2002 that I began researching for this volume. A number of responses were received after appeals for information and photos were put out in the local Press. Input from locals is valuable and allows the human element to shine. If only each week brought twice as many working hours, I could do what I love most and talk to just about every local person who can remember Teignmouth before the war. I sincerely hope this volume will bring back happy memories for everyone who loves Teignmouth Pier and generate interest for pier enthusiasts across the country.

DEDICATION

To my friend Pauline Rossi for her unfailing support and encouragement through all the trials involved in giving birth to a book.

Foreword

I look back now at my 50 years in Teignmouth and consider myself lucky to have lived in such a beautiful and interesting place. I was born in Torquay and in 1954, at the age of 13, moved to Teignmouth with my family and attended Teignmouth Grammar School. In the summer holidays, I helped my father George, who was already established on Teignmouth Pier with a few amusement machines of his own manufacture. He gradually took over other concessions, then built and operated the Midnight Chimes, an exciting race game for twelve players. I joined the family business just before my 16th birthday. After becoming Pier Manager, my father eventually bought it in 1961.

The Pier has been my whole working life, in fact, Elizabeth whom I married in 1966, considers it to be my real wife as I spend far more time with it than with her. She has been an immense support to me, bringing up our three children virtually single-handed for six months every year while I worked a 96 hour week each season. I could not have survived without her. Things are a bit easier now that two of our children, Lucie and Nik, have joined the firm and made themselves totally indispensable and a great pleasure to work with.

I am very lucky to have had such loyal and hard working staff through the years who have contributed in no small way to the longevity of both the company and the structure. I pay tribute to them all.

The Pier has featured somewhere in the lives of so many people, both visitors and locals. From those dancing days and promenading, to childish fun or working on it, and I thought that it should all be recorded in a book. Dear Viv agreed, having been one of those children with fond memories of her own of the Pier. I could not have been happier when she agreed to accept the task.

I hope you enjoy reading this book and that it brings back some happy memories. I have enjoyed being the Pier's most recent custodian and hope that I have contributed in some small way in maintaining a piece of our seaside heritage.

By the way - I haven't finished yet!

Anthony R. Brenner

The Advent of Seaside Piers

Early in the 1800s, the popularity of inland spas was eclipsed by a rising interest in seaside watering places. When Queen Victoria ascended her throne in 1837, disease was still an ugly, fearful shadow across England. Only the wealthy had the ability to try to escape from rampant cholera by resorting to the coast where they had to overcome their distaste of rubbing shoulders with the ill-bred seafaring communities. Seawater and ozone were perceived as health-giving and it was not long before coastal resorts came into their own. Taking the air in their finery along the promenade and mingling with others of their ilk was an essential component of the lifestyle. It was not easy to reach the coast in the early days when travel was limited to stagecoach or sailing boats, both slow and uncomfortable. The advent of fast and reliable steamboats around 1815 dramatically changed the picture. However, the question of getting passengers on and off these large vessels had to be addressed. It was tricky in many places and Ryde had more than its share of problems. It is hardly surprising to learn that in 1813, the first pier in Britain was constructed at Ryde, Isle of Wight. Stretching 1250 feet out into the water, it was an instant success story. Brighton followed suit and before long our coastline was spiked with piers of varying length and design. The most practical means of handling large numbers of people on and off vessels had arrived. A total of 84 piers were constructed during the next 143 years. Teignmouth was 13th in line and the only post-war pier was built at Deal in 1957.

Commercial strength broadened during the latter half of the 19th century and holidays became reality for untold thousands. For the first time in history, working class people had chance to indulge in a little leisure time and the advent of the railway network served to speed travellers to their destinations. Entrepreneurs bought a stake in amusement machines and other attractions, creating a new leisure industry. As the 19th century hurtled towards its turn, the working classes came in far greater numbers than the wealthy. Their quest was for fun rather than bodily restoration and piers, with an array of entertainment, drew the masses like a magnet.

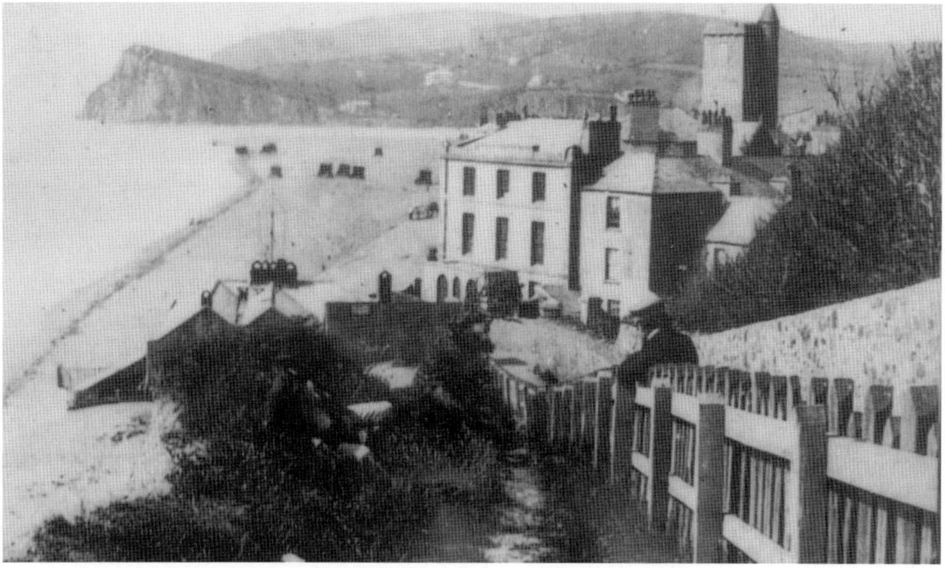

Teignmouth before the building of its pier. This rare, early photograph records the rooftops of the Public Baths at the foot of Eastcliff. A sea wall has yet to be built and beach features are nil except for bathing machines

Joseph William Wilson

Engineer of Teignmouth Pier

Joseph William Wilson's early training was as a cleric but his ambition was to be an engineer. His father was persuaded to allow him to take an apprenticeship with Fox & Henderson, an engineering company where his cousins were able to tutor him. By the time the company was contracted to build the Crystal Palace for the Great Exhibition of 1851, Joseph had risen to the position of Assistant Manager. His innovative skills were applied to improvement of the machinery used during construction of the palace. In later years, he was to become President of the Crystal Palace School of Practical Engineering. Joseph set up Oldbury Engineering Works in partnership with his brother-in-law but ill health forced him to change course and become a Consultant Engineer in Banbury. His first pier design was for Bognor Regis in 1864 and shortly afterwards, his services and those of his son were engaged for the construction of Teignmouth Pier. He was also responsible for Hunstanton Pier of 1870-1, an overlap of work with his ill-fated Westward Ho! Pier. The latter took three years to build, yet was demolished two years after completion. Joseph William Wilson died in 1898.

Chapter 1

Earliest Days - 1865 to the Great War

Recorded Owners during this period
Samuel Kerkawich Esq 1869
Teignmouth Pier Company 1871
A.H. Dendy & I. Woodridge Esqs 1887
W.C. Jones Esq 1891 : Devon Steamship Company 1898

The Earl of Devon drove in the first of a series of piles for Teignmouth Pier in 1865. Two years passed and £8000 spent before completion of J.W. Wilson's design. The wood and iron structure marched 600 feet out into the sea supported by cast iron piles. Simplistically, screw blades were fitted to the piles, iron castings allowing them to be twisted down through the sand to clay level. Earth pressure on both top and bottom surfaces of the pile blades and frictionally through the pile-body created a rigid foundation. The Chairman of the Local Board performed the official opening in 1867 and the pier commenced its life as a landing stage for summer steamboat passengers voyaging between the coastal resorts of Lyme Regis, Sidmouth, Exmouth, Teignmouth, Torquay and Dartmouth. Few features lined the deck apart from seats running the whole of its length and the eventual enhancement of gas-lit globes mounted on elegantly curved iron arches. Four pagodas with a turnstile tollhouse stood sentry at the entrance. Victorians who loved the idea of being at sea without the discomfort of a sea voyage, paid one penny to promenade the deck and drink in the ozone and panorama. Commercial possibilities did not pass unnoticed and profits through the provision of entertainment and refreshment soon became a reality. The first machines offering a peep of "What the Butler saw" were installed on the deck. Teignmouth Pier became the UK's second oldest amusement machine park after following the lead of Blackgang Chine, Isle of Wight in 1842. At the end of its first decade, the pier failed to impress a contributor to the Teignmouth Journal of 1875:

"We Teignmothians are naturally proud of our scenery, beach, river, bridge, and - I had almost written the pier, but no, the least said of that the better. In its present state there is little to be proud of."

Commercially, however, it must have been doing extremely well and a 250-foot pavilion was added at the shore end towards the end of the 1880s. The extended new entrance was shrouded with advertisements for local businesses. Mr Dendy purchased the pier in 1887 with the idea of removing it lock, stock and pile to Paignton but discovered it would be too costly. A tent was erected at the seaward end for the 1888 season where a concert by the band of the 1st

Rifle Volunteers was followed by dancing to the strains of a string band. Clearly, the tent was to test the market and two years later, the 300-seat pavilion was constructed. The pier was stretched further out into the sea by the 35 foot long footbridge built to connect to the new 60 x 40 feet landing stage. Magic lantern shows were staged in an inner space in the new pavilion. Technology progressed through a family named Mack who introduced cinematic moving images, usually of cowboys and Indians. The original oval-shaped dance floor was of sprung maple and claimed to be one of the finest in the area. An orchestra played popular melodies twice daily in the early 1900s when attractions included tea dances, dance competitions, charity balls and gala dinners. On Boxing Day, the tradition was for locals to roller-skate in the ballroom. Teign Corinthian Yacht Club established a clubhouse on the deck before the turn of the century.

The new pier was subjected to the sea's relentless attempts to triumph over man-made structures and through the years, it suffered many severe assaults. It held strong through a notable storm in 1894 but succumbed in January 1908 when heavy waves breached the sea wall. The entrance pavilion folded and collapsed on the beach leading to costly repairs. There was a silver lining - the redesigned hall included the addition of a tea verandah at first-floor level but the toll doubled to two pence. During the Daily Mail Air Race in 1912, a 70hp Farman water plane landed on east beach and the deck rail was crowded with excited onlookers. Teignmouth Swimming and Lifesaving Society used a wooden building on the deck beyond the entrance pavilion as their headquarters. Burly swimmers made spectacular entrances on to the beach via a trap door in the pier deck. The swimmers staged water polo matches drawing enormous crowds to the deck whilst others viewed from pleasure boats. Ordinary mortals were allowed to bathe from the end of the pier at all tides and use the changing cabins and companionway in exchange for a 6d ticket. The pier rapidly became a focal point for visitors, artists and photographers and featured in numerous postcards.

Four pagodas mark the entrance of the new 600 foot-long structure of wood and iron

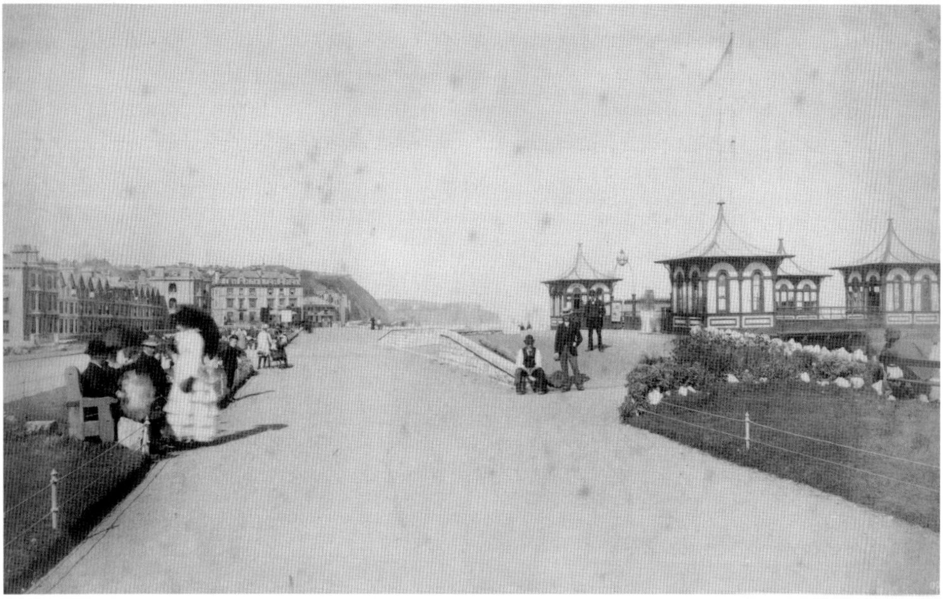

The low wall on the right marks out the boundary of the pier forecourt, punctuated by the upright feature

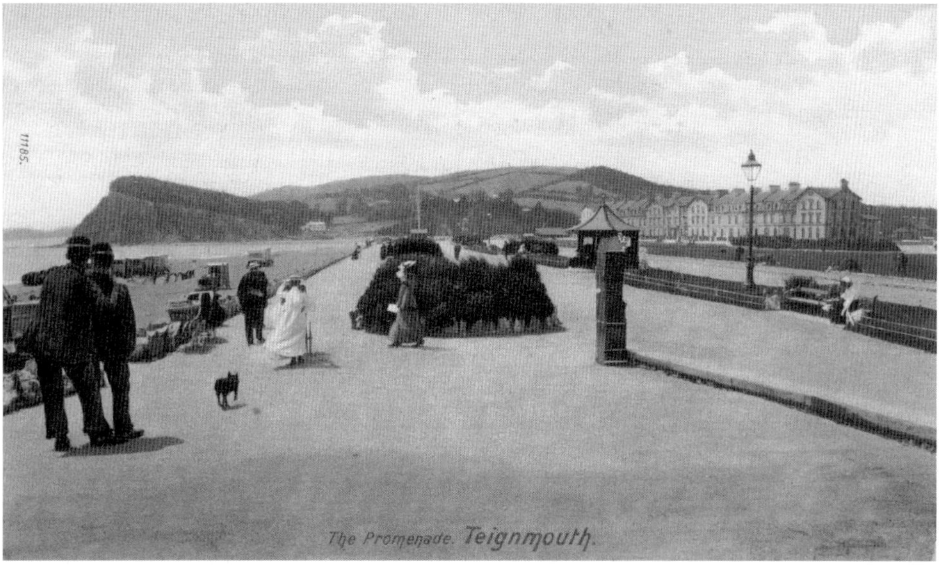

A narrow first section led down to a double width deck

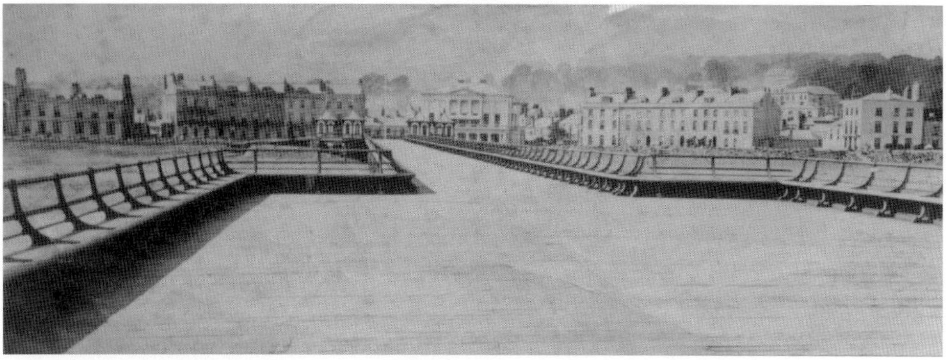

Seats ran the length of the deck and gas globe lamps added later

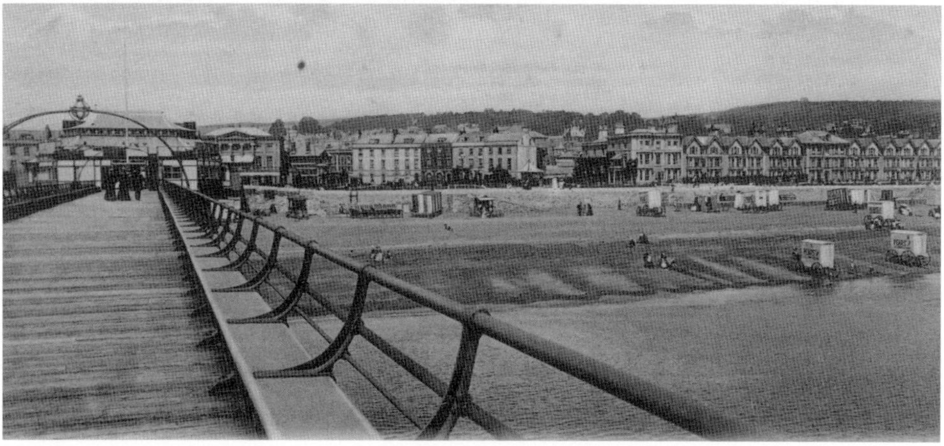

Elegant arches led to the ballroom and landing stage added in the final decade of the 19th century

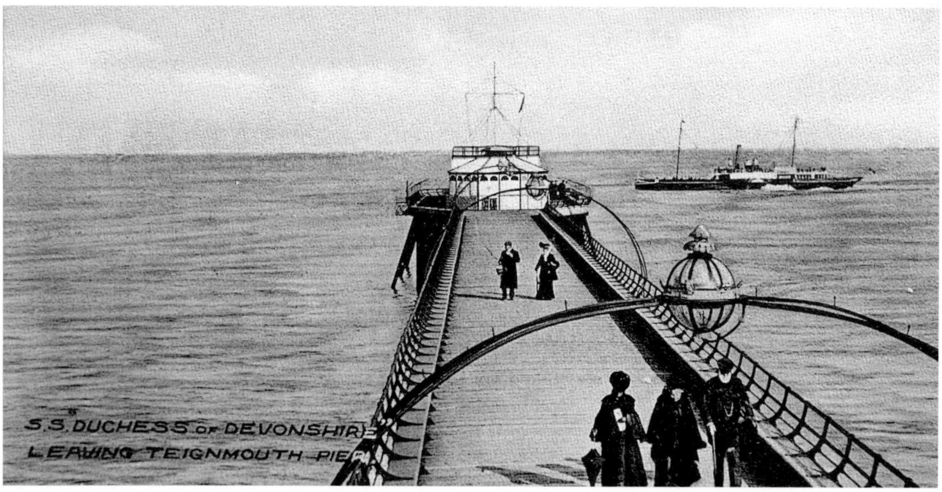

Turn of the century overview

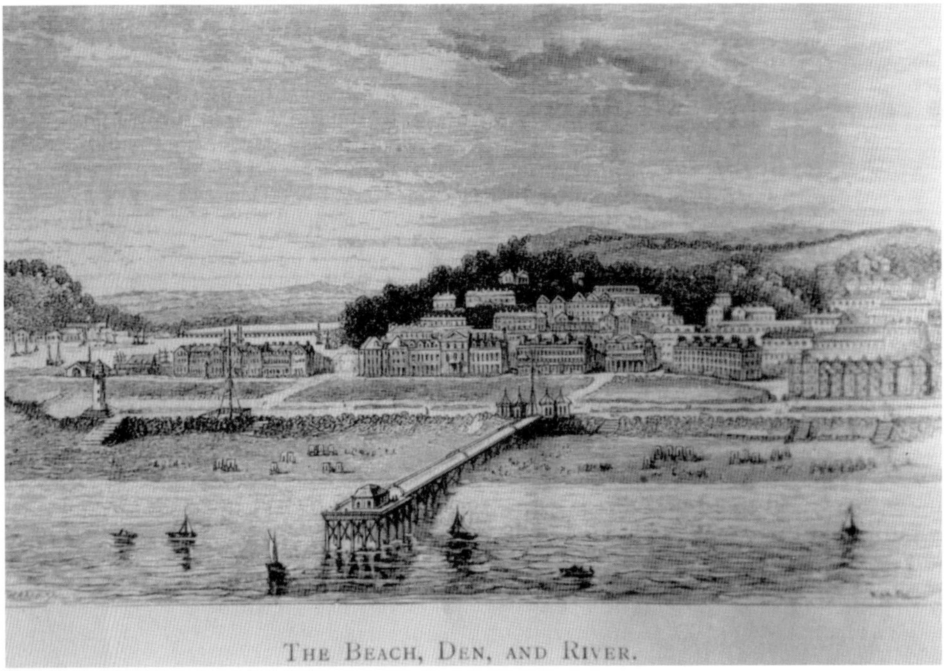

Rides with pony, donkey and goat cart were available on the Prom beside the pier

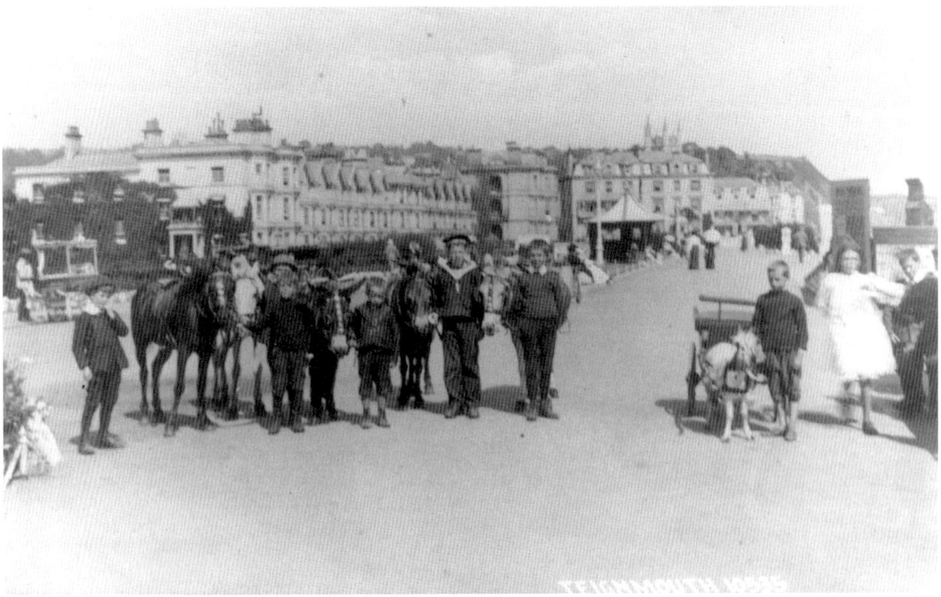

Donkey carts and invalid carriages await the arrival of boat passengers who were conveyed to their lodgings or off on jaunts

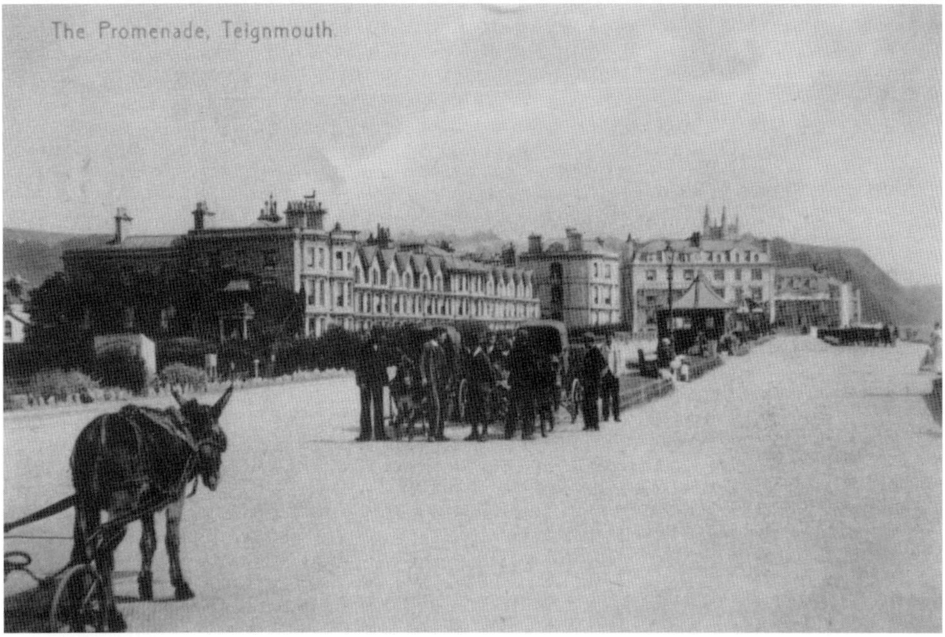

Paddle-steamer Duchess of Devonshire disgorging passengers beside the new pavilion at the pier head

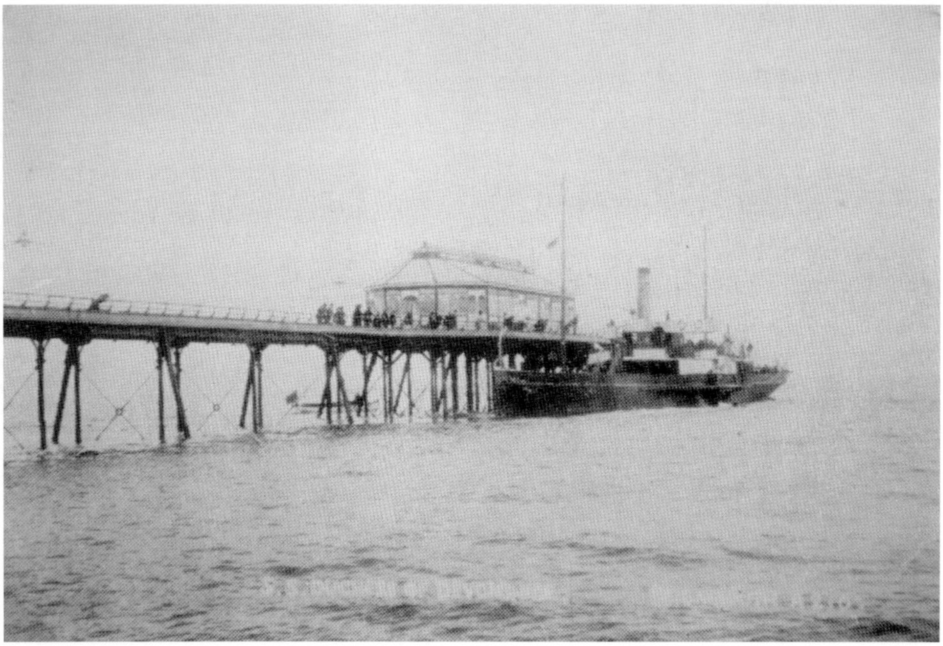

Both paddle-steamers Duke and Duchess of Devonshire conveyed day trippers between Weymouth, Exmouth, Torbay and Plymouth

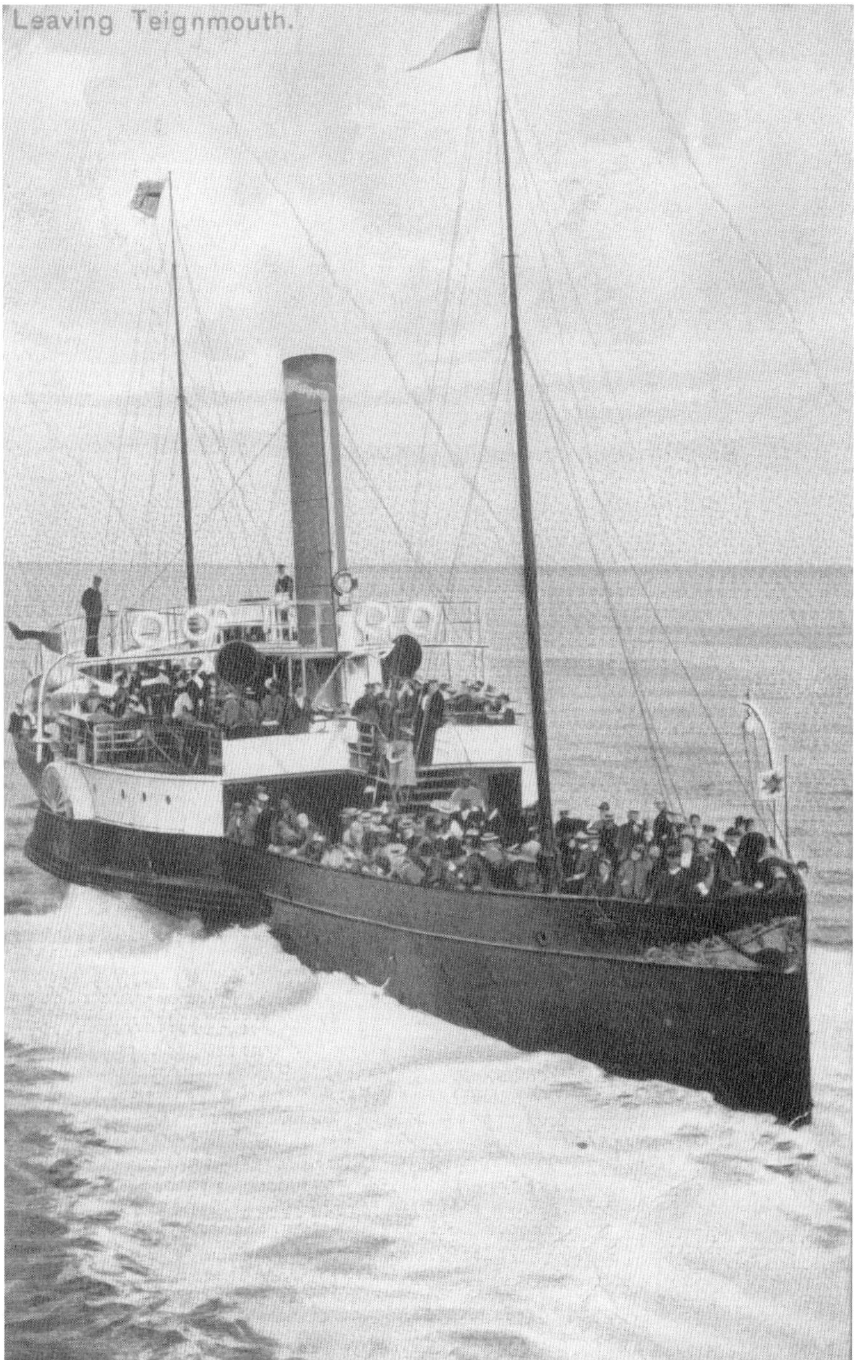

Every opportunity for advertising was taken at the pier entrance around 1900

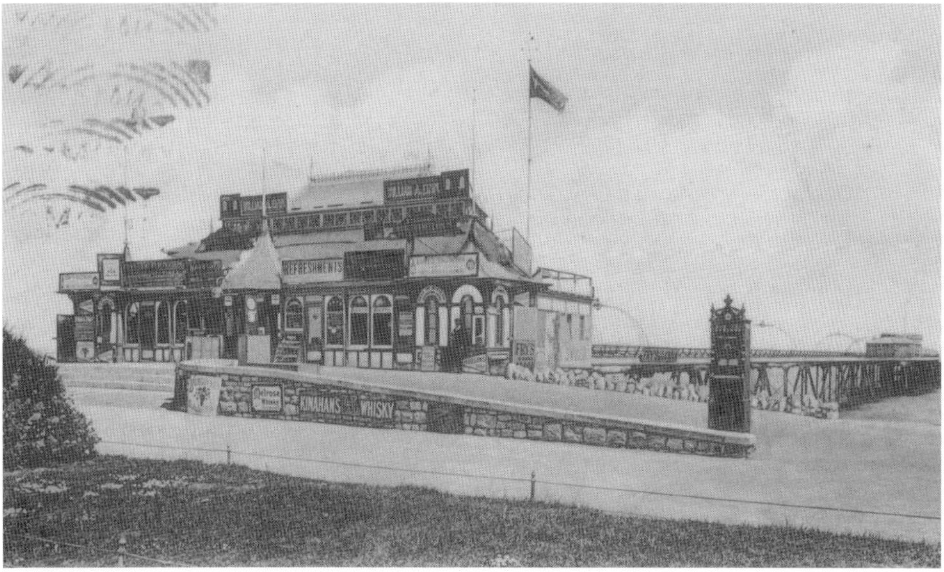

Baby's first time in a saddle beside the bathing machines on east beach reserved for ladies' bathing in the late 1800s

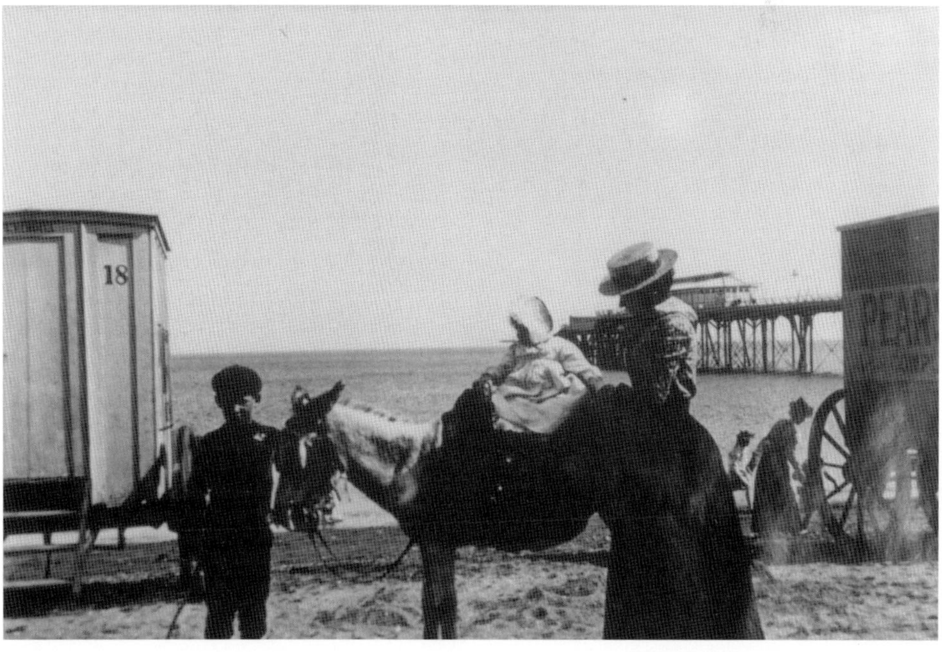

Seafront shelters mirror the pagoda style of the original pier entrance, swallowed up into the new larger structure

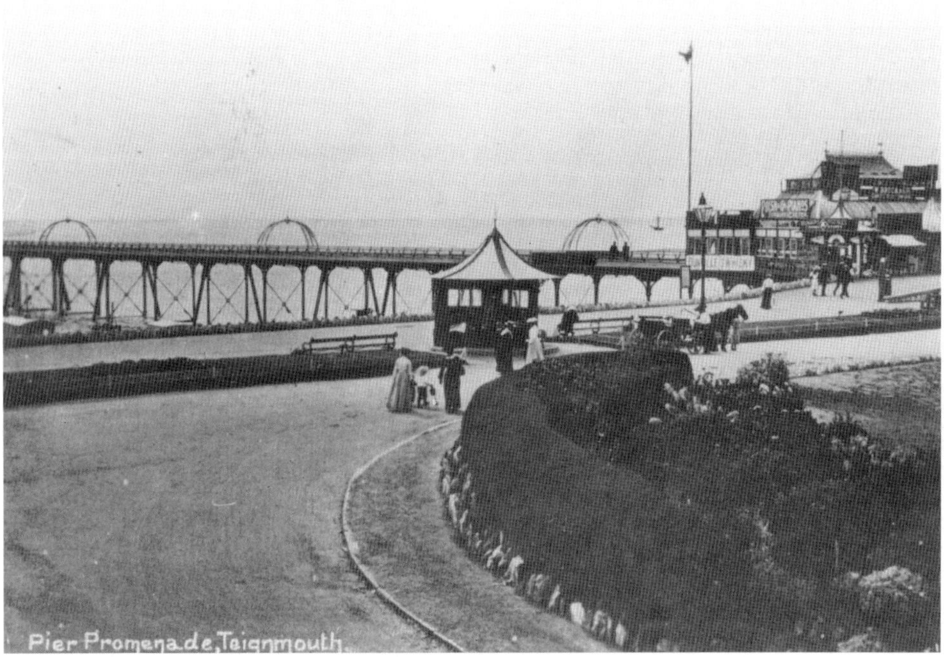

Bath chairs and invalid carriages on standby outside the entrance

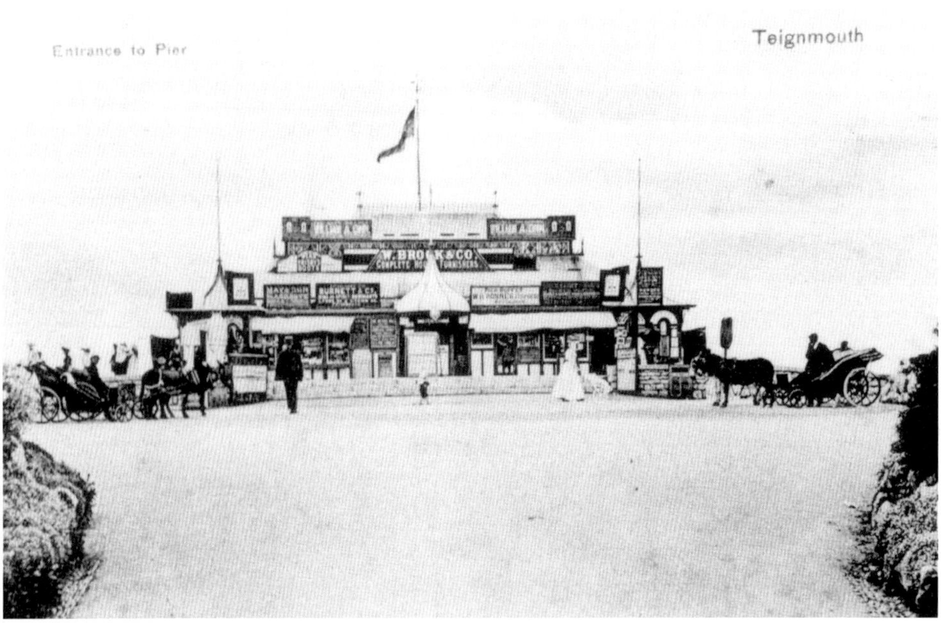

Hordes of onlookers push against the fence surrounding the Den to watch a spectacle

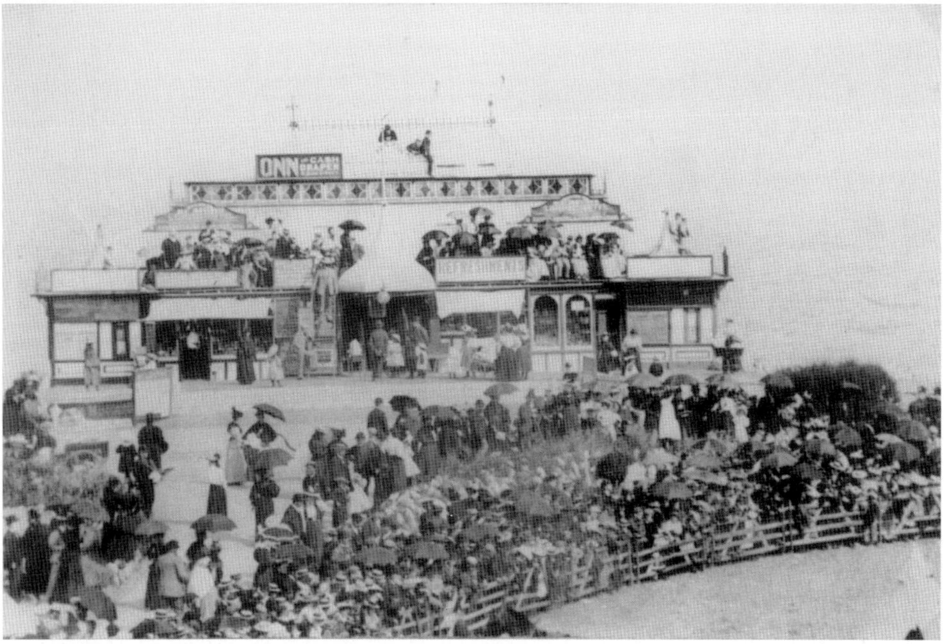

Disaster on January 3rd and 4th 1908. A devastating storm and heavy seas breached the protective wall built only a decade earlier. The raised concrete plinth and other sections further along the sea wall collapsed. Note the Swimming & Lifesaving Society HQ along the deck marked by the town's coat of arms

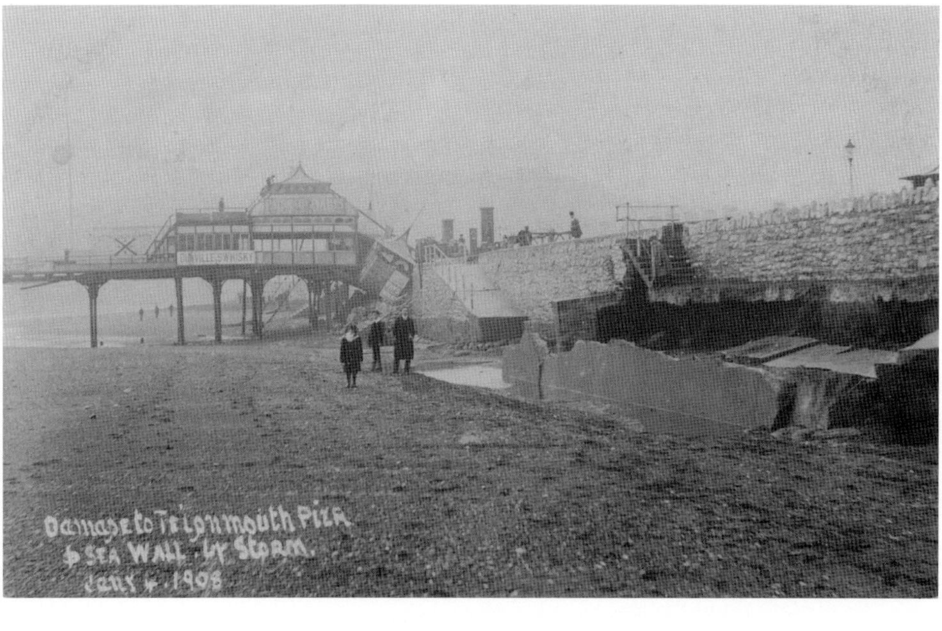

The wall crumpled beneath the entrance. A workman is at the top of the ladder and a delivery boy with his huge basket takes time off to watch proceedings

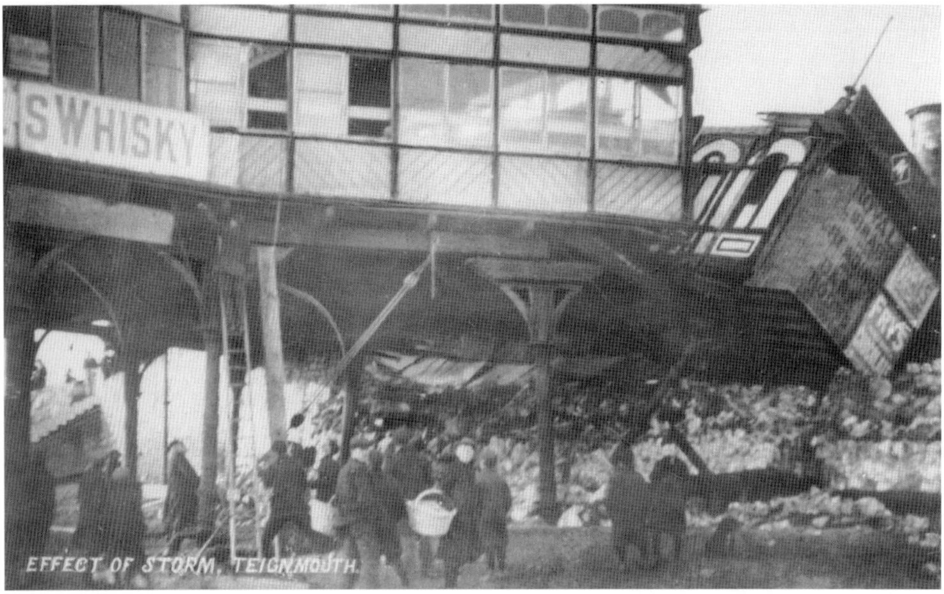

The end of the pagodas covered in advertisements for the reading rooms and dark room at the Royal Library and Poole's pianos

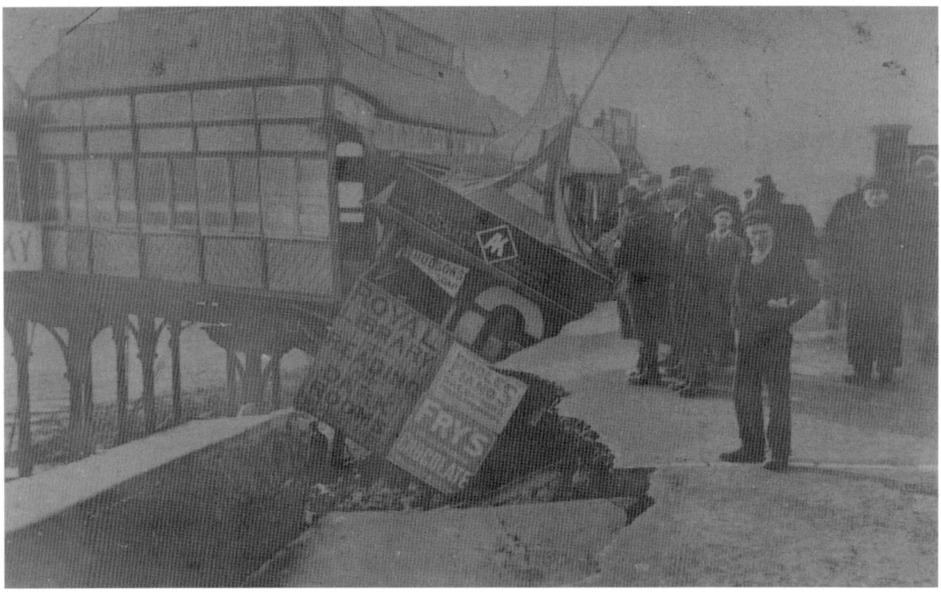

The eastern-style pagodas were swept away after this disaster

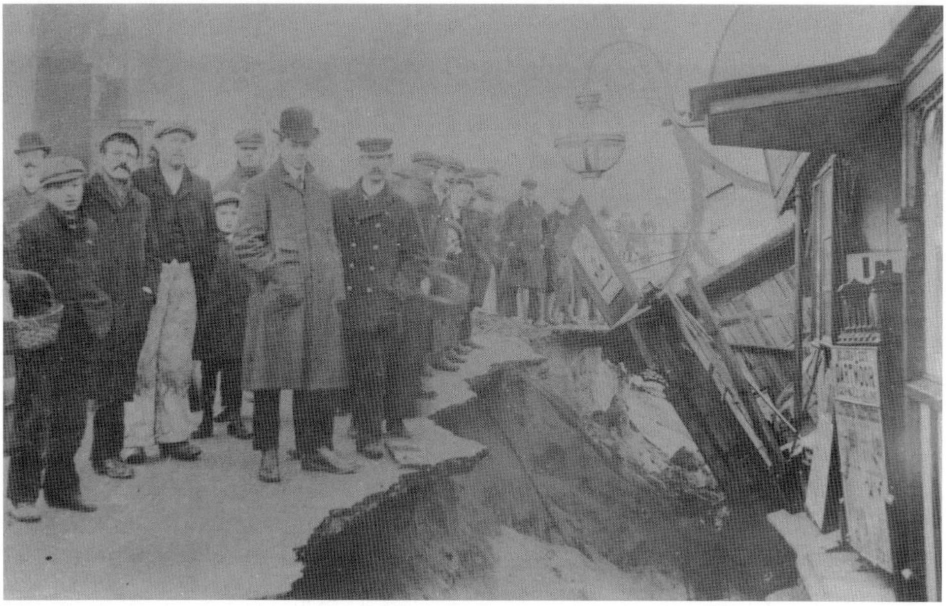

Removal of the roof panels. A poster offers brine baths and roller skating rink, almost certainly at the Winter Gardens, Carlton Place

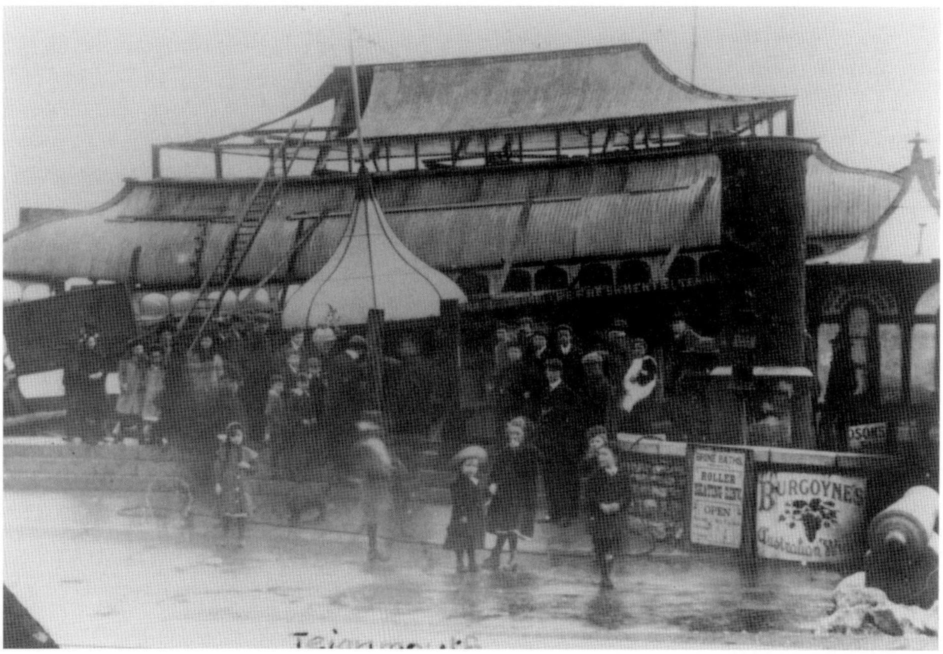

Building of the New Parade 1909

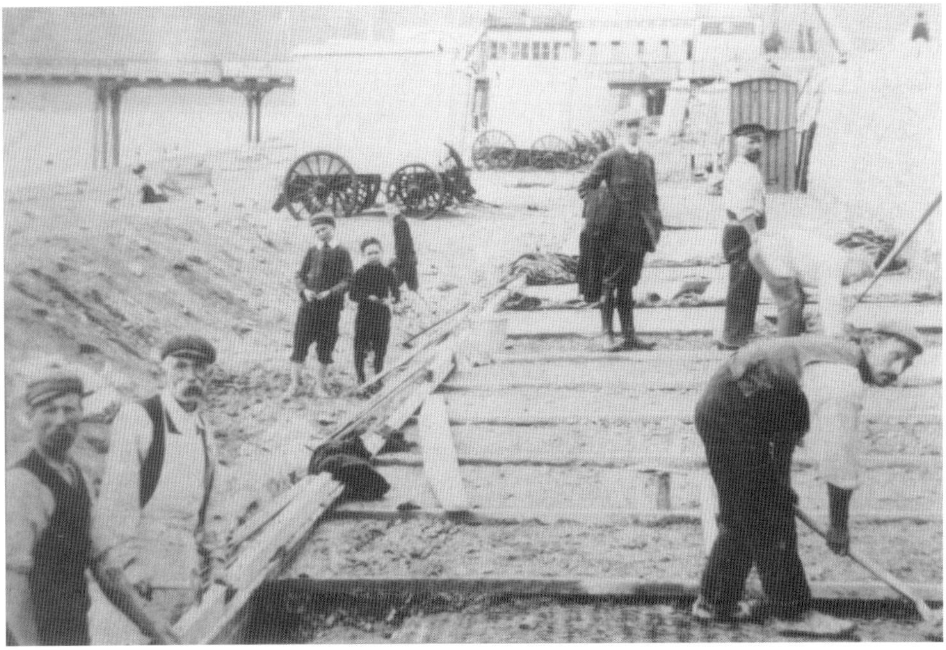

George Denney recorded this construction site in 1909. Contractor was W.E. Blake of Plymouth with local stonemason, J.J. Hayman as Clerk of Works

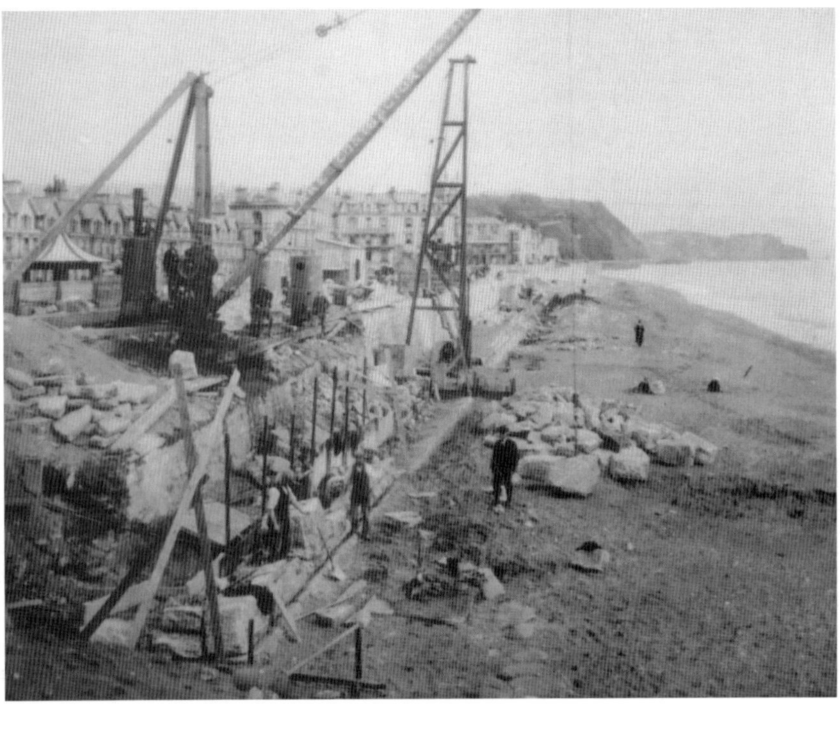

Henry Farman 70hp water plane in the 1912 Daily Mail Air Race. Huge crowds occupy boats, beach and pier for their first view of a flying machine

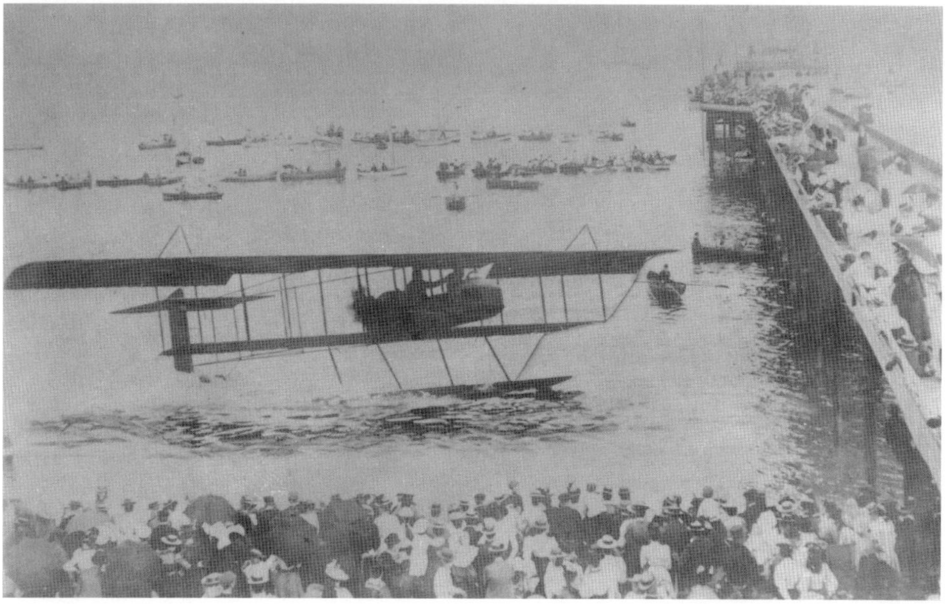

Enlarged and more elaborate, the new pier's entrance has become the most imposing feature on the seafront

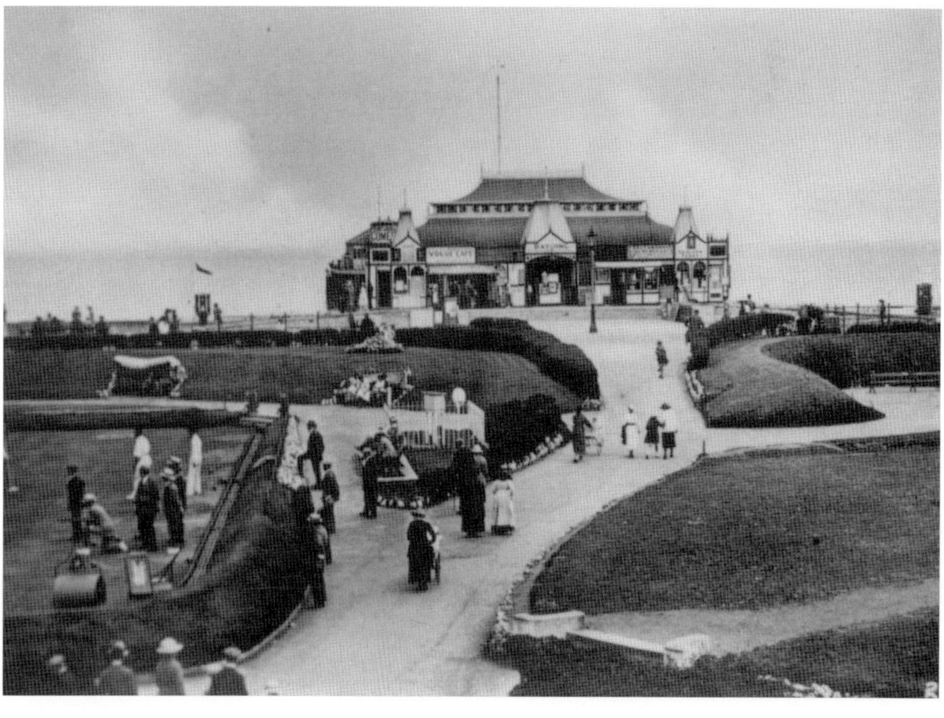

Members of Teignmouth Swimming & Lifesaving Society about 1930. Their member's card allowed them to avoid paying a 2d toll. A trap door in the deck had a ladder attached allowing swimmers easy access to the beach below

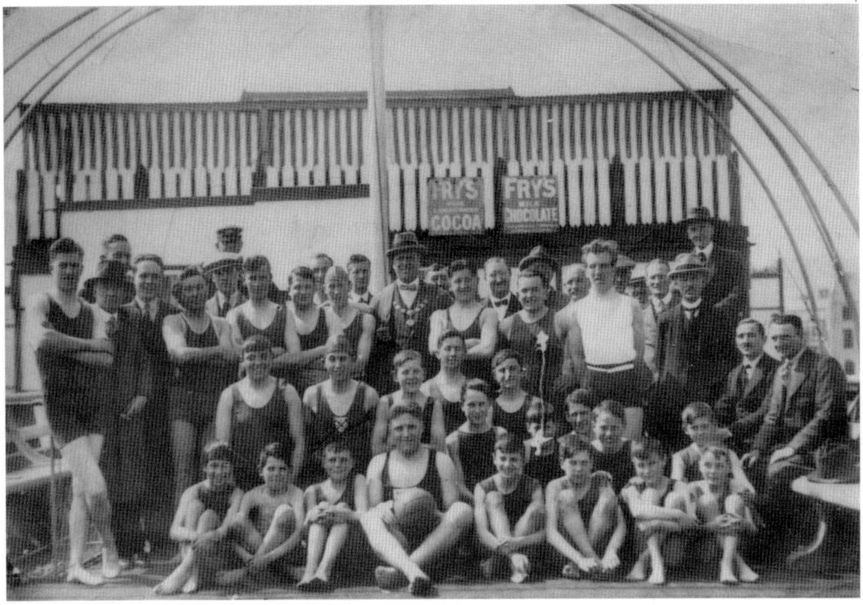

Huge crowds supported the water polo matches played during the summer months on Saturday afternoons and some evenings when acetylene flares, used to illuminate the scene, added to the excitement

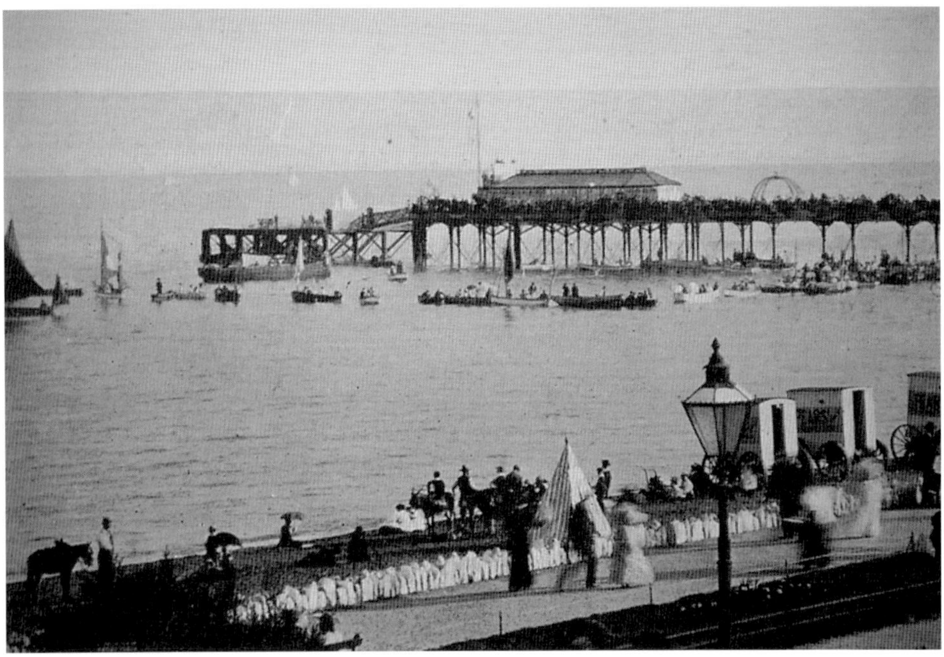

Water polo matches attracted a multitude of local boats filled to the gunwhales with spectators and crowds on the beach and the pier

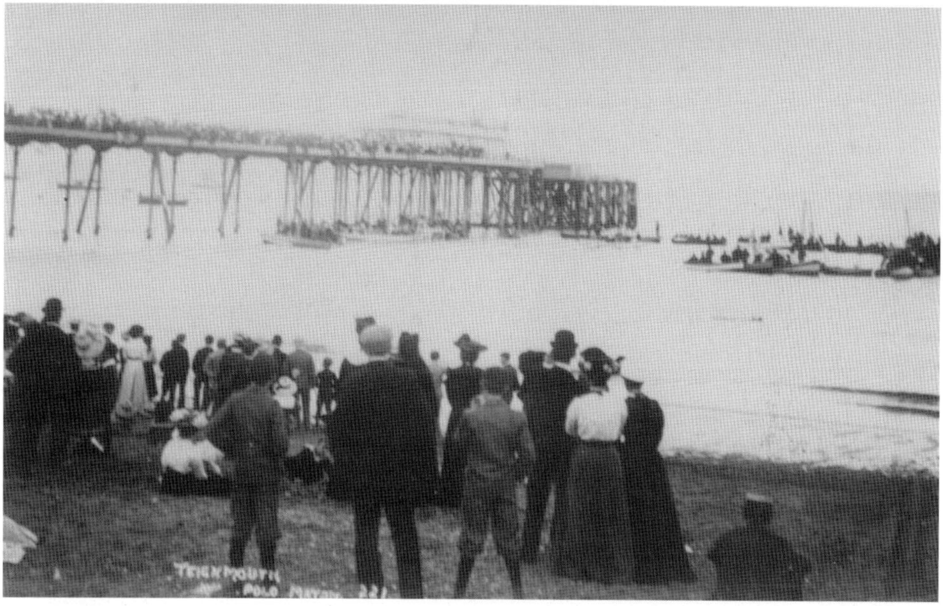

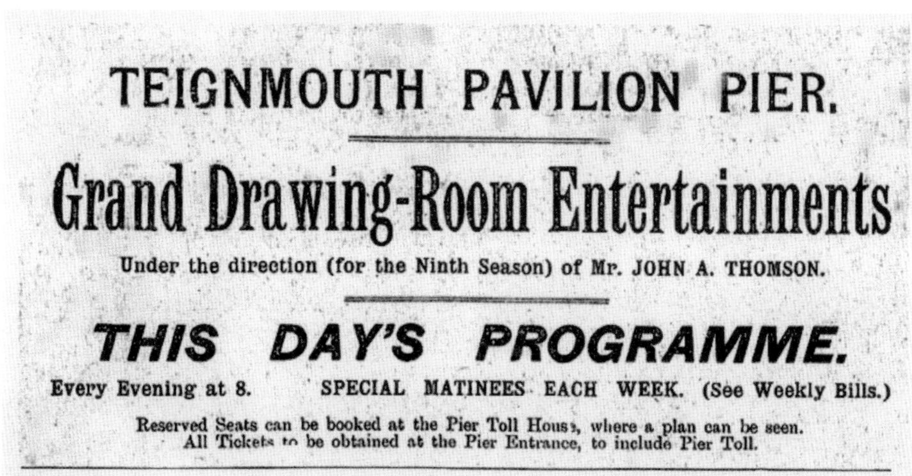

TEIGNMOUTH PAVILION PIER.

Grand Drawing-Room Entertainments

Under the direction (for the Ninth Season) of Mr. JOHN A. THOMSON.

THIS DAY'S PROGRAMME.

Every Evening at 8. SPECIAL MATINEES EACH WEEK. (See Weekly Bills.)

Reserved Seats can be booked at the Pier Toll House, where a plan can be seen.
All Tickets to be obtained at the Pier Entrance, to include Pier Toll.

CHAPTER 2

The 1920s and on into World War Two

Recorded Owners during this period
Devon Dock & Steamship Company 1898 -1930
Auto Rides Ltd 1931
General Amusements Corporation Ltd 1932
Mr Albert Snape, Mr Bramwell Collinge & J.A. Matthew 1935 -1961

The two decades of the '20s and '30s marked a period of intense development. The next group of images is testimony to additional attractions and improvements of those years between the wars. Additions included glass panel windbreaks down the centre of the deck and extra kiosks became shops for gifts and toys as well as photography. Another was occupied by Captain Victor Mayne, masquerading as a teller of fortunes, Mr E. Palmist. Paddle-steamer trips continued to be enormously popular and both the Duke and the Duchess of Devonshire, with their red ensigns, continued to call daily up until 1934. The Duke ran onto eastern beach in 1930 and had to be floated off at high tide. Both steamers ended their days at Exmouth after one of them went aground. Transport options were expanding and the resort could now be reached by rail, motorcar, omnibus or charabanc and even through the aerodrome at Haldon in the late '20s and early '30s.

In 1935, J. Arthur Rank Company used the pier as inspiration for the film about a company of actors involved in an end-of-the-pier show. Rushes from "Return to Yesterday" were viewed in the newly updated Riviera Cinema. The film reflected an era of "frightfully English" accents and chaste good sports playing the game of life with long-forgotten decency and good manners.

Locals have vivid recollections of spectacular feats performed by stuntmen such as one-legged, high-diving Peg Leg Pete, who climbed a ladder and set himself alight before diving into the sea. Dreadnought Stanley and Dare Devil Curly carried out similar stunts using a motorcycle. Scores achieved on the pinball games in the entrance's Amusement Grotto were kept and end-of-season prizes awarded. In 1933 the Chairman of the Council presented the highest male and female scorers with a bicycle each and runners-up received consolation prizes of fruit bowls, biscuit barrels and cigarettes. The success of this period allowed for investment in innovative amusement machines of the type being played in Blackpool and Coney Island.

Cultural Sunday night concerts often featured local vocalists such as Miss Lorna Smallcombe "whose reputation in south Devon is sufficient to ensure a good audience" and Gertrude Bennett, alias Trudie Iveson, with her "pleasing stage manner". Dancing was at its most popular during the 1930s, when the National Society of Amateur Dancers staged many events. Jack Mercer's Band from the north brought up-to-date ideas in the latest styles to the "Hall over the Sea". Local clubs arranged their own themed dances and people dressed appropriately. Informal Flannel and Holiday Dances had just as strict a dress code as the so-called Old-fashioned Dance and the more formal Grand Dance. Tea Dances were also enjoyed along with End-of-the-Pier variety shows and concert parties included The Scamps. A gipsy violinist who played on the pier was often heard practising on Haldon moor where the family home consisted of a tent and a London taxi.

The Teignmouth Post newspaper carried editorial about the pier every week through the season. It was invariably full of praise for the manager, Joe Angliss, who worked diligently in his post from 1931 to 1955. Problems were inevitable at times. At the Carnival Dance in 1936, a drunken fisherman tried to get into the ballroom without a ticket. After being ordered off, he attacked Joe, who fell and injured his eye. It ended in 14 days hard labour in prison for the fisherman, a sharp reminder of how anti-social behaviour was once dealt with.

Fear of invasion by the enemy reached its highest during the summer of 1940. A 60-foot wide breach was made between the middle pavilion and the ballroom and the bridge between the ballroom and landing stage was removed. It is said to have taken place the day before Teignmouth's first air raid on Sunday 7th July, when two bombs fell in the sea close to the pier at 18.55pm. There was one death and injuries to twelve people. The following day, five more bombs were dropped in the sea nearby at 14.19 hours but no damage was done. The pier entrance shop remained open for trade although the remainder of the pier was closed until the advent of the American servicemen in 1943. One Seabee of the 82nd battalion recalls that his unit straddled the gap and put on a dance in the ballroom. During the war years Joe Angliss acted as MC at a Home Guard social and dance in the Assembly Room in the London Hotel and helped recreate the appearance of the Pier Pavilion in its glory days. The Press reported the ambience was reminiscent of soirees of half a century earlier run by the now defunct 1st Rifle Volunteers.

The pier archive contains sheaves of letters of gratitude to Joe from TUDC, Royal Navy, King George's Fund for Sailors, RN Air Station at Haldon, National Savings Wings for Victory Week, Bishopsteignton British Legion, Carnival Committee, Rugby Club and Teignmouth Hospital for lending automatic machines for fetes at Eastcliff. With the wisdom of hindsight, it is clear that those years between the wars were favoured with the sweet smell of success and were truly the halcyon days.

BANK NIGHT

ARRIVES AT THE

PIER, TEIGNMOUTH

When the Pier opens at Whitsuntide, anybody over sixteen years of age, can go to the **PIER TOLLS OFFICE,** and register as a Bank Night Member, when he will be allotted **a NUMBER,** for which he will not pay anything. On the following Thursday during the Dance Interval at 9.30 p.m. a Numbered Ticket will be taken from a drum on the Ballroom Stage. This Number will be announced by Loud-Speakers in the Ballroom, and also in all Pavilions on the Pier.

The Bank Night Member holding the Number must make the claim within **THREE MINUTES** of the Announcement, when the Member will be presented with £1. Should the prize not be claimed, as stated above, it will be carried over and added to the next week's Draw.

NO MEMBER OF THE PIER STAFF
WILL BE ALLOWED TO ENTER

CORNISH-HOBART, TEIGNMOUTH

Overview 1920s

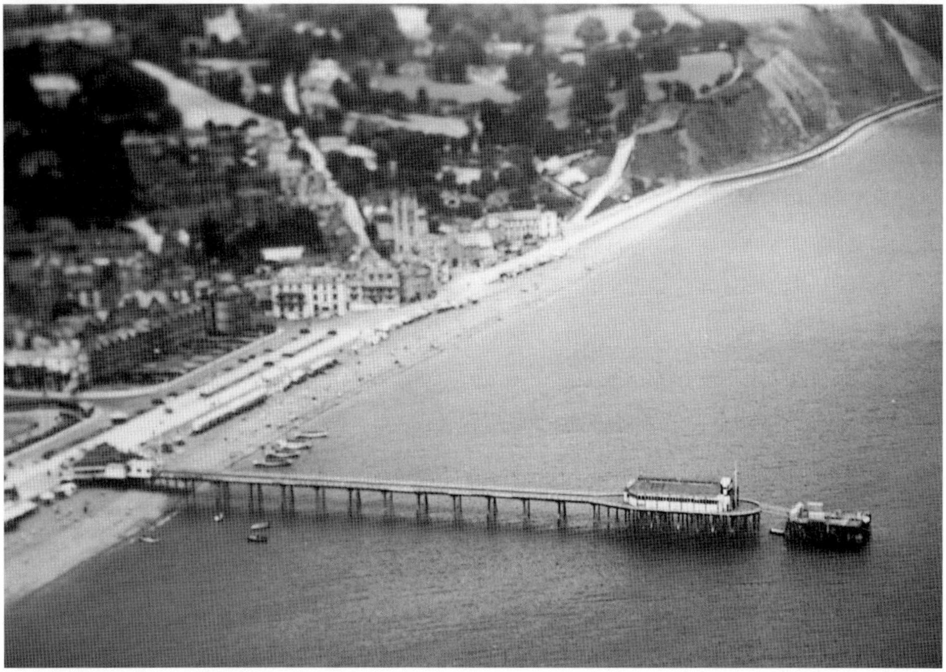

Black Prince pleasure boat approaches

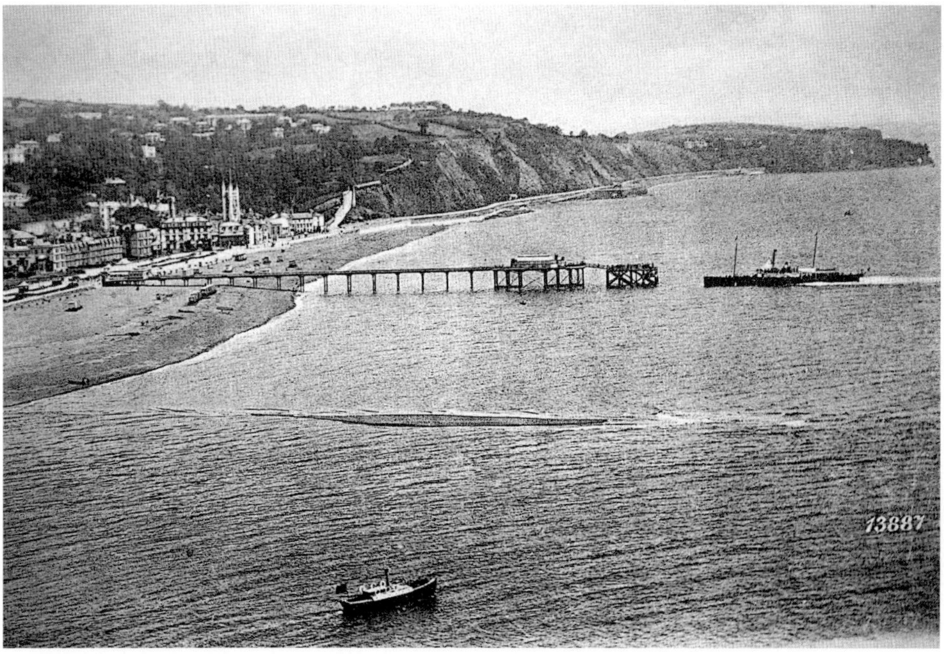

Bustling day of high summer in the '20s when there was bathing from facilities on the jetty and concert parties in the pier pavilion with The Aristocrats

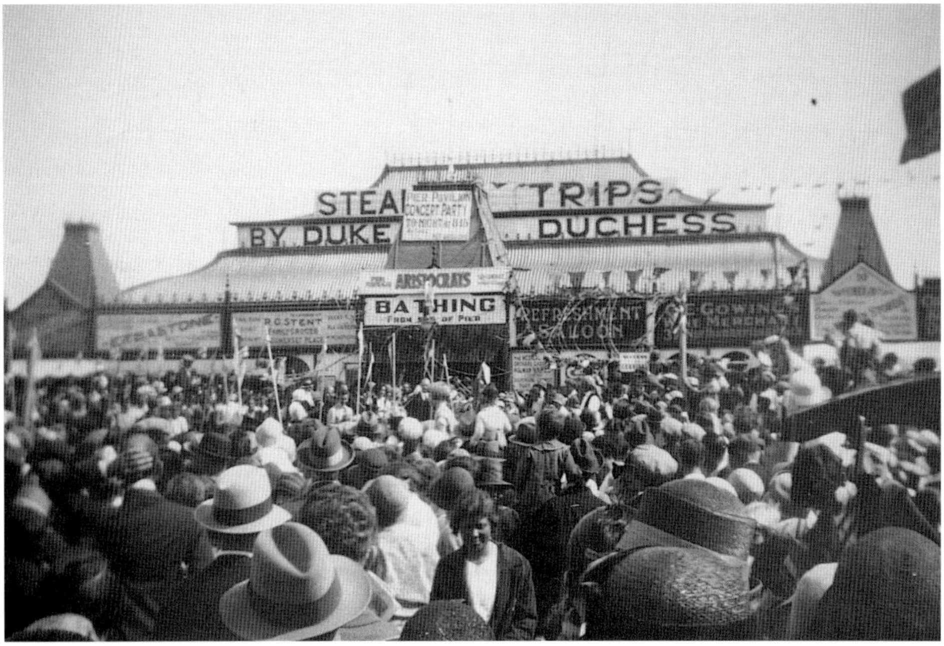

A stroll along the prom was just as popular as it had been during the last half of the previous century

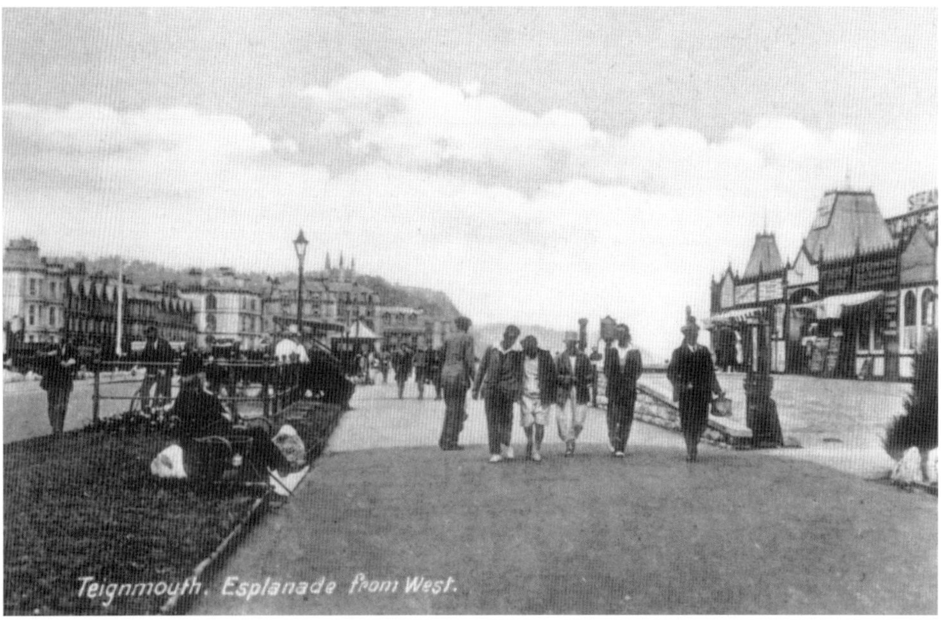

TEIGNMOUTH CARNIVAL, 1936.

The Carnival Committee desires to express to you its sincere thanks for your help in connection with the Carnival on August 20th.

Your valuable assistance was much appreciated and we are indeed grateful to you for your services, which contributed in no small measure to the success of the effort.

Thank you very much.

A Meeting will be held at the Old Council Chamber, Town Hall, on Tuesday next September 29th, at 8 p.m., when your presence will be esteemed. Please come.

T. H. Aggett.

Hon. Secretary.

Caxton House,
Teignmouth.

Beach tents mark a changing trend away from George English's orange and blue bathing machines dating from the days of segregated bathing

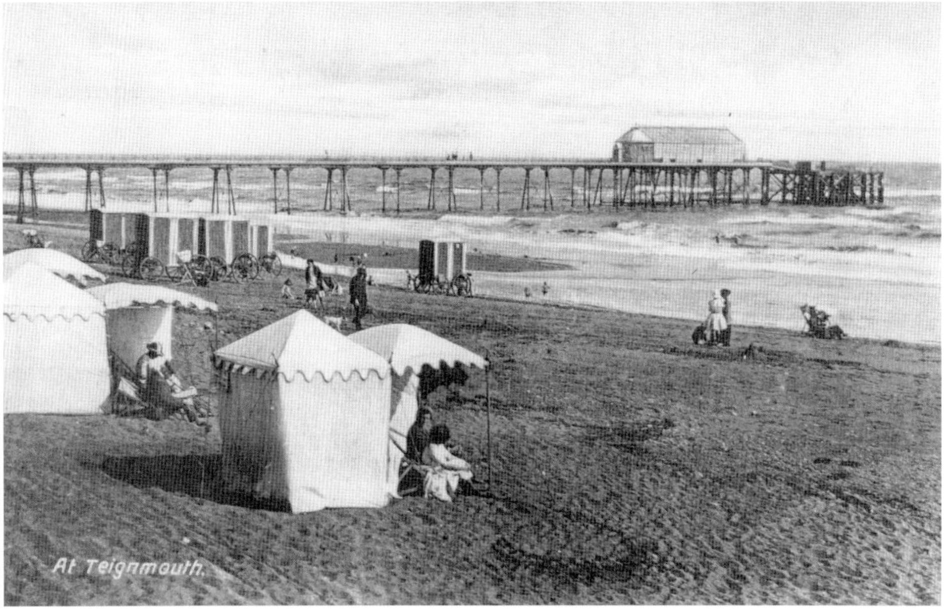

New kiosks with a country cottage look were erected between the entrance and middle pavilion. Decking in pre-war days was laid across the width

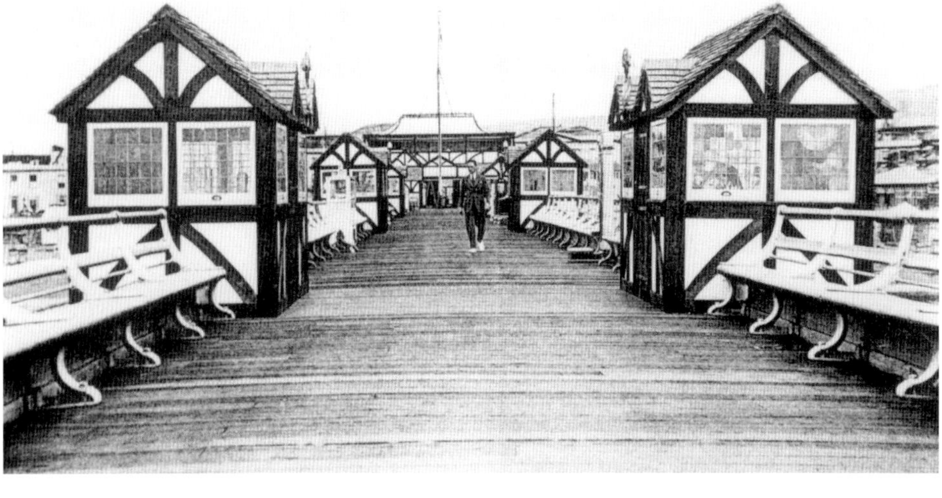

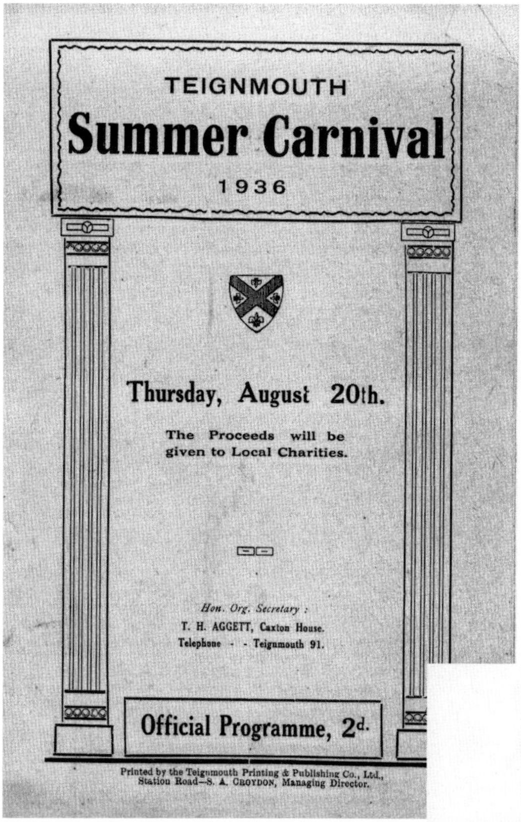

TEIGNMOUTH

Summer Carnival

1936

Thursday, August 20th.

The Proceeds will be given to Local Charities.

Hon. Org. Secretary :
T. H. AGGETT, Caxton House.
Telephone - - Teignmouth 91.

Official Programme, 2d.

Printed by the Teignmouth Printing & Publishing Co., Ltd., Station Road—S. A. CROYDON, Managing Director.

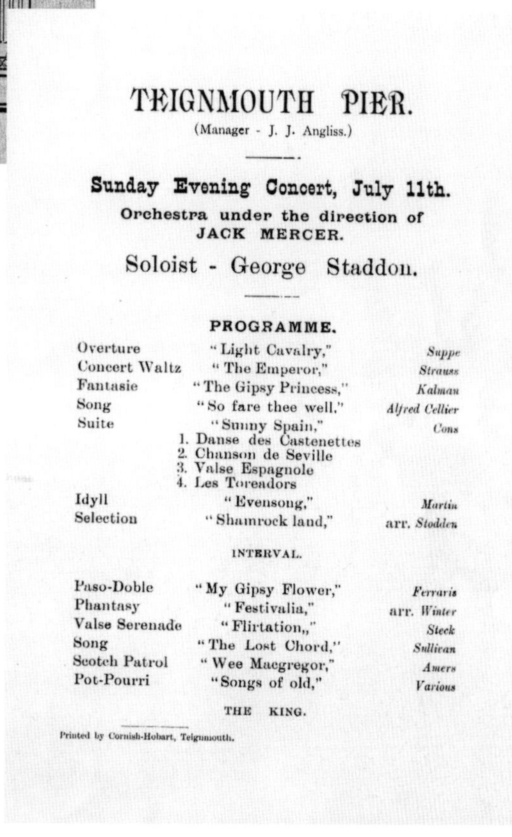

TEIGNMOUTH PIER.

(Manager - J. J. Angliss.)

Sunday Evening Concert, July 11th.

Orchestra under the direction of JACK MERCER.

Soloist - George Staddon.

PROGRAMME.

Overture	"Light Cavalry,"	*Suppe*
Concert Waltz	"The Emperor,"	*Strauss*
Fantasie	"The Gipsy Princess,"	*Kalman*
Song	"So fare thee well,"	*Alfred Cellier*
Suite	"Sunny Spain," 1. Danse des Castenettes 2. Chanson de Seville 3. Valse Espagnole 4. Les Toreadors	*Cons*
Idyll	"Evensong,"	*Martin*
Selection	"Shamrock land,"	arr. *Stodden*

INTERVAL.

Paso-Doble	"My Gipsy Flower,"	*Ferraris*
Phantasy	"Festivalia,"	arr. *Winter*
Valse Serenade	"Flirtation,,"	*Steck*
Song	"The Lost Chord,"	*Sullivan*
Scotch Patrol	"Wee Macgregor,"	*Amers*
Pot-Pourri	"Songs of old,"	*Various*

THE KING.

Printed by Cornish-Hobart, Teignmouth.

Stuntman Peg Leg Pete is remembered for his daring feats from the pier

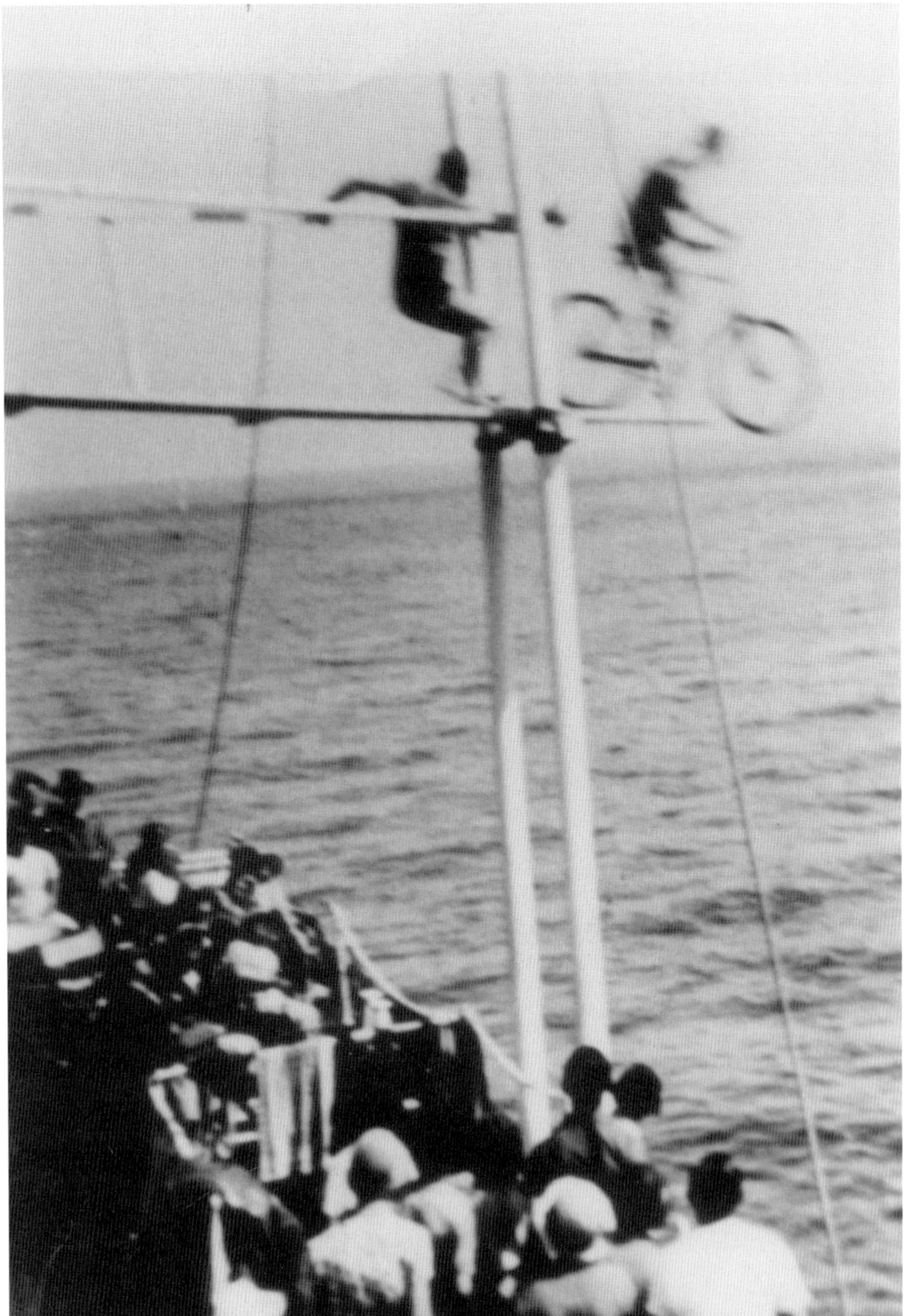

The Piermaster and others working with boats at the jetty wore a white peaked cap

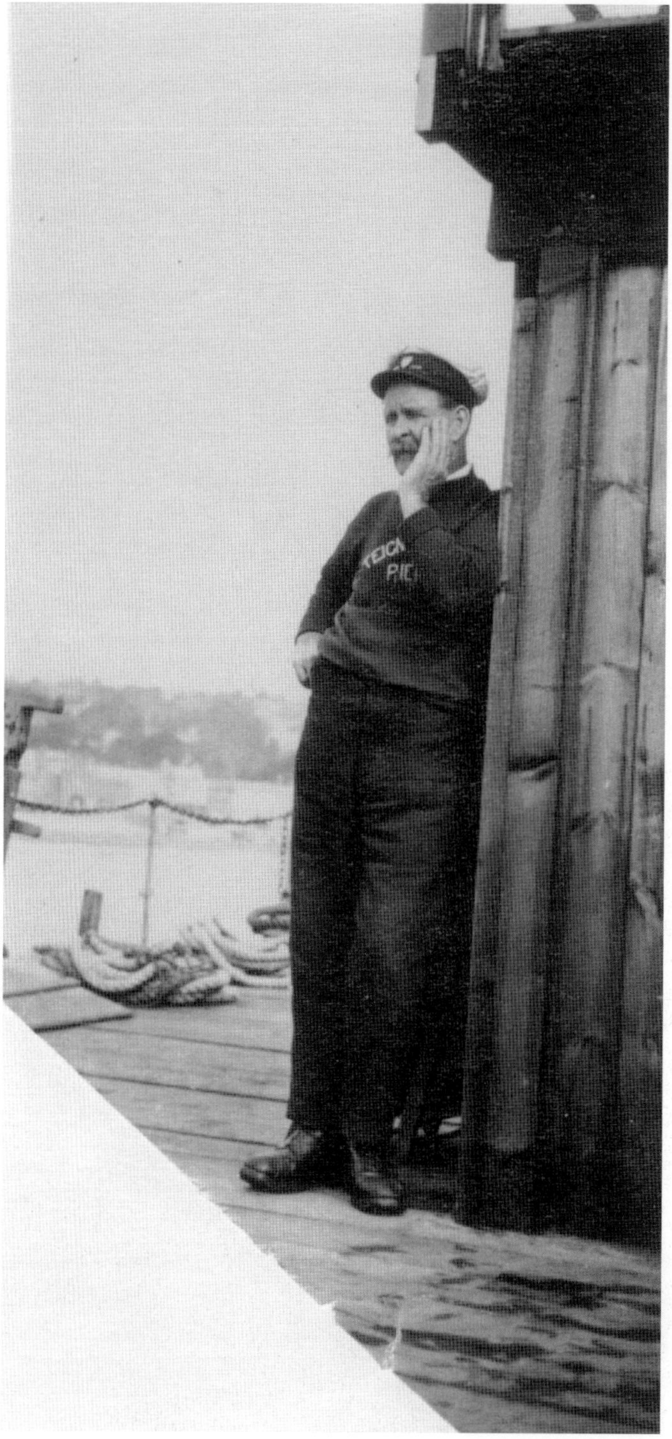

A banner blazes out the title 'Merrie England' above the entrance amusement grotto and tents line the beach

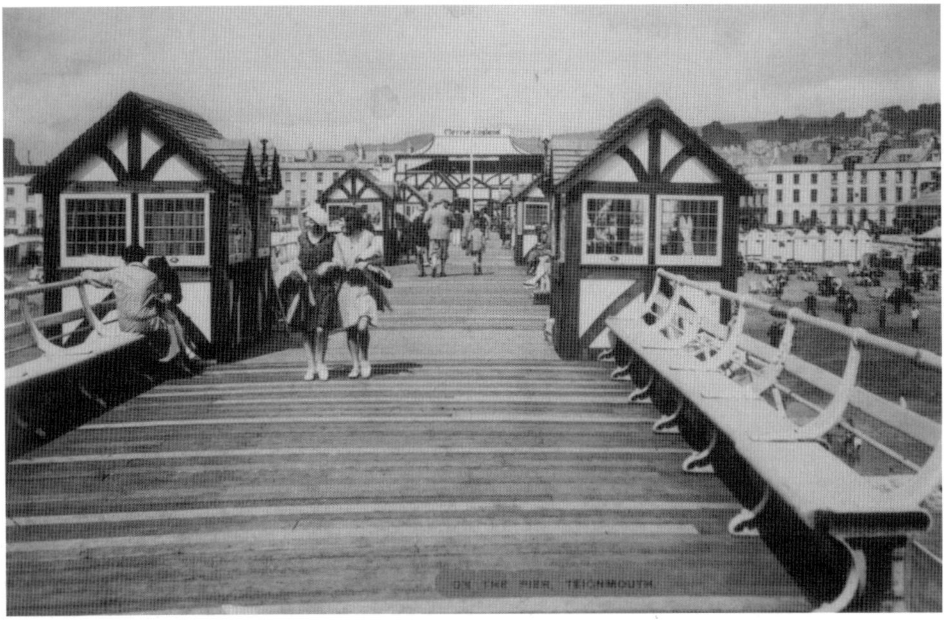

Looking towards the pavilion at the pier head. Amusements include the round machines giving visitors chance to see what the butler saw! The palmist machine on the left remains in use to the present day

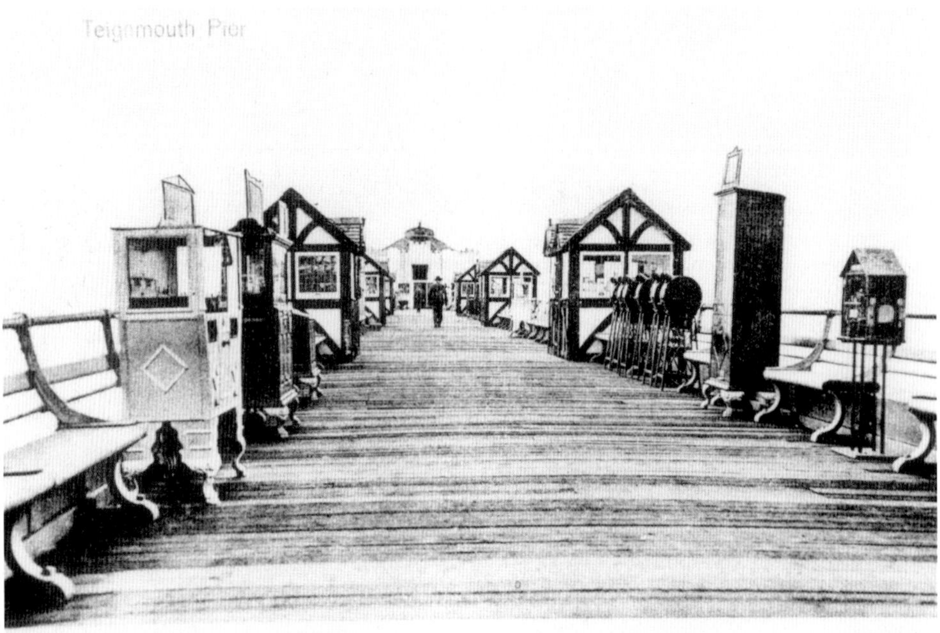

Teignmouth's pleasure boats basking in the best of times with Britannia, White Heather, Princess Mary and Sea Belle

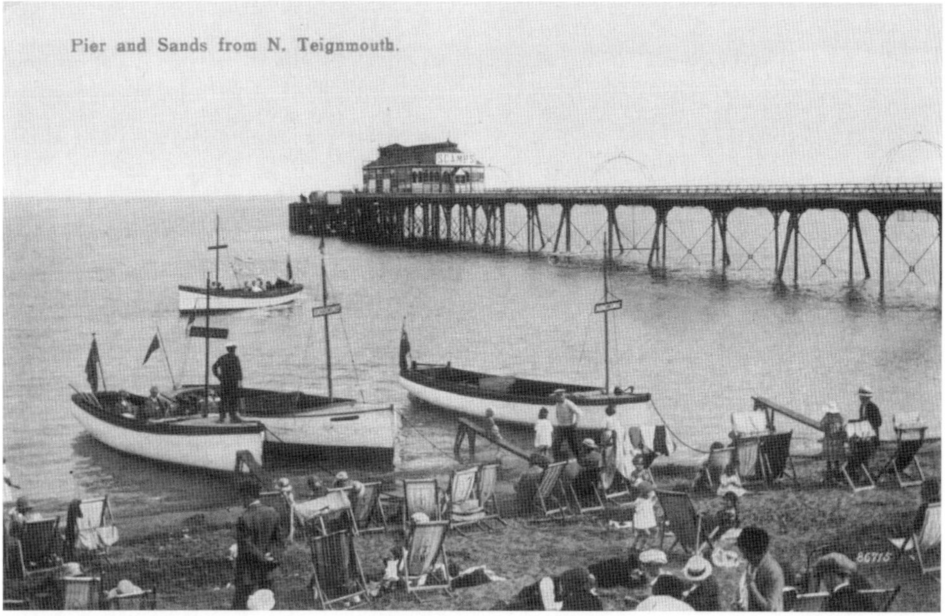

Local boatmen plied their trade from both sides of the pier

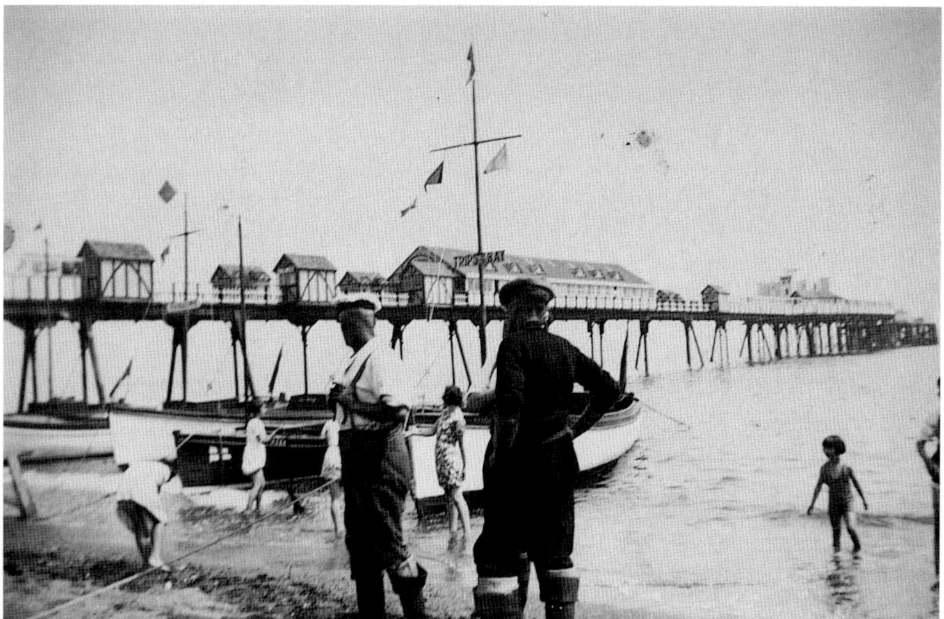

At some point in its 70-year lifespan, it was called the Castle Pavilion. Could it have been a temporary addition to celebrate 70 years since the start of the pier's construction as well as the silver jubilee of King George V and Queen Mary in 1935?

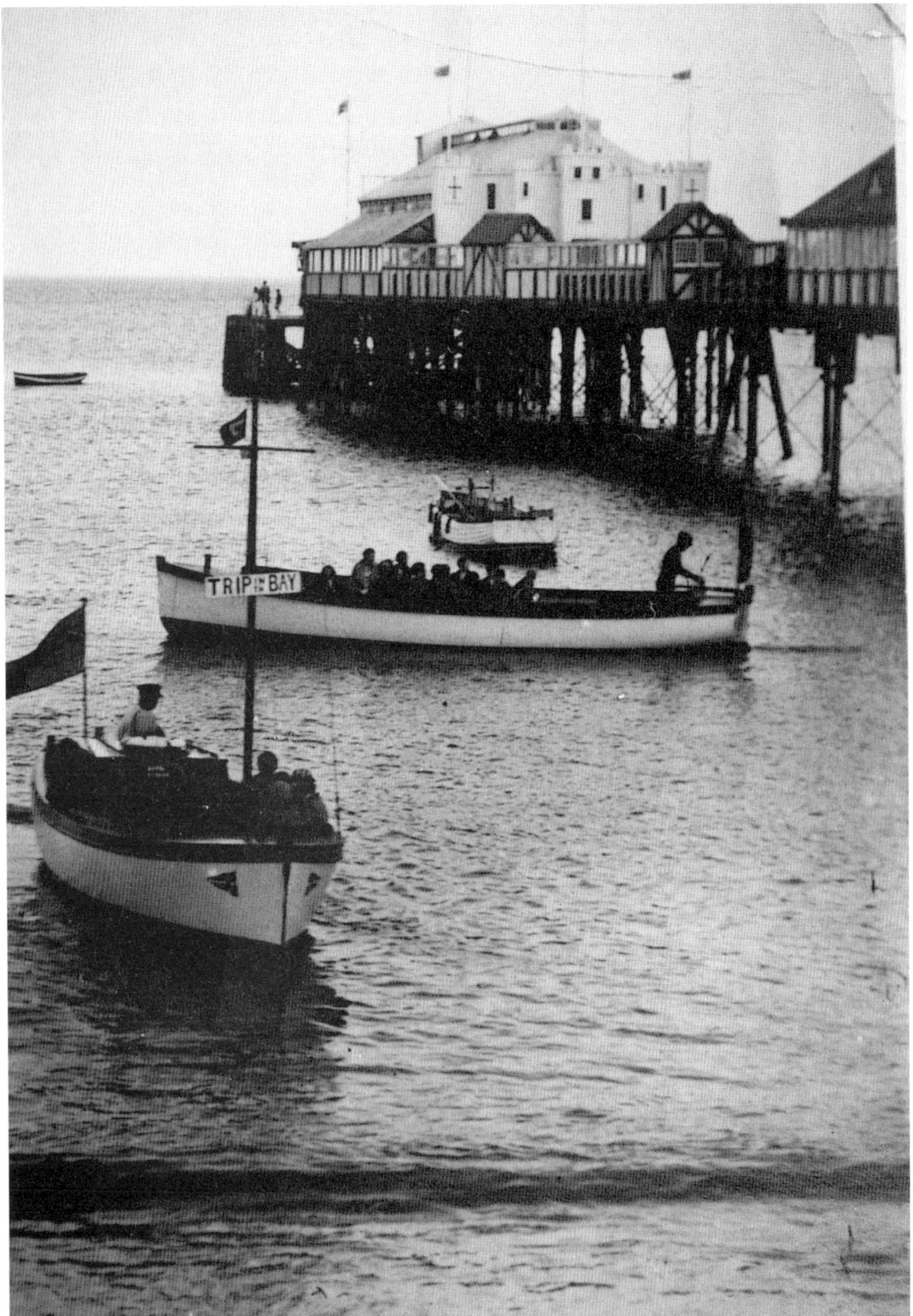

Overview from Jubilee Shelter enlarged in 1935 to commemorate the Royal Silver Jubilee

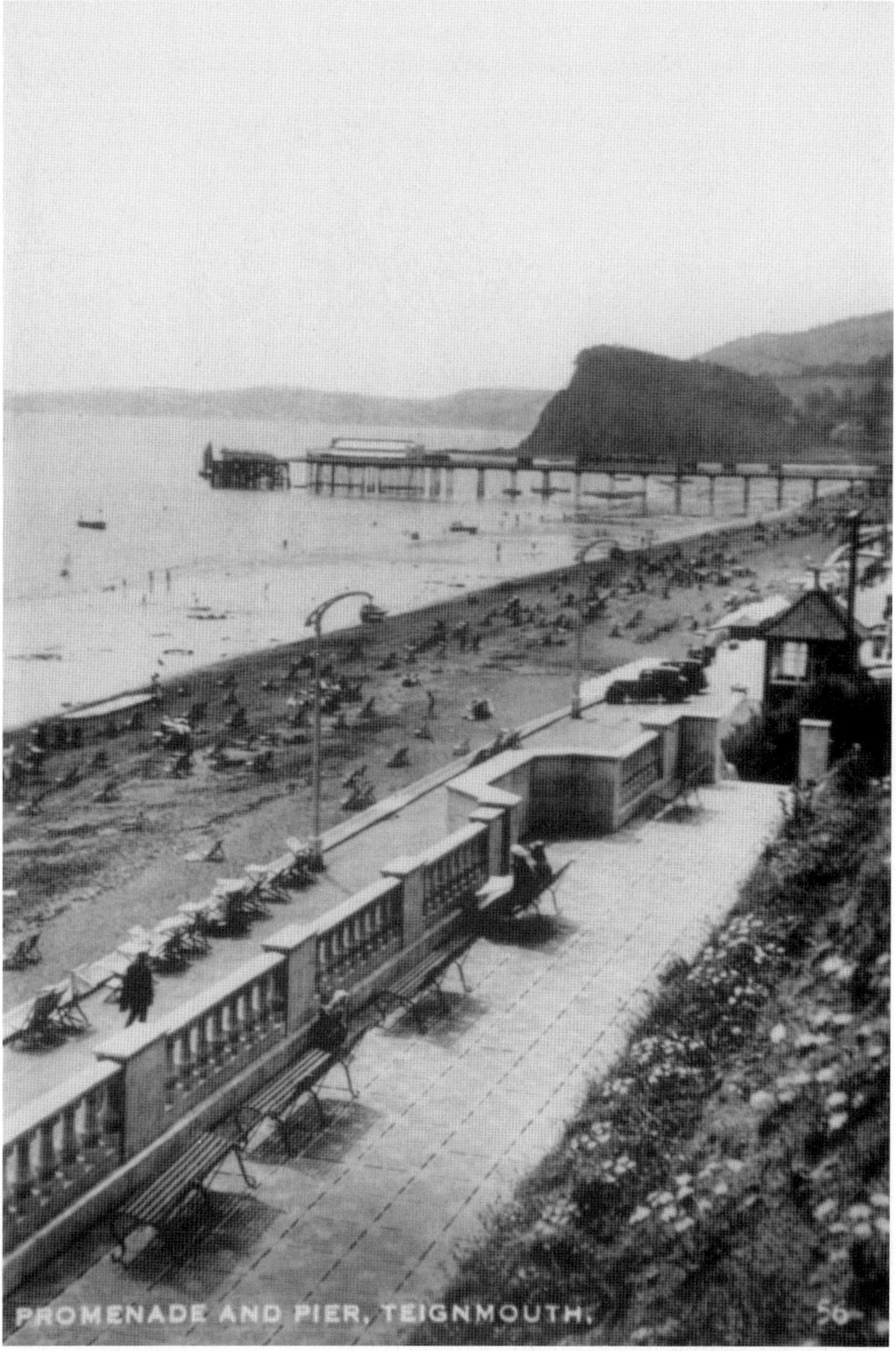

Two children peep at the sea through the barriers whilst the overall-clad shop assistant conveys supplies to the ballroom beyond the line of elaborate amusement machines. In later years, this trolley broke through the deck when thieves used it in an attempt to haul away a huge stack of coins. The trolley survived and remains in use

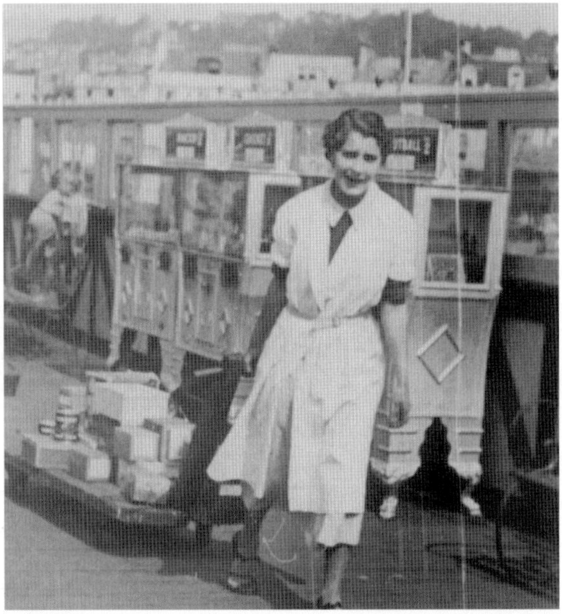

Cyril and May Boatfield (L), who ran the café kitchen, and hard-working waitresses of the '30s

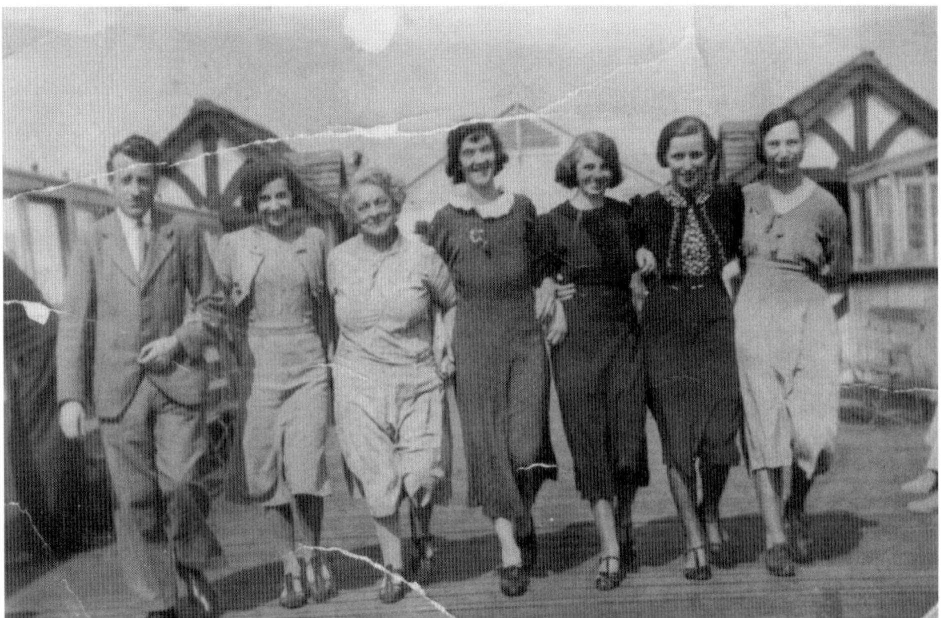

Local photographer J.J. Payne recorded this group of staff and bandsmen and centre, Manager Joe Angliss

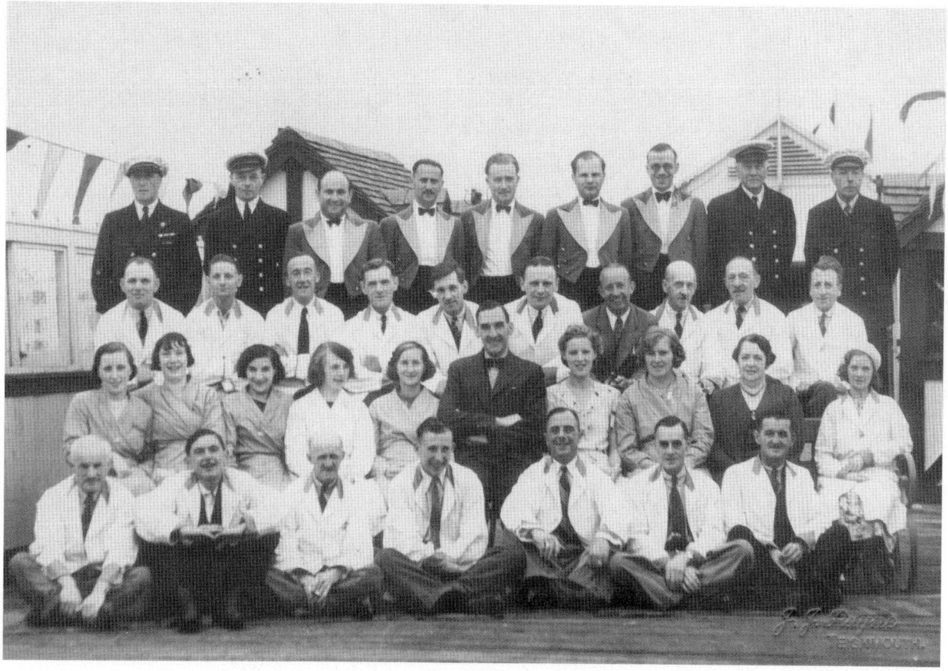

Franked 1930, this postcard shows the whalebone arch donated by Mr Pike Ward, a local fish dealer trading in Iceland around the turn of the 19th century

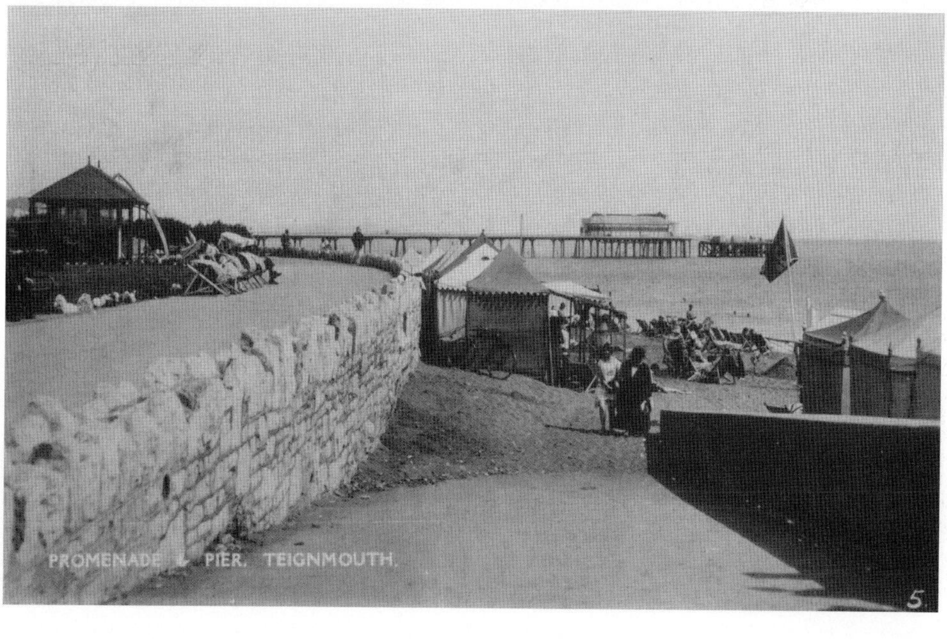

The pier at its height of popularity. A wooden hut amongst the tents marks the progression in beach use

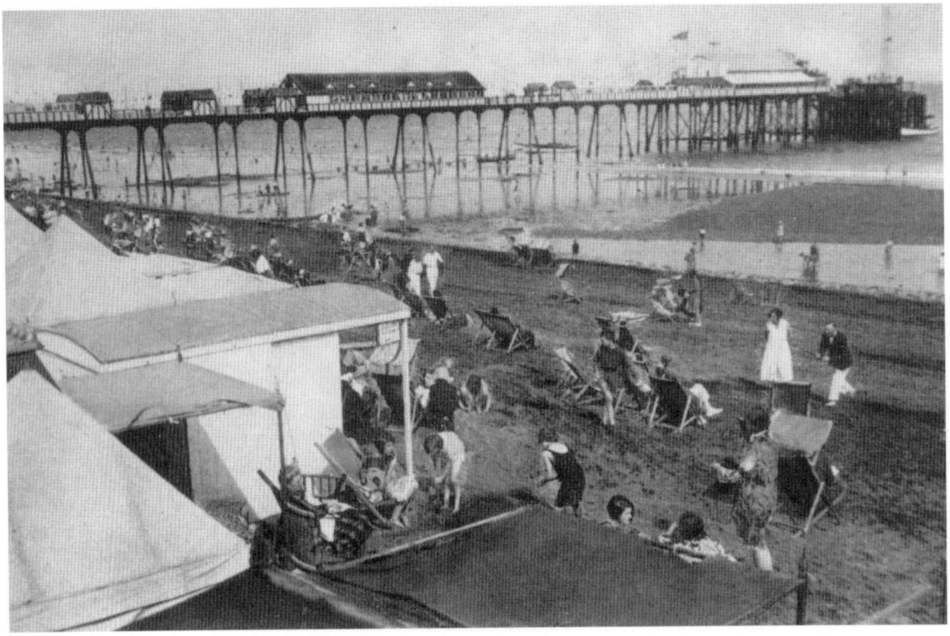

There was no other time in its history that the pier was so full of variety and style

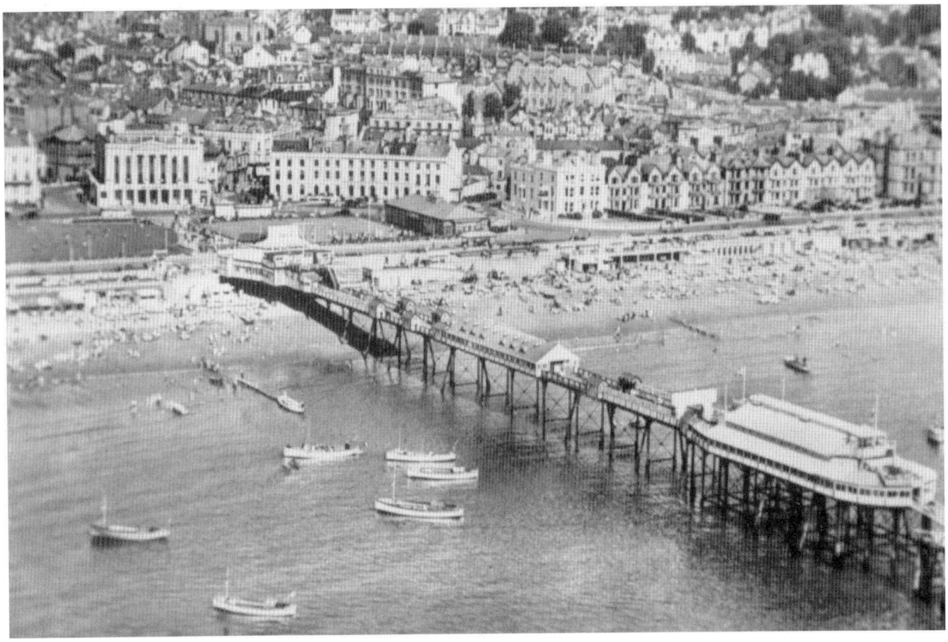

A meticulous Den and promenade with fairy lights introduced in 1937

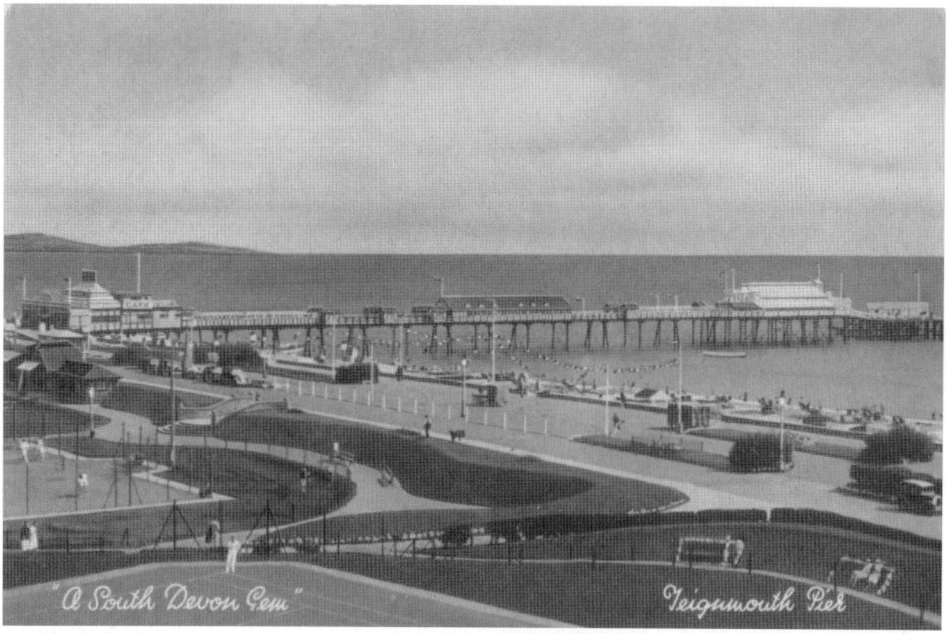

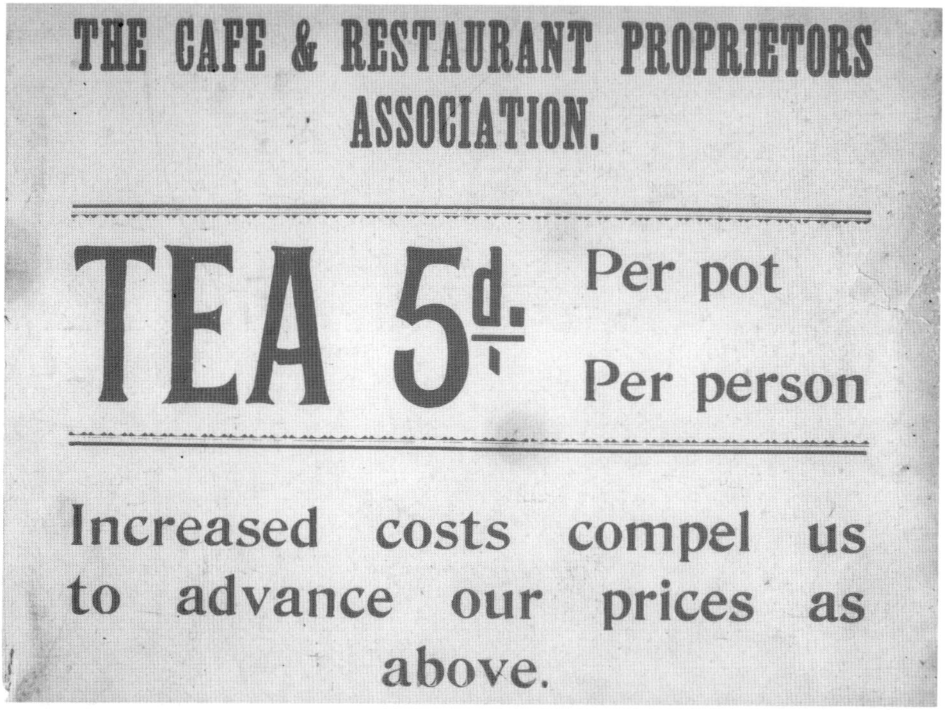

THE CAFE & RESTAURANT PROPRIETORS ASSOCIATION.

TEA 5d. Per pot Per person

Increased costs compel us to advance our prices as above.

Local girl Joan Hill next to pier's advert tower on the prom in the halcyon years before the world erupted into war

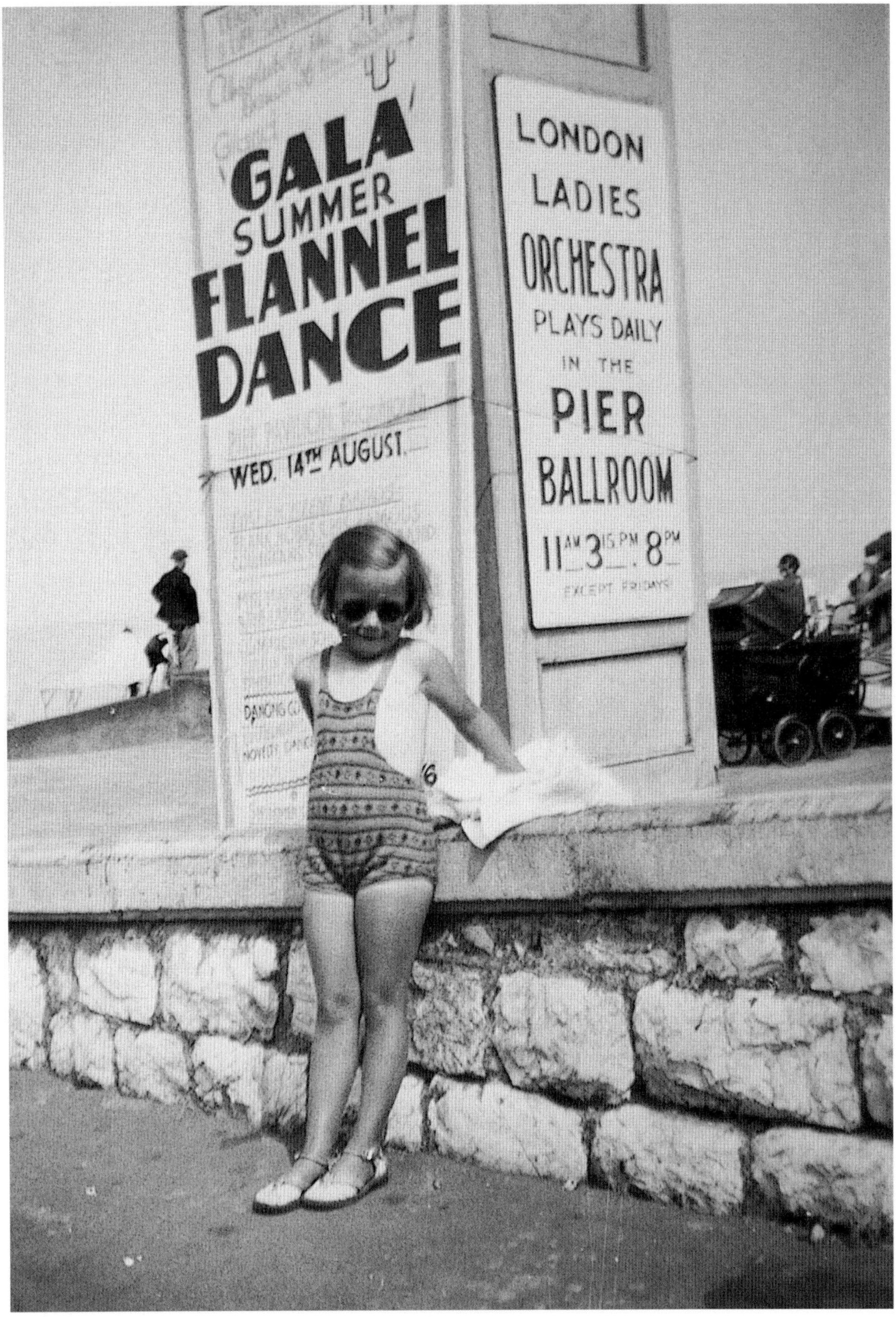

The jetty was multi-purpose as a ships' landing stage, bathers' diving board and changing rooms as well as a haven for anglers

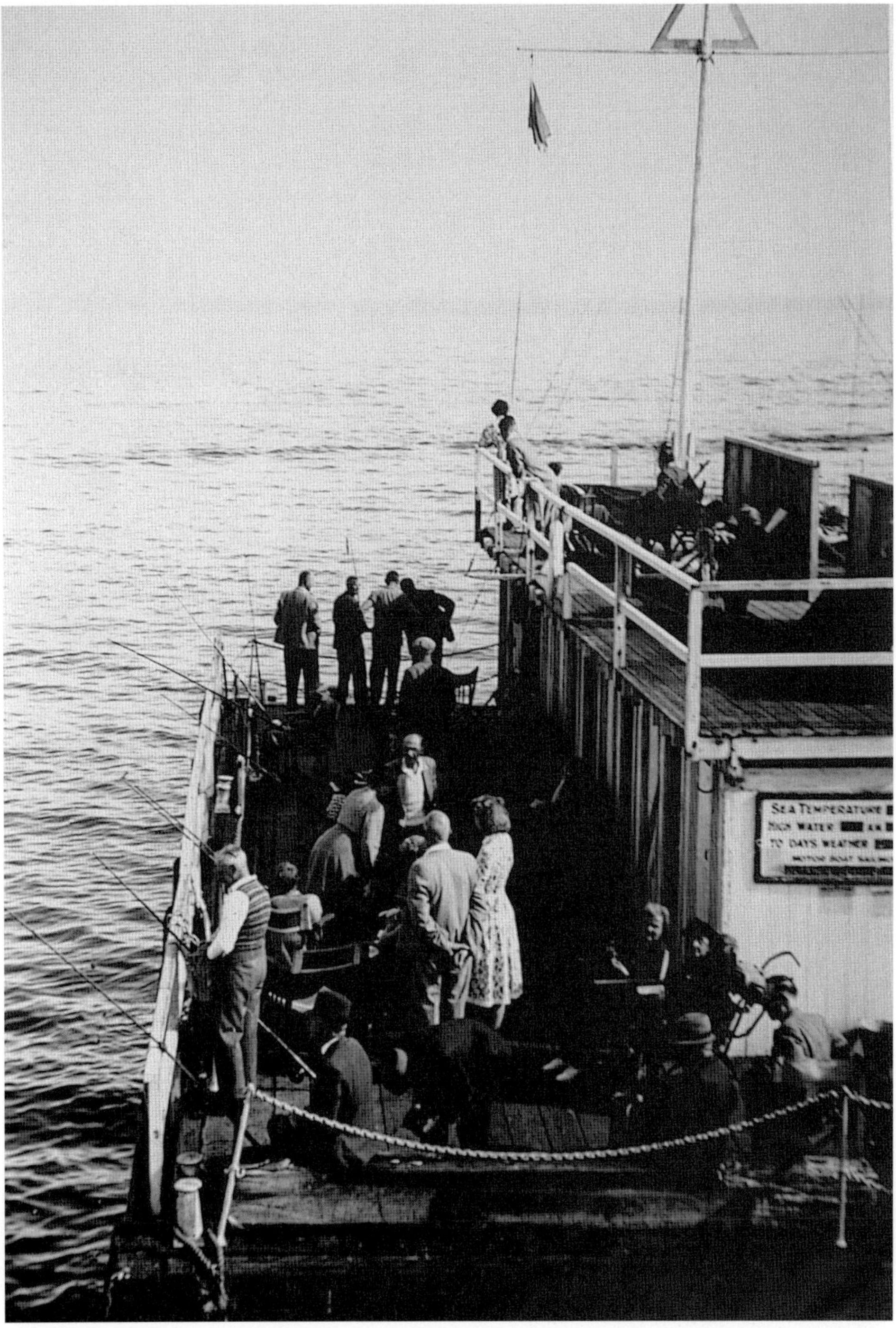

Steamer chairs grouped around tables set for tea on the sprung-maple ballroom floor

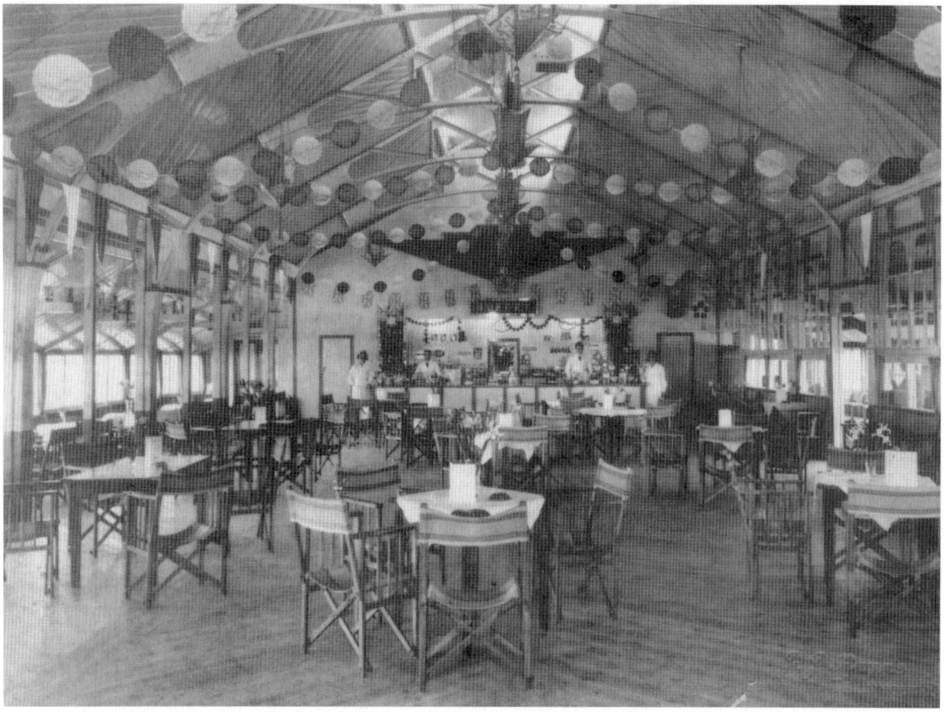

The last waltz? War clouds loomed when J.J. Payne took this photograph. The two white-capped gentlemen on the left appear in the earlier group photo

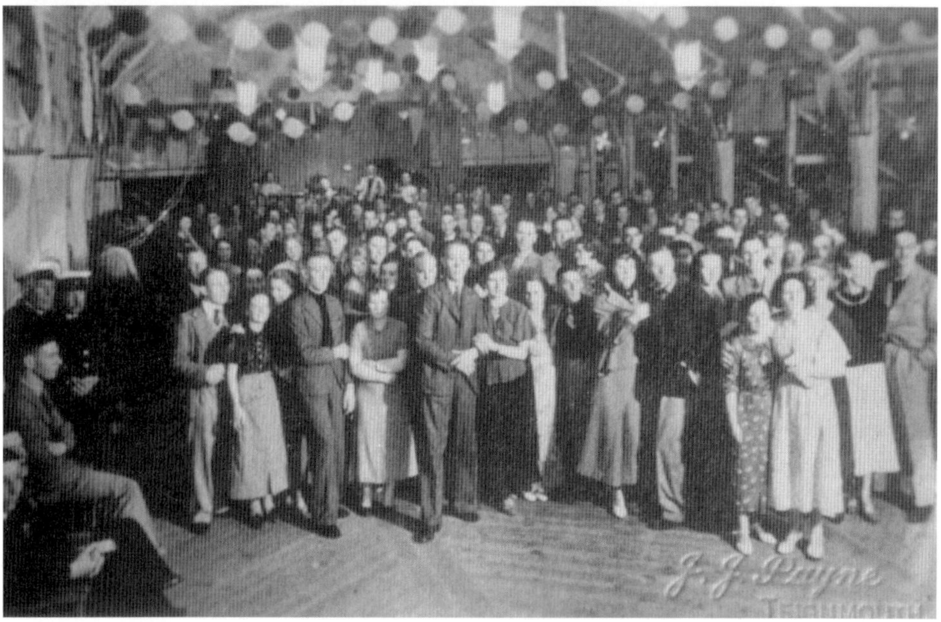

On July 7th 1940, two bombs landed in the sea close to the pier. The following day it was subjected to machine gun fire, a bullet lodging in a roll of tickets and another 5 bombs dropped

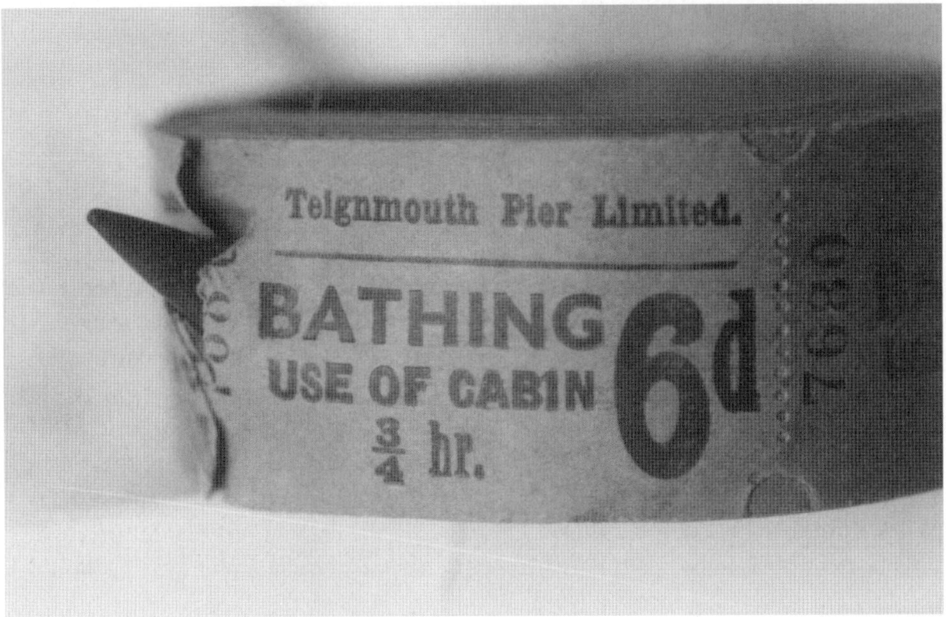

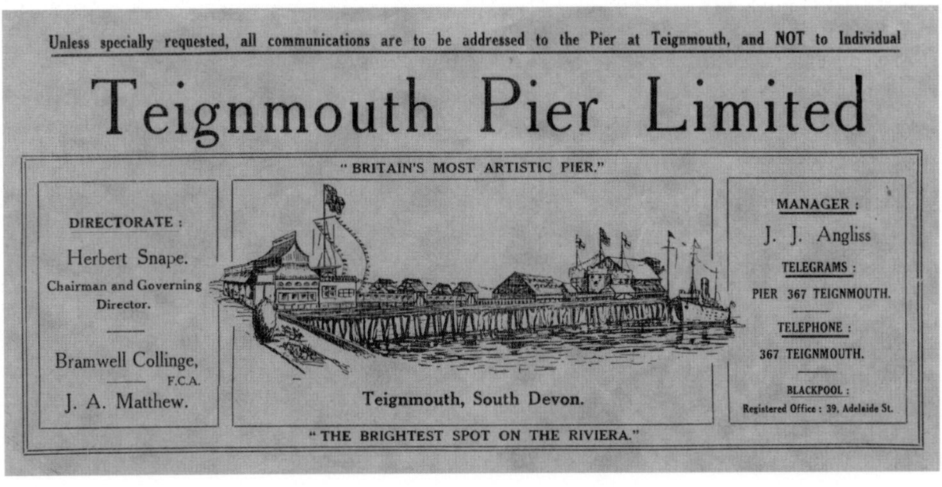
Unless specially requested, all communications are to be addressed to the Pier at Teignmouth, and NOT to Individual

Teignmouth Pier Limited

"BRITAIN'S MOST ARTISTIC PIER."

DIRECTORATE :

Herbert Snape.
Chairman and Governing Director.

Bramwell Collinge, F.C.A.

J. A. Matthew.

Teignmouth, South Devon.

MANAGER :

J. J. Angliss

TELEGRAMS :
PIER 367 TEIGNMOUTH.

TELEPHONE :
367 TEIGNMOUTH.

BLACKPOOL :
Registered Office : 39, Adelaide St.

"THE BRIGHTEST SPOT ON THE RIVIERA."

Chapter 3

War over, the unrepeatable '50s

Recorded Owners during this period
Mr Albert Snape, Mr Bramwell Collinge & J.A. Matthew 1935 -1961

A vision of snow on the sea was one of the extraordinary experiences etched on the minds of local people during the winter of 1947. Their memories and those of six years of conflict were stowed away in a determined bid to get life back to normal. The introduction of a 2d toll was no barrier to having fun on the pier and both cafés did a roaring trade. A large staff was employed for sales and maintenance as the pier regained its position as Teignmouth's premier pleasure palace. Boy Scouts held swimming galas in the sea off the pier and speedboat trips turned into the most exciting five minutes of the day. Pleasure boats, including Dumbo from Exmouth, brought in hordes three times a week. The days of paddle-steamers were over. Hugin, a replica Viking ship, moored off the pier for one hour in August 1949 and only Council members were allowed to board her. It was a different matter when visiting Royal Navy ships dropped anchor in the bay. The pier's landing stage was a thronging through-point for both sailors and sight-seers with huge queues of people waiting to go aboard the 22,000-ton US destroyer Borie. If sailors missed the liberty boat back to their ship, they were allowed to sleep on the ballroom floor until 6am, a privilege that was never abused. Sailors from HMS Volage visiting in 1955 were given the freedom of the pier with free passes to concerts and dances all week. Some of the other visiting HM Ships were Tremadoc Bay 1948: Battleaxe 1949: Swiftsure, Burghead Bay, Agincourt and Barrosa 1950 and Orwell 1953.

Lunches and teas were served in the ballroom café and food demonstrations by the Co-op Wholesale Society and flower and fashion shows were popular. People flocked to Sunday Celebrity Concerts featuring, amongst others, broadcaster Organists Robin Richmond and Brian Rodwell and rising stars Pearl Carr & Teddy Johnson, Cyril Fletcher, Roberto Cardinale, Hypnotist Henry Blyth and the acclaimed ventriloquist Terry Hall with Lenny the Lion. Up-coming local singers, including Tiny Knight and Betty Bace, got a chance to show off their skills and win five shillings on Talent Night and local Baritone Peter Prince won many fans in concerts. Miss Teignmouth was selected at the annual Beauty Contest when proceedings followed a traditional programme of politeness and decorum. The previous year's winner was always escorted in by the Chairman of TUDC and a judge. The 1948 judge represented Oldway Film Studio, Paignton. Contestants paraded, suffered elimination and witnessed the proclamation, enthroning and investment ceremony. After the prizes were presented, everyone danced until midnight and the evening rounded off in patriotic manner with the singing of God Save the King.

Life was breathed back into the ballroom with its newly-laid floor but rationing inhibited the catering. When clouds pushed people off the beach and on to the pier for refreshments, Joan Wharton, Manageress of the ballroom café was sent down to the Ministry of Food Office based at Channel View. Her powers of persuasion usually resulted in a permit to get extra tea and sugar from International Stores, Bank St. There were no shortages on the dancing front with afternoon tea dances twice a week and five nights out of seven the ballroom was full of couples tripping the light fantastic. Olde Tyme with Bob Aggett teaching the steps to as many as 500 people on Tuesdays and Fridays. It cost 2/- for the Saturday night dance and half-a-crown (12.5p) on special occasions. Dance bands included Les Bayliss, Wally Dewer, Gregory Beale, Ritzer Sixers, Bill Greenhalgh and Don Cavalo, whose wife played drums. Local affection for Evelyn "Post Horn Gallop" Hardy and her all-girls' band knew no bounds. Pianist Harold Lusher and his popular band were residents for the seasons of 1951 and '52, when the cost of hiring bands was rising. Profits were by no means certain so it was suggested that various local clubs take over the running of the dances for a season - and they did!

In the early '50s George Brenner acquired a concession to run machines in the front pavilion. The roll-a-penny, spinning arrow, climbing monkeys and laughing clown games run by pier staff were superseded by George's new Midnight Chimes Race Game. Next, he came up with the Devon Belle game. His wife, tired of staying at home alone in Torquay took over a deck shop and sold toys and gifts. It was not long before he also took over the photography shop.

Pier ownership at the time was a triumvirate of Snape, Collinge and Matthew. Albert Snape visited three times each season and was a dapper man with a liking for striped blazers, Oxford Bags trousers and brown and white golf shoes. It took him three days to drive down from Lytham St Annes in his Rolls Royce. He always put up at the Royal Hotel and a mechanic from Bobbetts Garage, who had been trained at Rolls, collected his precious car and took it to the safety of their premises on Eastern Quay. Mr Collinge was an older businessman who kept a very low profile. Mr Matthew, a Coal Merchant in Orchard Gardens, was sometimes wheeled out in his bathchair by his wife for afternoon tea on the pier.

Towards the end of the afternoon in April 1955, Joe Angliss was about to leave for home when he suffered a heart attack and died. George Brenner took over as Manager until 1961 when he bought it.

The cost of upgrading accounted for about £20,000 in the late '50s. Another worry was the discovery of rotten piles beneath the landing stage. Replacement piles had risen from £60 or £80 each to as much as £600-a-piece. Upkeep costs were endless.

J. Arthur Rank filmstar Tony Wright selected the winner of the Press Queen competition in the pier ballroom in 1957. Swimming, even skinny dipping, after dances was all the rage, youngsters thinking nothing of walking home across town in wet clothes. The Great Western Railway immortalized this tradition by designing a poster called Midnight Swimmers in 1957, an original copy selling for £1000 by Christies 40 years later. This period proved to be the final peak of popularity for social dancing. Television was making its mark and the days of live shows were numbered. If concerts ran at a loss in the council-run Den Pavilion, the bill was met by the public purse but the privately-owned pier had to stand its own losses. George Brenner bought the pier in 1961 and let his son, Anthony, organize the first dance of the following season. Sadly, due to storm damage and closure of the ballroom, it was the last dance ever held.

Summer dances in the hall over the sea seem far off as snow covers the beach in winter 1947

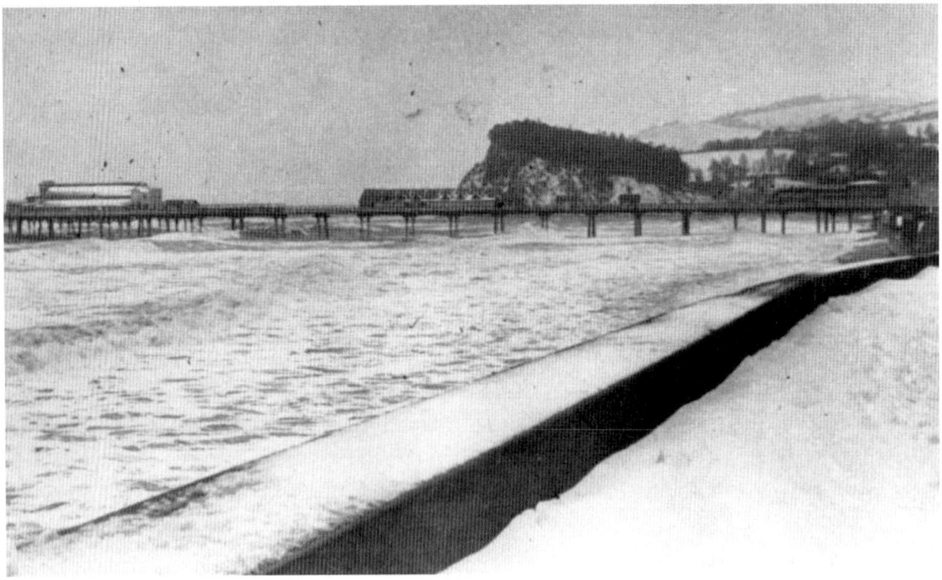

HMS Tremadoc Bay visiting summer 1949

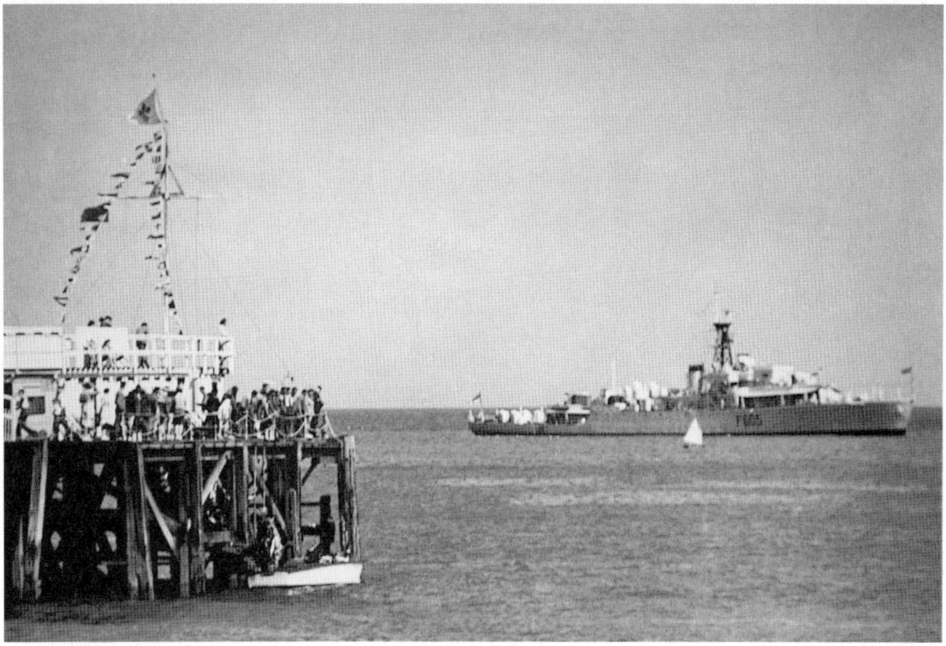

Photographer B.J. Wareham captured the scene as VIPs board a motor cruiser

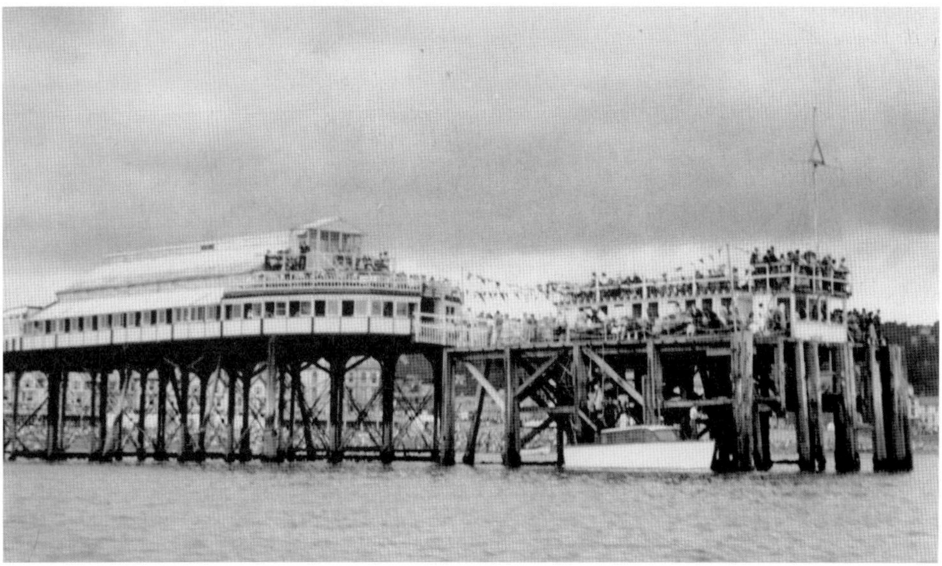

The cruiser conveys VIPs out to HMS Tremadoc Bay

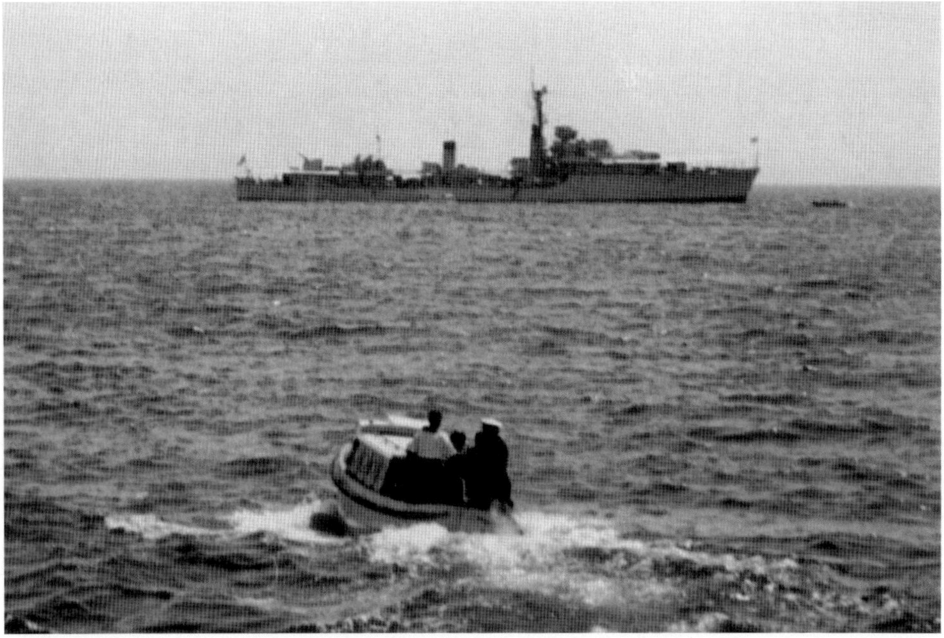

Cllr Alan Etherton, TUDC Chairman, accompanied by his wife, prepares to fire the miniature cannon to start Regatta Week 1949

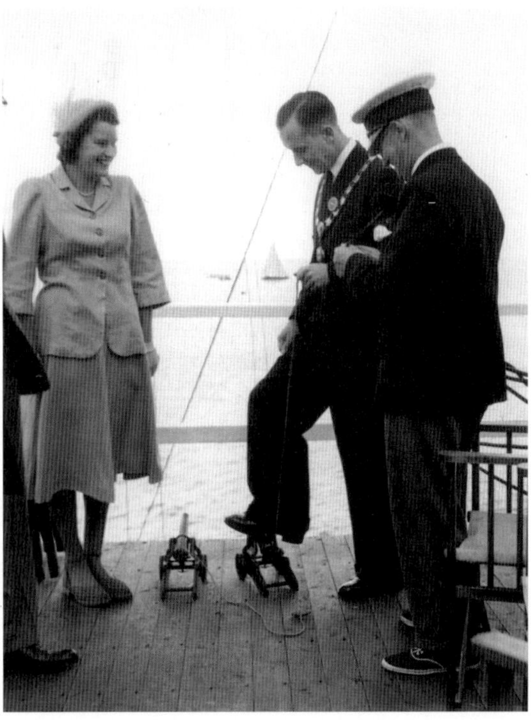

Urban District Council of Teignmouth.

CHAIRMAN'S PARLOUR.

TELEPHONE Nº 743 (5 LINES).

Council Offices,
Bitton House,
Teignmouth.
Devon.

November 26th 48

J.Angliss Esq.,
Manager. Teignmouth Pier Co.Ltd.,

Dear Mr Angliss,

This is just a personal note to say thank you for the very friendly and helpful manner in which you assisted with the various entertainments during the past season. I can assure you that your friendly cooperation was very greatly appreciated.

I would also like to mention how grateful we are to Miss Evelyn Hardy and her band for all their assistance. Their readiness to assist at all times in such a cheerful manner was an example which has doubtless increased their popularity in the hearts of the citizens of Teignmouth. Please convey to them my warmest thanks.

May I take this opportunity of wishing you all the compliments of the Season.

Yours sincerely

F.E. Davidson

Chairman.Teignmouth U.D.C.

"LIFE IS NOTHING WITHOUT MUSIC"

EVELYN HARDY

The Celebrated Lady Trumpeter

and her ORCHESTRA

play in the

PIER BALLROOM & CAFE

Daily — (Except Mondays)

Any number played by them can be obtained either as a record or music from

EVELYN HARDY'S MUSIC SALON

Handel House - Teignmouth

Also H.M.V records, Instruments, Pianos (TUNED, Bought or Repaired), Accessories, and for everything in Music

R.N. Air Station,
Haldon,
Bishopsteignton,
S. Devon.

5th August 1943.

Dear Mr. Angliss,

On behlaf of the Wrens at this Station, I wish to thank you very much indeed for your kindness in loaning us the Roll-the-Penny canvas which we used at the H.G. Fête at Bishopsteignton House last Monday, and we hope that we may be able to repay you at some future date.

Again thanking you.

Yours sincerely,

A. M. Story

Leading Wren.

J.J. Angliss Esq.,
23, Northumberland Place,
Teignmouth.

Hon. Treasurers:
Irvine C. Geddes, Esq.
Sir James P. I. M. Corry, Bart.

Hon. Secretary:
Sir T. Harrison Hughes, Bart.

Telegraphic Address:
"Seaserver, Knights, London."

Telephone: SLOane 0331.
(5 lines)

KS

G R

KING GEORGE'S FUND FOR SAILORS

(Incorporated Under Royal Charter.)

Patron:
HIS MAJESTY THE KING

President:
Rear-Admiral the Earl Mountbatten of Burma,
K.G., P.C., G.M.S.I., G.M.I.E., G.C.V.O.,
K.C.B., D.S.O.

Chairman of the General Council:
Vice-Admiral Cedric S. Holland, C.B.

General Secretary:
Lieut.-General Sir Gerald R. S. Hickson,
C.B., C.B.E., D.L., R.M. (Retd.).

1, CHESHAM STREET,
LONDON, S.W.1.

21st July, 1948.

-. Angliss, Esq.,
The Pier,
Teignmouth.

Dear Mr. Angliss,

I have had the most enthusiastic report from our Area Secretary, Miss Walker, of the Garden Fete held in Teignmouth on July 8th.

Miss Walker tells me that you very kindly provided the side-shows and the prizes to go with them, and I am sure that your generosity and kindness contributed a great deal towards the success of the event.

Thank you very much for all you did.

Yours sincerely,

Geoffrey Webb

Lieut. Commander, R.N.,
Deputy Secretary.

BATTLE OF BRITAIN WEEK

The President, Chairman and members of the Teignmouth branch of the Royal Air Forces Association offer their very sincere thanks to

J. J. Angliss Esq.

for the generous help and co-operation during the "Battle of Britain Week," 1948.

W. A. Parkhouse
Chairman, Teignmouth Branch, R.A.F.A.

Stanley Dayton
Chairman, Battle of Britain Week General Committee

Teignmouth Beauty Queen Contest.

Choosing of
MISS TEIGNMOUTH
1948

THURSDAY, MAY 20th
in the
PIER PAVILION.

Souvenir Programme
4d.

Evelyn Hardy All Girls' Band. L-R: Evelyn Hardy : Rosie : Josie : Vera : Lottie

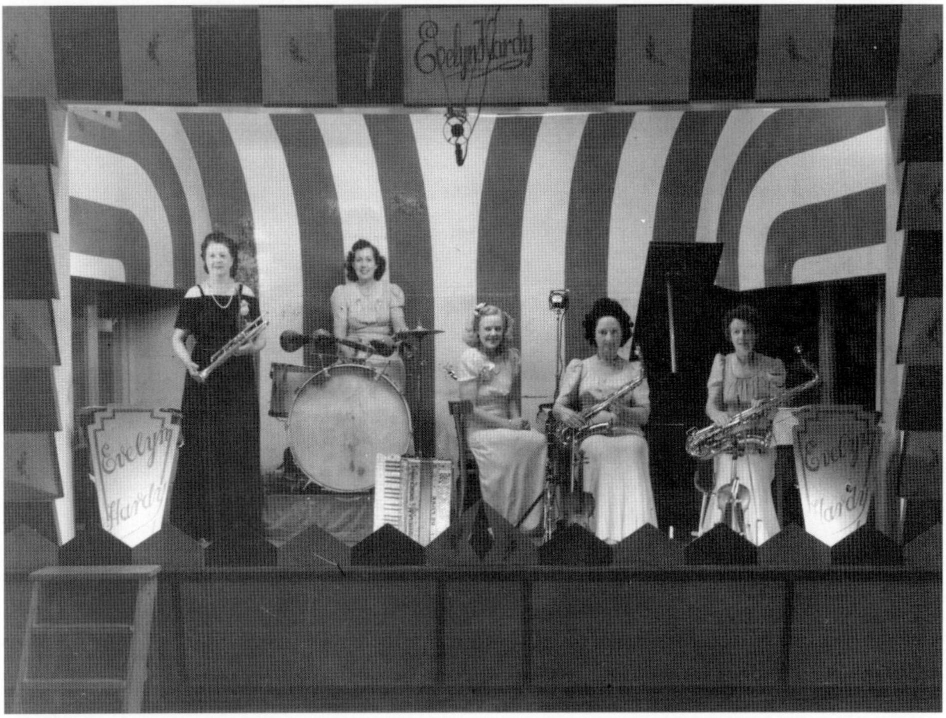

Relentless and untameable, the sea builds up more problems for the future

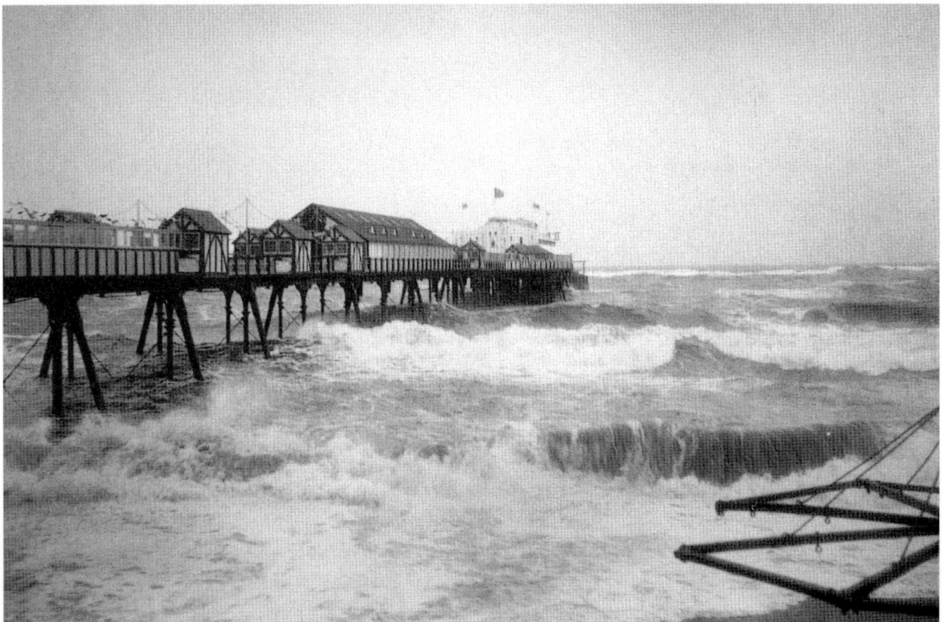

Refreshment huts lashed to the sea wall to prevent being swept out to sea

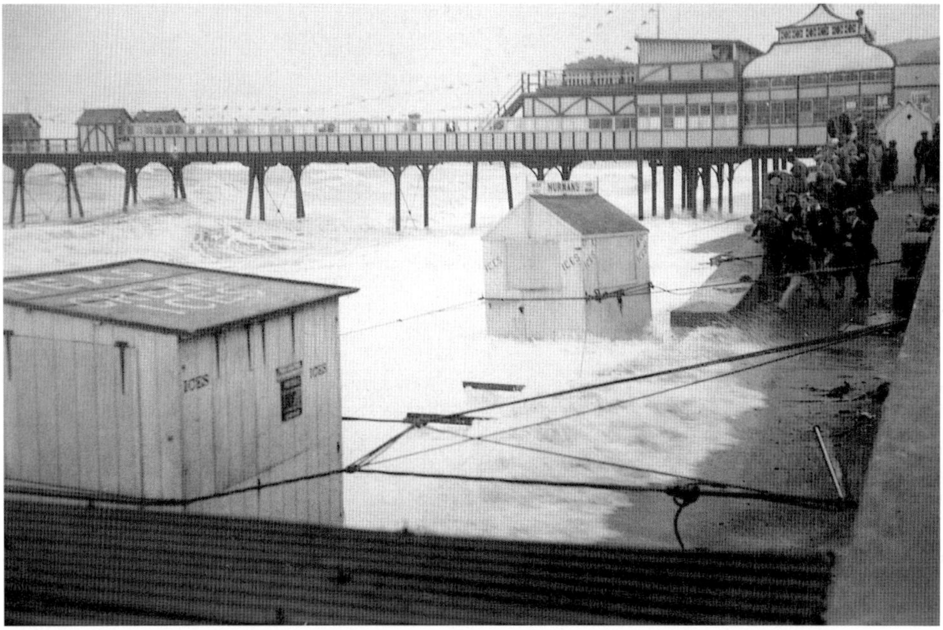

Scaffolding and ladders in place for the annual inspection and repair programme

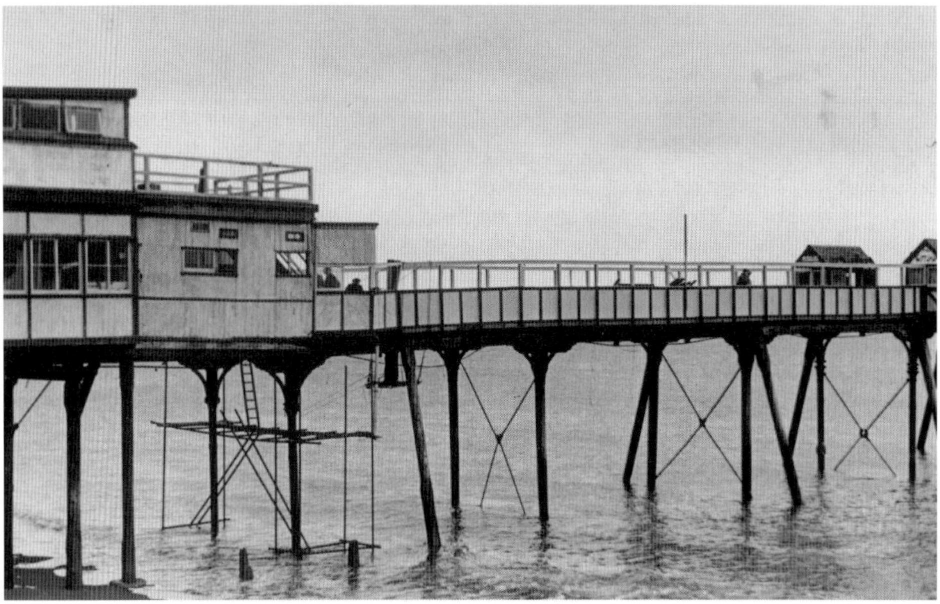

Manager Joe Angliss (R) inspecting the underside with a workman

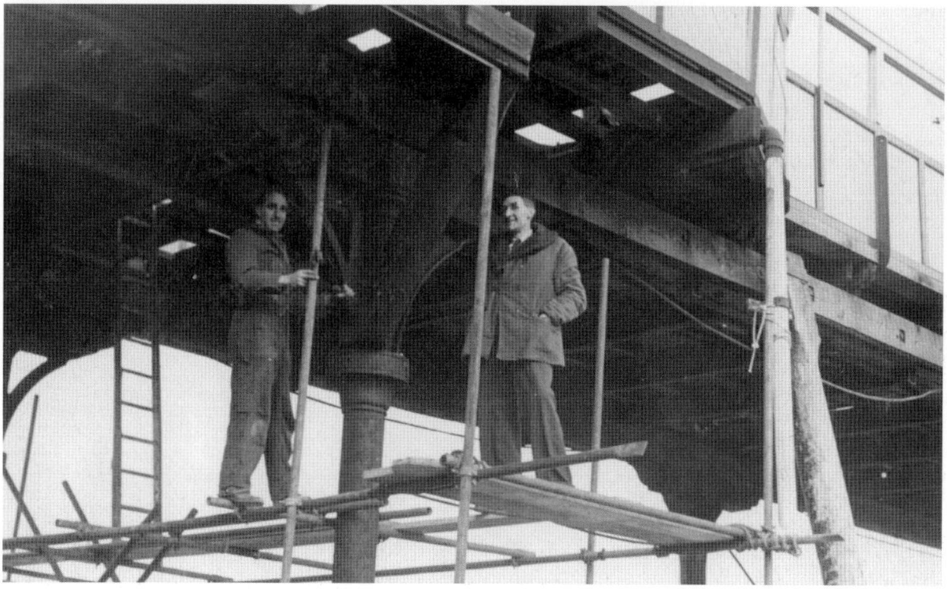

Relaxing in the balmy breezes beyond the middle pavilion

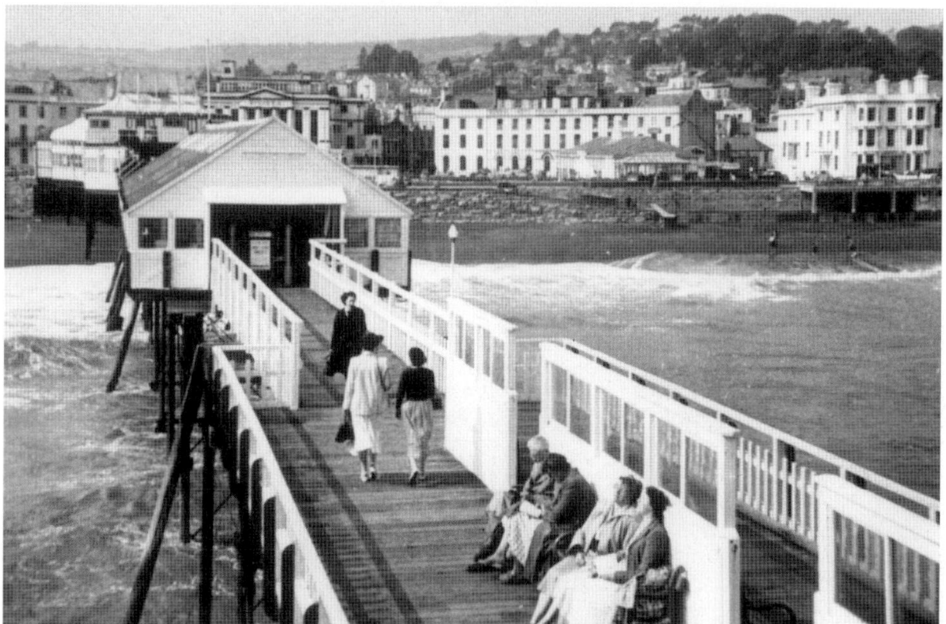

Safety measures were at a minimum

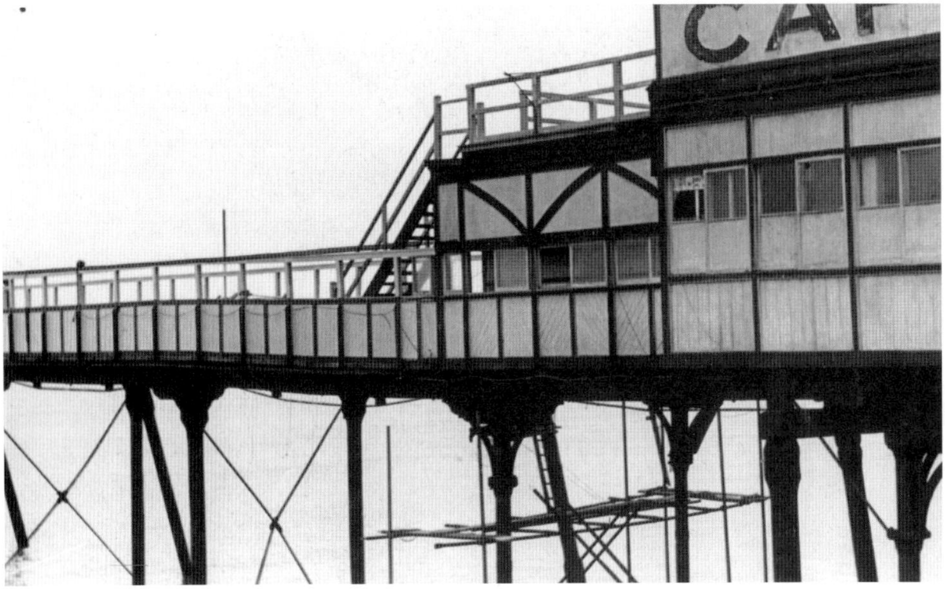

Pauline Roberts (L) and Minnie Steer at ease on the trolley used for conveying coinage along the deck to the cashier

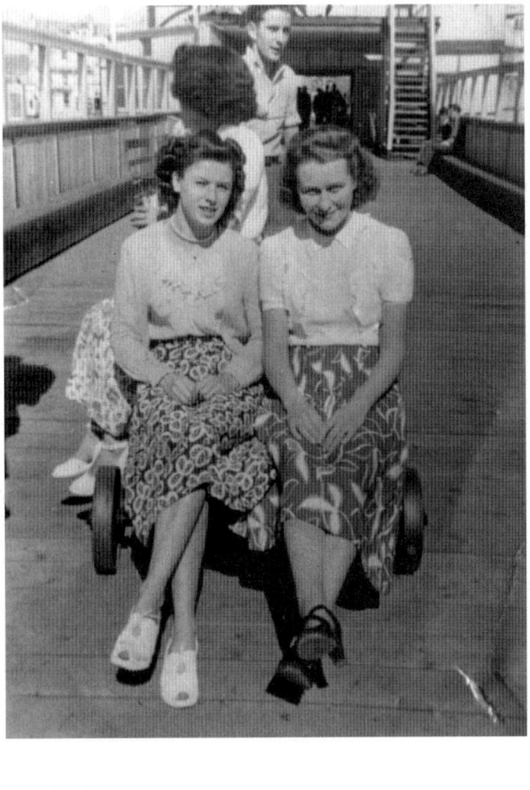

Metal stacking chairs and matching tables are laid out for morning coffee in the ballroom just after the war. The bandstand is set up ready for Evelyn Hardy's resident band

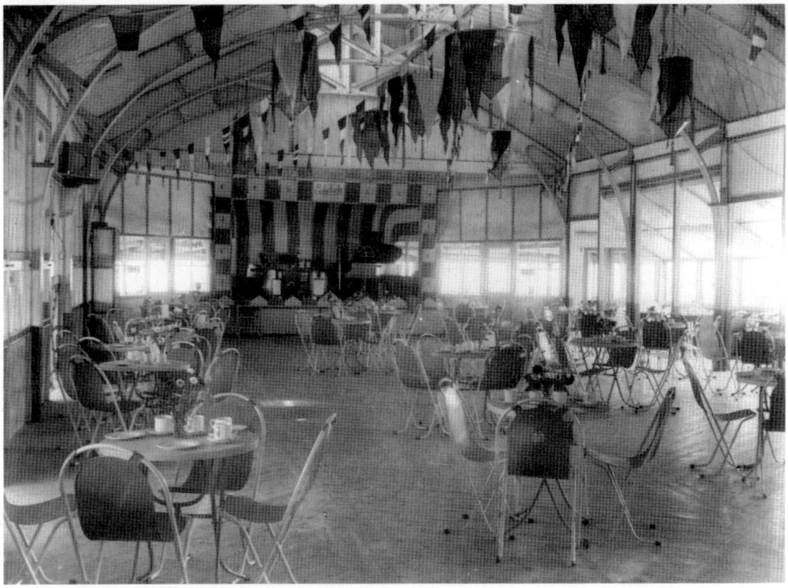

Civic Ball 1949. L-R: Betty Tanner as Miss Teignmouth : Mrs Etherton : Cllr Etherton Chairman of TUDC : Miss New Zealand : Unknown couple

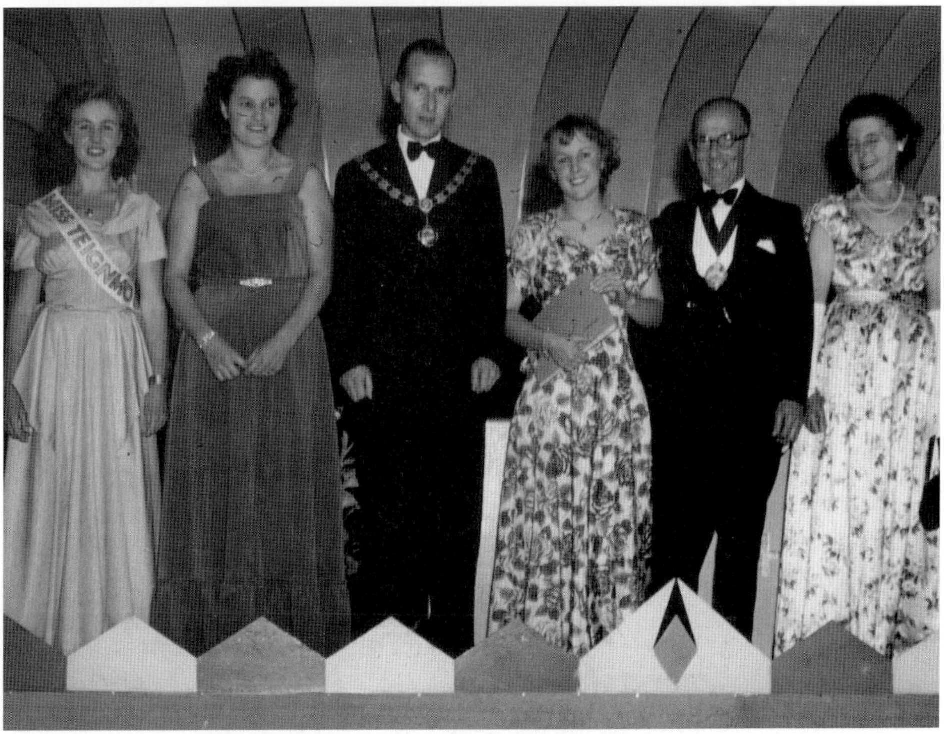

Miss New Zealand 1949 is treated to a slice of humour from the inimitable Cyril Fletcher, performing at the pier early on in his career

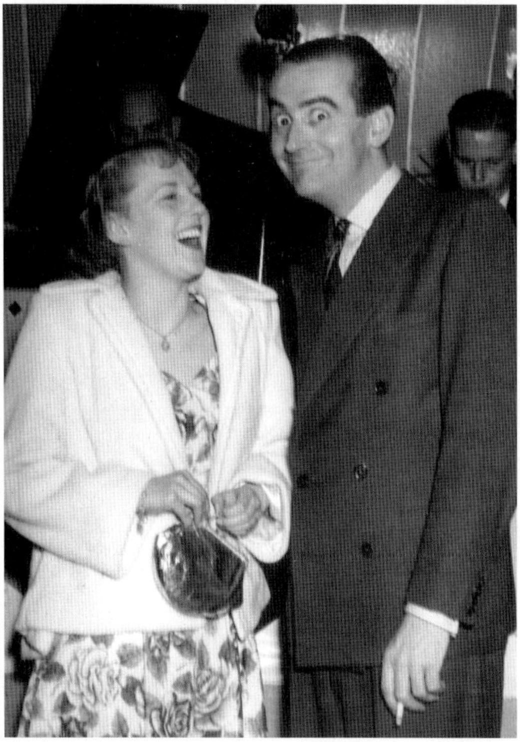

L-R: Pauline Roberts : Phyllis Steer : Ballroom Organist : Minnie Steer and Mavis Hook

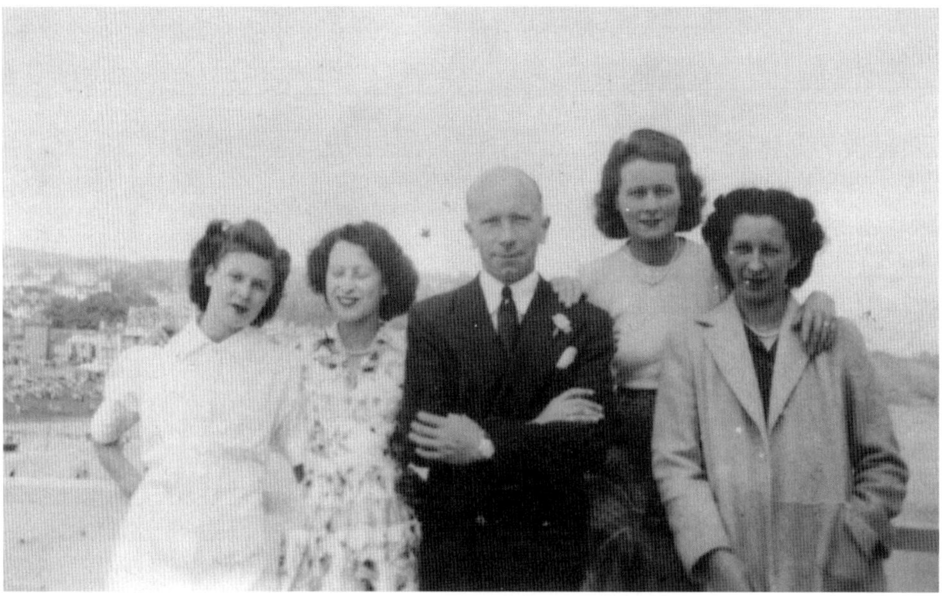

ATTRACTIONS IN THE PIER BALLROOM

WEEK COMMENCING 27TH AUGUST

SATURDAY **THE PIER'S POPULAR DANCE**

8 p.m. to midnight ADMISSION 3/6

MONDAY **REQUEST NIGHT**

LES BAYLISS AND HIS ORCHESTRA PLAYS YOUR REQUESTS

8 p.m. to 10 p.m ADMISSION 1/-

TUESDAY TEIGNMOUTH SWIMMING & LIFE-SAVING SOCIETY

Annual DANCE

8 p.m. to midnight Buffet & Licensed Bar ADMISSION 3/6

WEDNESDAY

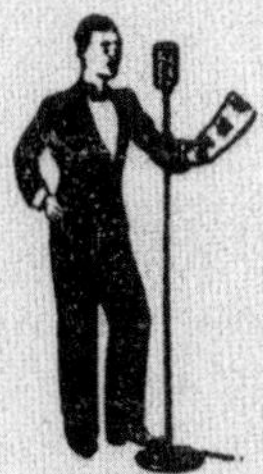

TALENT CONCERT

Open to Visitors and Residents £5 in CASH PRIZES

PLEASE SEND YOUR ENTRIES IN NOW.

8 to 10 p.m. Booking Office open Monday 10 a.m.

ADMISSION 3/- reserved; and 1/6 unreserved

THURSDAY ROYAL AIR FORCES ASSOCIATION

DANCE

8 p.m. to midnight Licensed Bar ADMISSION 3/6

FRIDAY

Olde Tyme Dance

8 p.m. to 11-30 p.m. ADMISSION 2/6

M.C. G. W. FRETWELL, M.B.A.T.D. (O.T.B.) Highly Comm. Hostess Mrs. V. WYLIE

LES BAYLISS & HIS ORCHESTRA PLAY DAILY

(Except Sunday)

at 11 a.m. and 4 p.m. IN THE BALLROOM CAFE

MORNING COFFEE. LUNCHES. TEAS served daily. Sundays included

The original 'Restless' built by Hook Brothers in 1947. While Syd Hook did trips round the Bay, his wife Mavis worked in the Ballroom Café

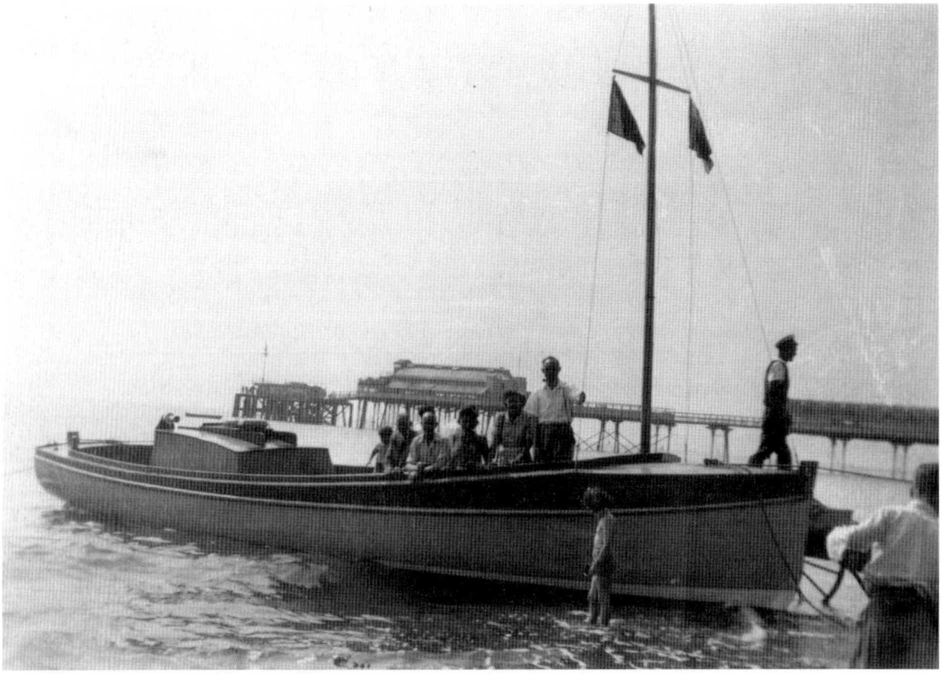

Late 1940s Fashion Parade photographed by Gordon C. Walker

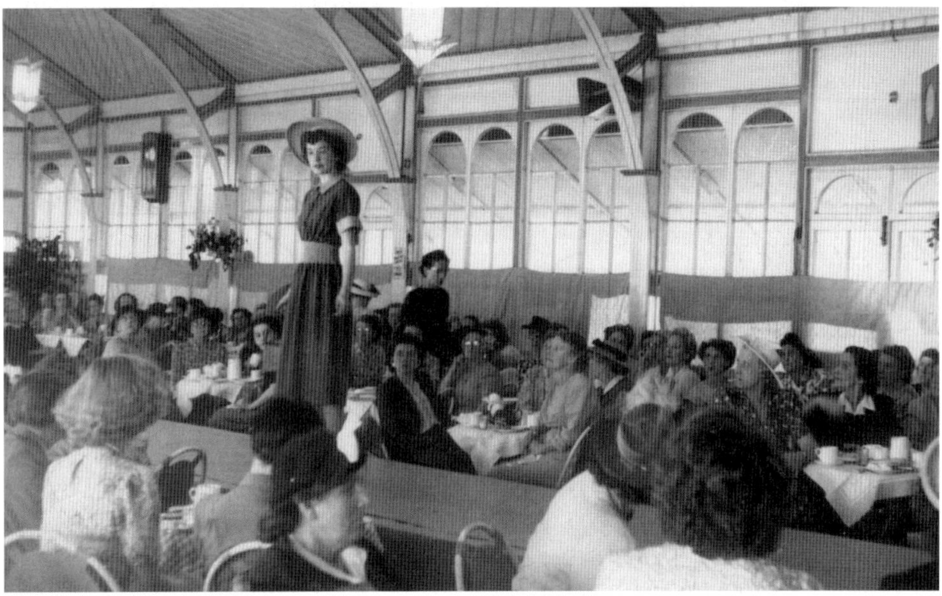

L-R: Unknown : Nora : Mrs Boyne : Pauline Roberts : Minnie Steer : Joan Wharton : Mavis Hook : Elsie Lakeman : Josie Rodwell : Nora's sister

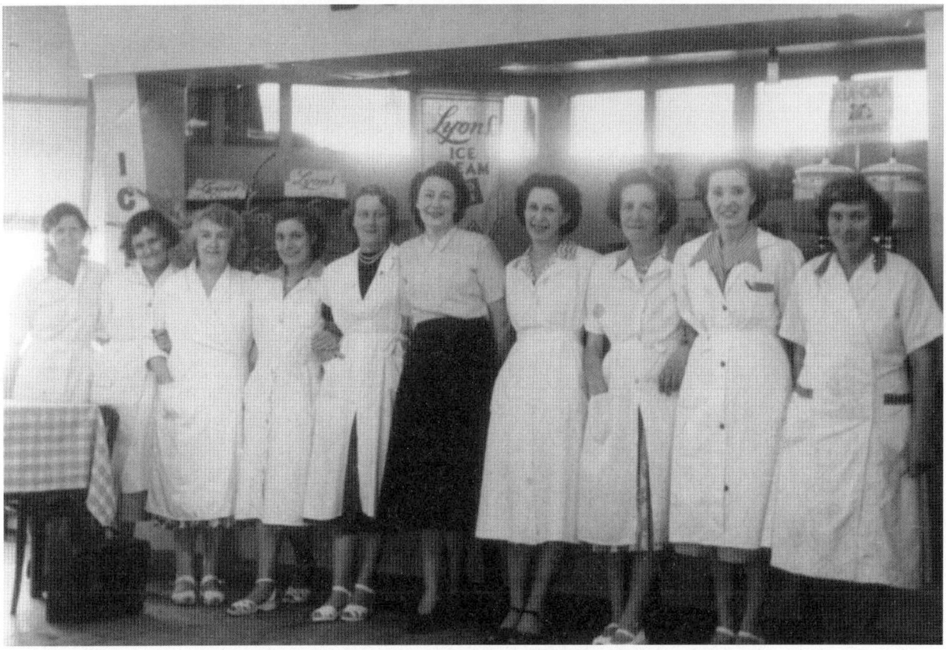

A break on the bandstand for three hardworking waitresses

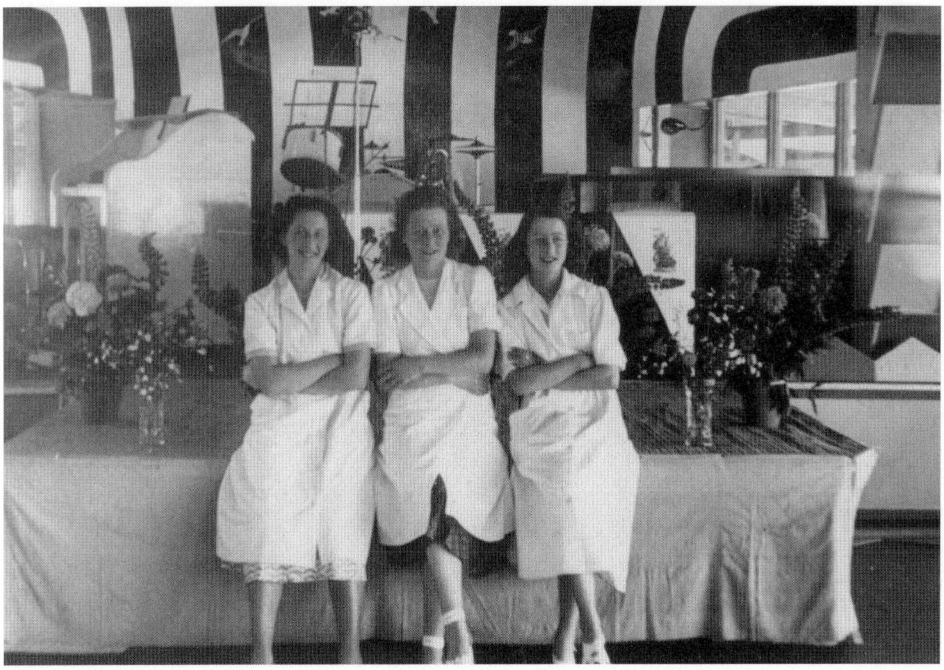

Harold Lusher Band on the new-look bandstand of 1950 playing for a Mannequin Parade

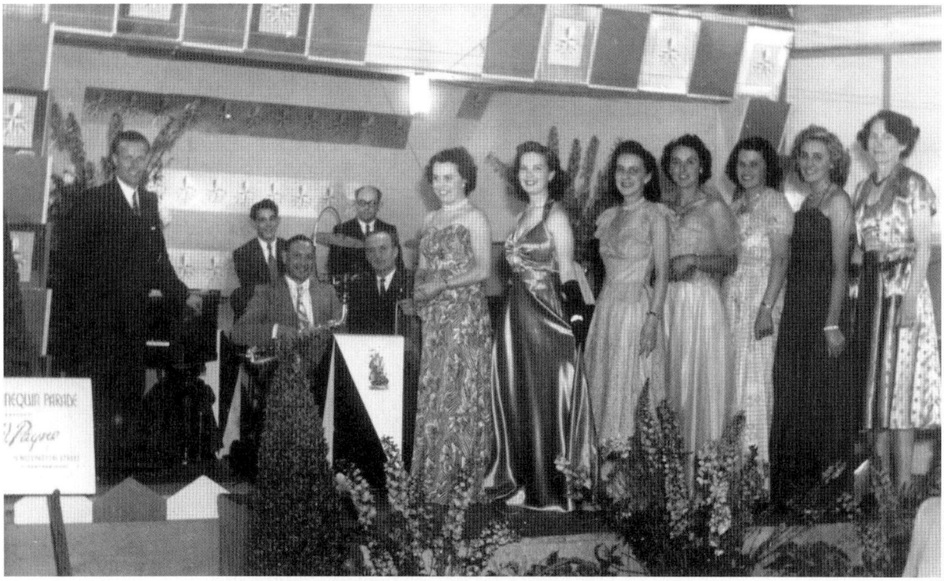

Brian Winstanley was a local boy who loved crooning in the Talent Contests and later became a TUDC Labour Councillor

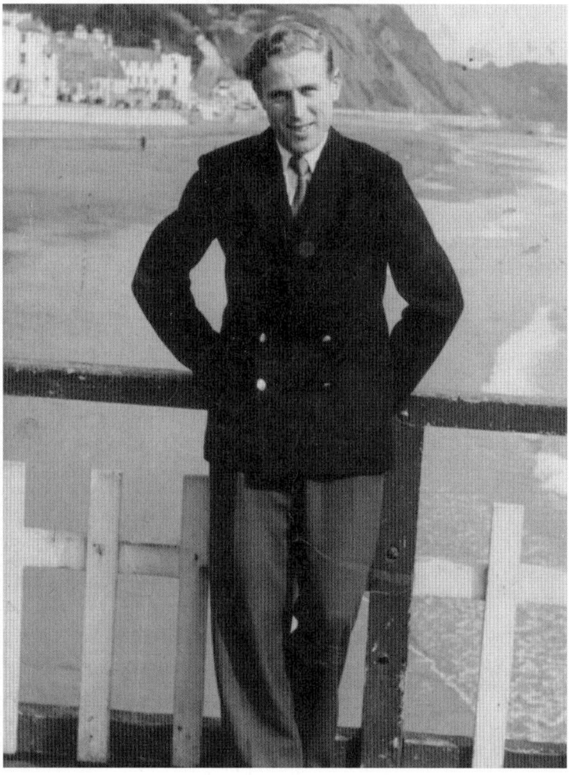

Gwynne East, who married Brian Winstanley's sister Joyce. Gwynne was called the Children's Friend because he always served the biggest and best Eldorado ice cream cornets. Before his death in 1956 he was assistant catering manager and worked in the large pier shop selling candyfloss and tobacconist goods. Note the rare glimpse of the short-lived camera obscura on the beach

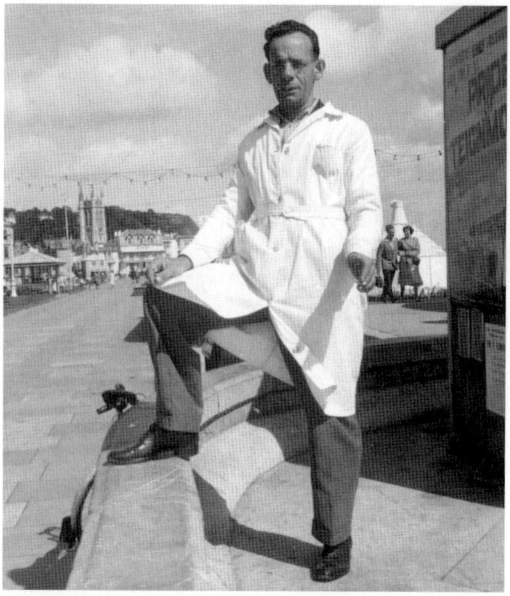

Staff from the busy shop at the pier entrance 1951. Back L-R: Roma Davies : Lil Brown : Dyliss Quantick.
Front L-R: Alice Northcott : Phyl Satchell and Bertha Herbert

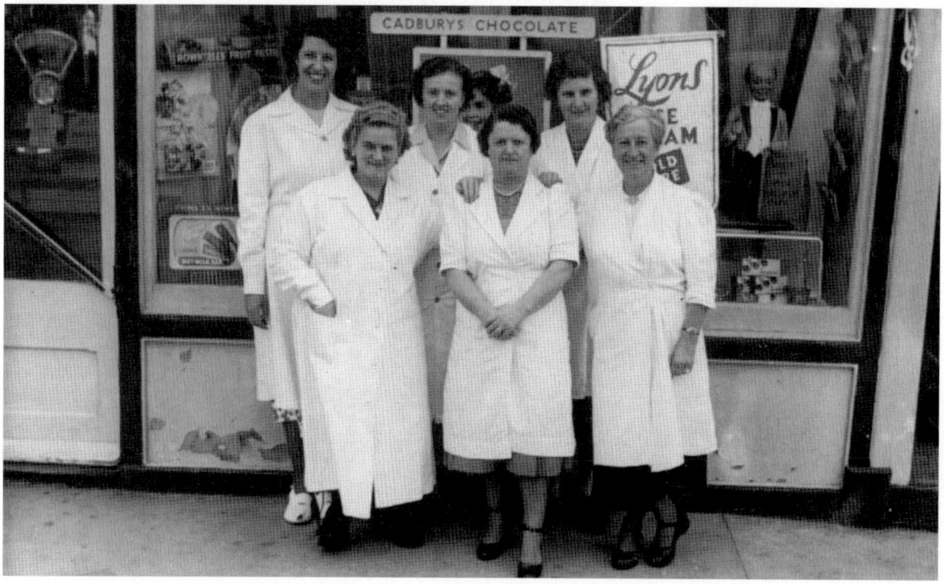

Staff Outing 1951. Names provided by Peter Mole.
Back L-R: Jack Nicks : Bill Steer : Phil Hook : unknown : Harold Lusher : Bus driver : Mr Hamlyn : Gwynne East : unknown : unknown : Peter Mole : unknown
Middle L-R: Mavis Hook : Alice Northcott : Mrs Davis : Mrs Quantick : Mrs Symonds : Minnie Steer : unknown : unknown : unknown
Front L-R: Mrs Boyne : Mrs Ware : Mrs Brown : Mrs Steer : Mrs Barnes : Joyce Symons : unknown : Elsie Lakeman

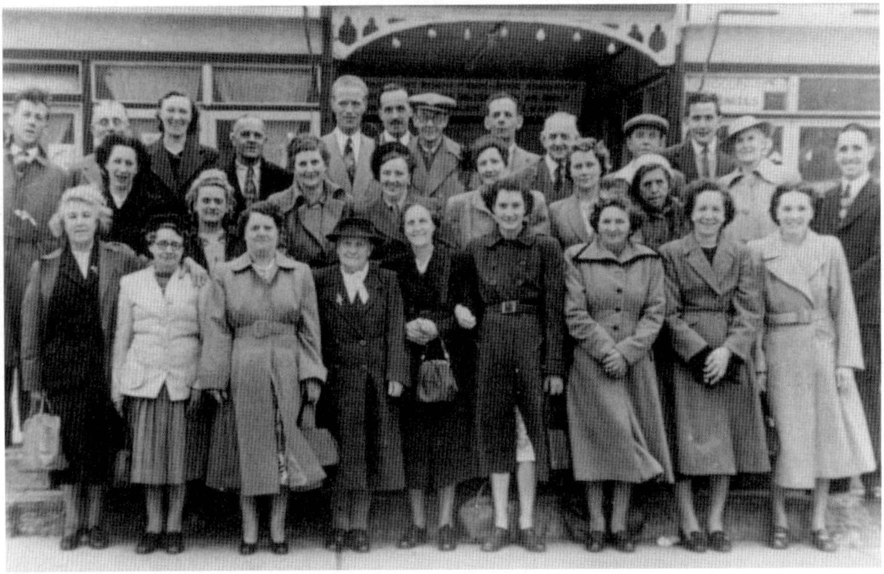

Annual Staff outing to Weston Super Mare where J.G. Brenner, owner of the Grand Pier Weston, bestowed the freedom of the pier upon them

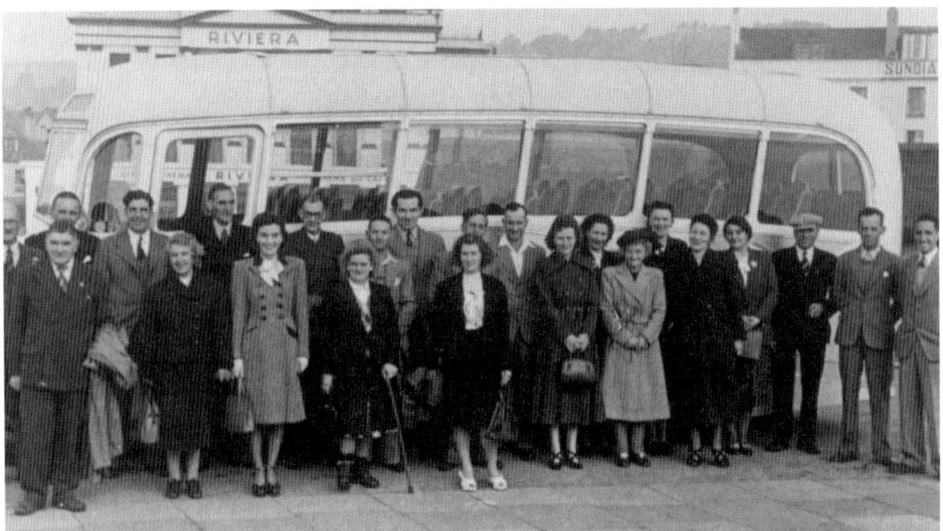

Postcard, franked 1950, shows the sunken gardens, a useful retreat from strong sea breezes. They were particularly attractive when illuminated at night

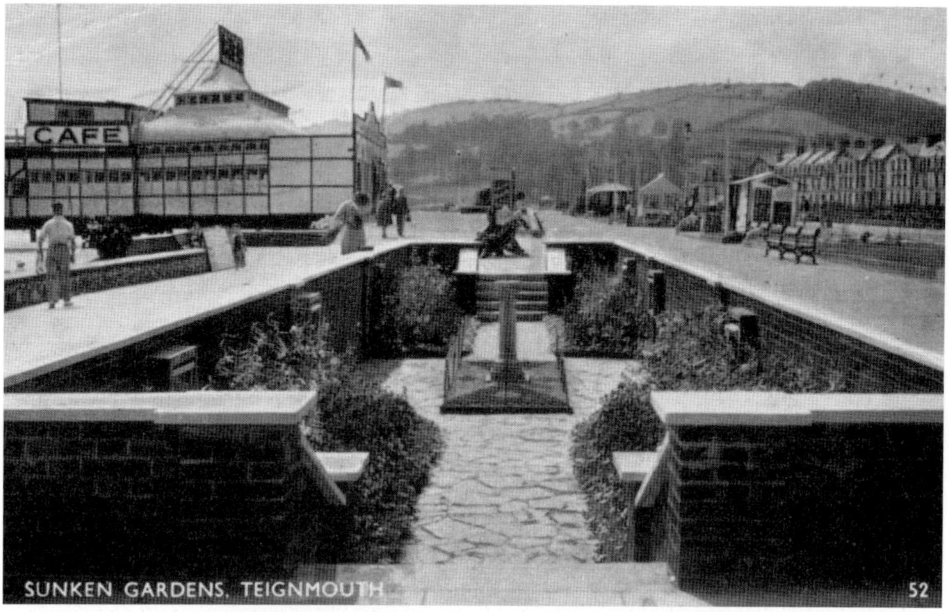

Overview from the Riviera Cinema balcony early 1950s

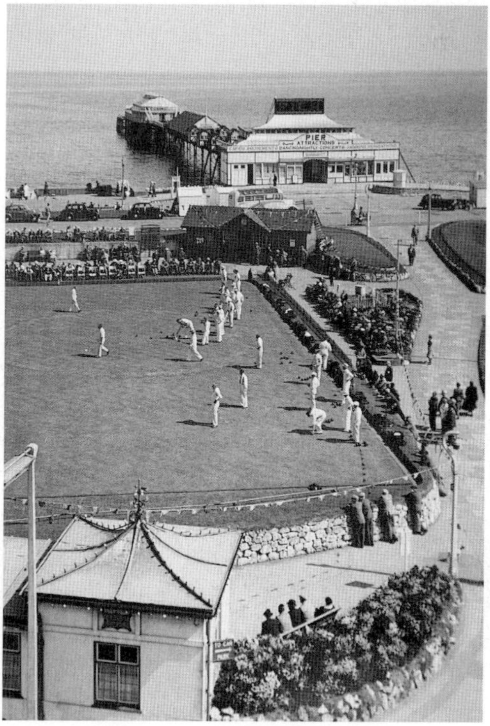

Overview from Eastcliff late 1950s by amateur photographers Elizabeth and Reginald Lewis

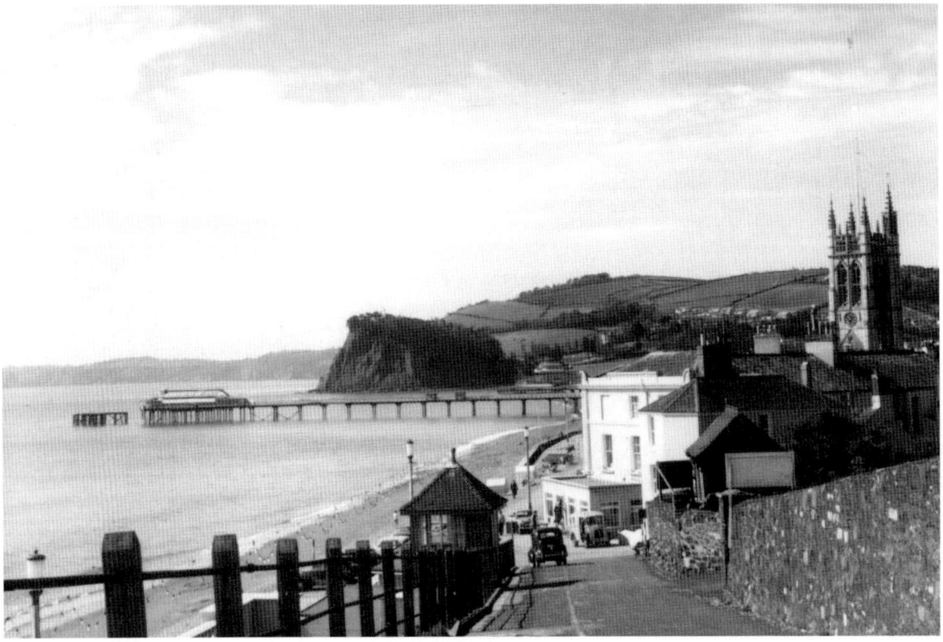

About 1955.
Back L-R: Harry Sessions : Mr Finch : Harold Rodwell : Mr Steer : Ted Sessions
Front: Young Terry Farleigh sits with two visiting workmen, billeted in his parents' house. Boatman Bill Boyne holds a large salmon on his knee.

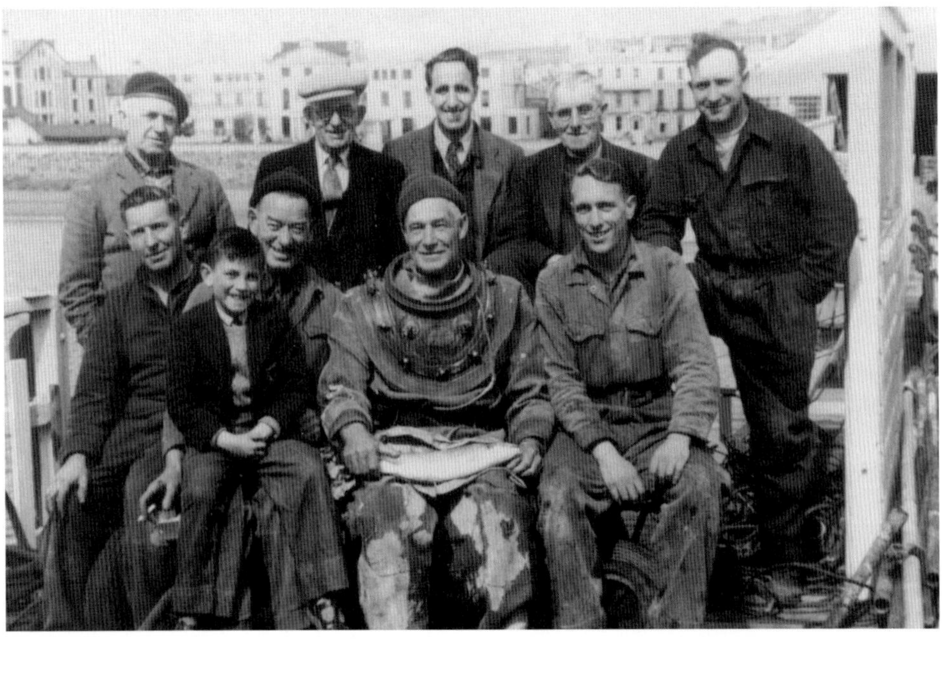

Bill Boyne dons a diving suit for publicity photographs

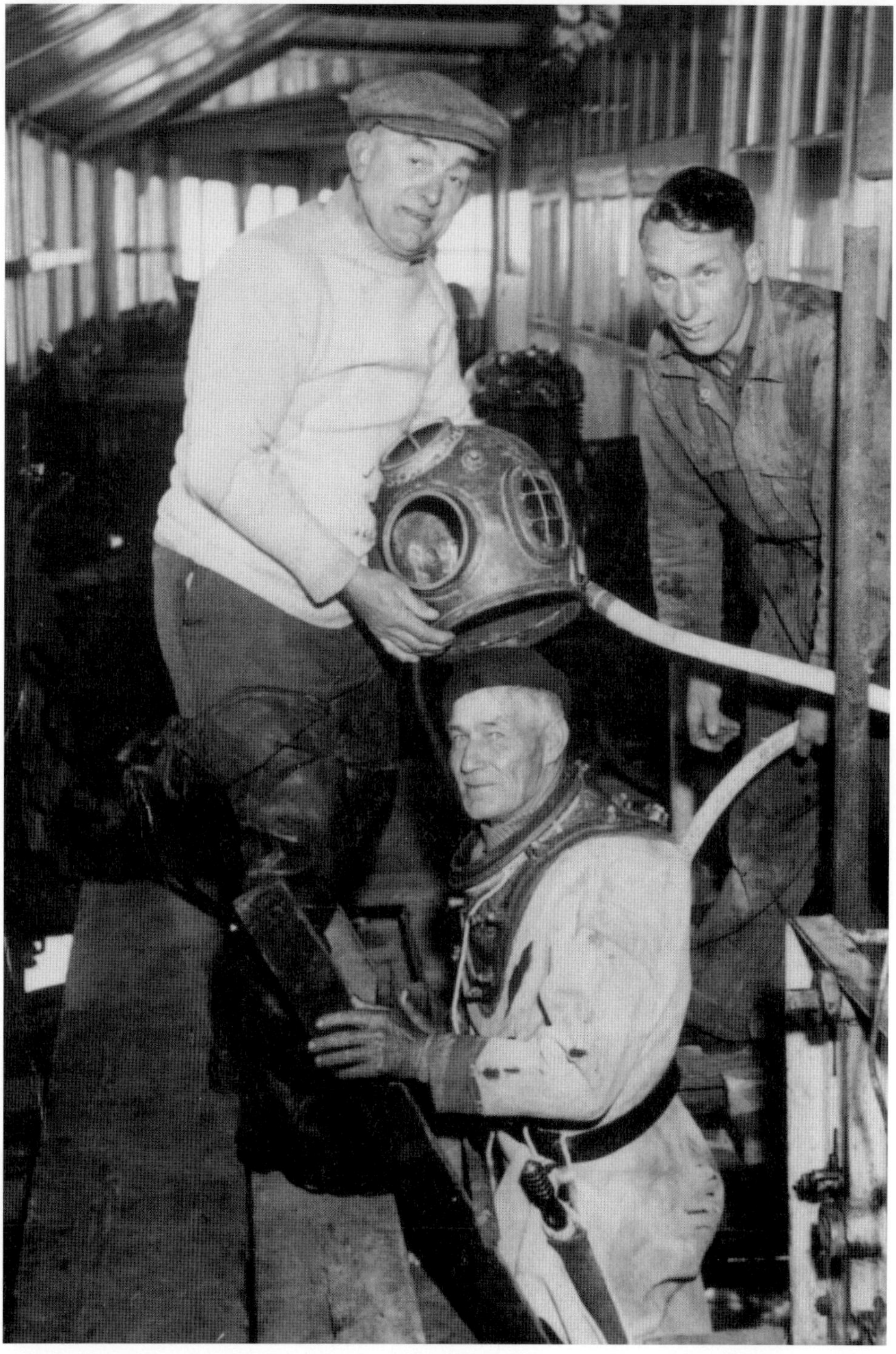

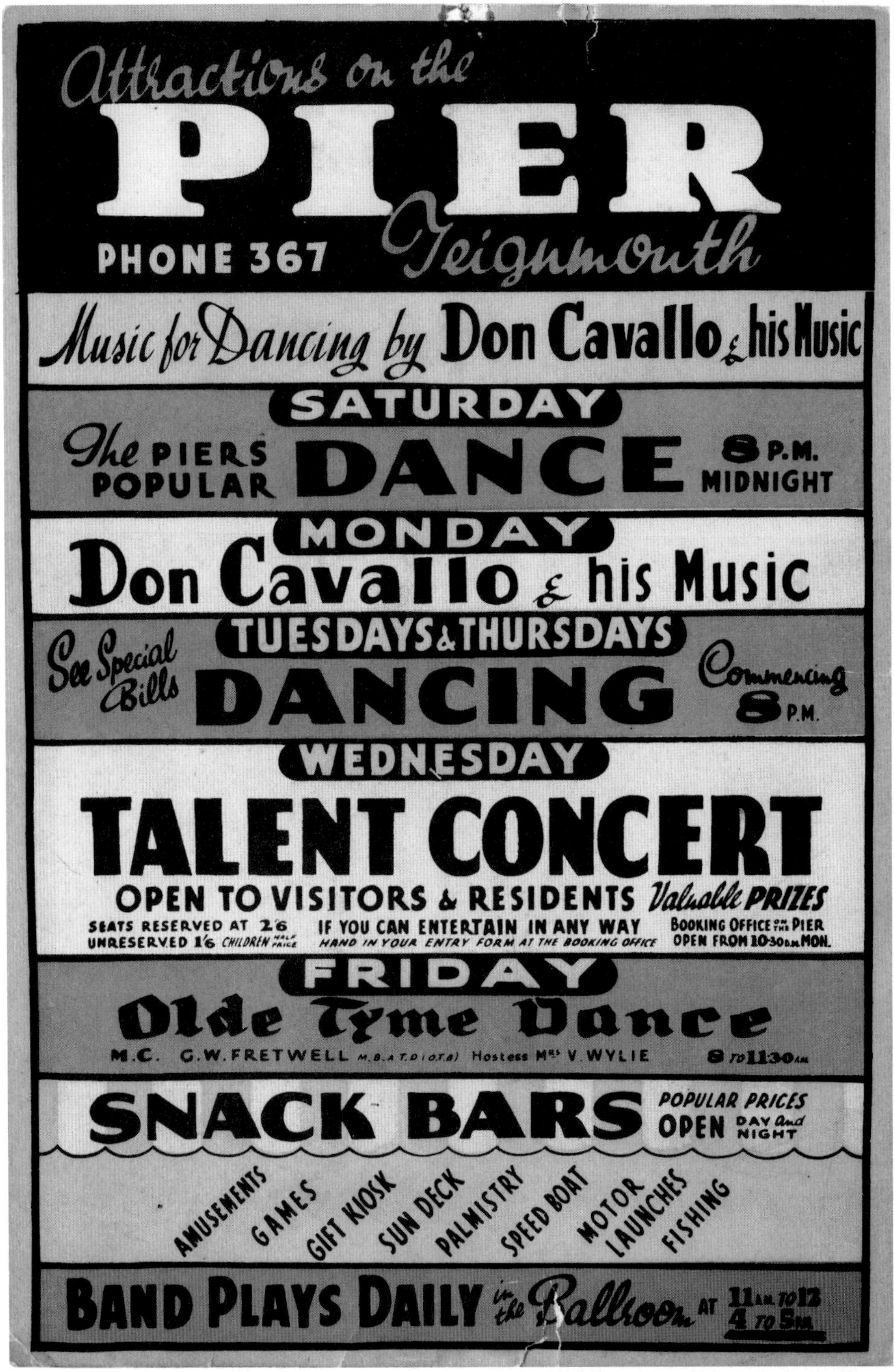

Attractions on the
PIER
PHONE 367
Teignmouth
Music for Dancing by Don Cavallo & his Music
SATURDAY
The PIERS POPULAR
DANCE
8 P.M. MIDNIGHT
MONDAY
Don Cavallo & his Music
TUESDAYS & THURSDAYS
See Special Bills
DANCING
Commencing 8 P.M.
WEDNESDAY
TALENT CONCERT
OPEN TO VISITORS & RESIDENTS
Valuable PRIZES
SEATS RESERVED AT 2/6
UNRESERVED 1/6 CHILDREN HALF PRICE
IF YOU CAN ENTERTAIN IN ANY WAY
HAND IN YOUR ENTRY FORM AT THE BOOKING OFFICE
BOOKING OFFICE ON THE PIER
OPEN FROM 10-30 A.M. MON.
FRIDAY
Olde Tyme Dance
M.C. G.W. FRETWELL M.B.A.T.D (O.T.B) Hostess Mrs V. WYLIE
8 TO 11.30 P.M.
SNACK BARS
POPULAR PRICES
OPEN DAY and NIGHT
AMUSEMENTS
GAMES
GIFT KIOSK
SUN DECK
PALMISTRY
SPEED BOAT
MOTOR LAUNCHES
FISHING
BAND PLAYS DAILY in the Ballroom AT 11 A.M. TO 12
4 TO 5 P.M.

George Brenner and his wife Paddy early 1950s

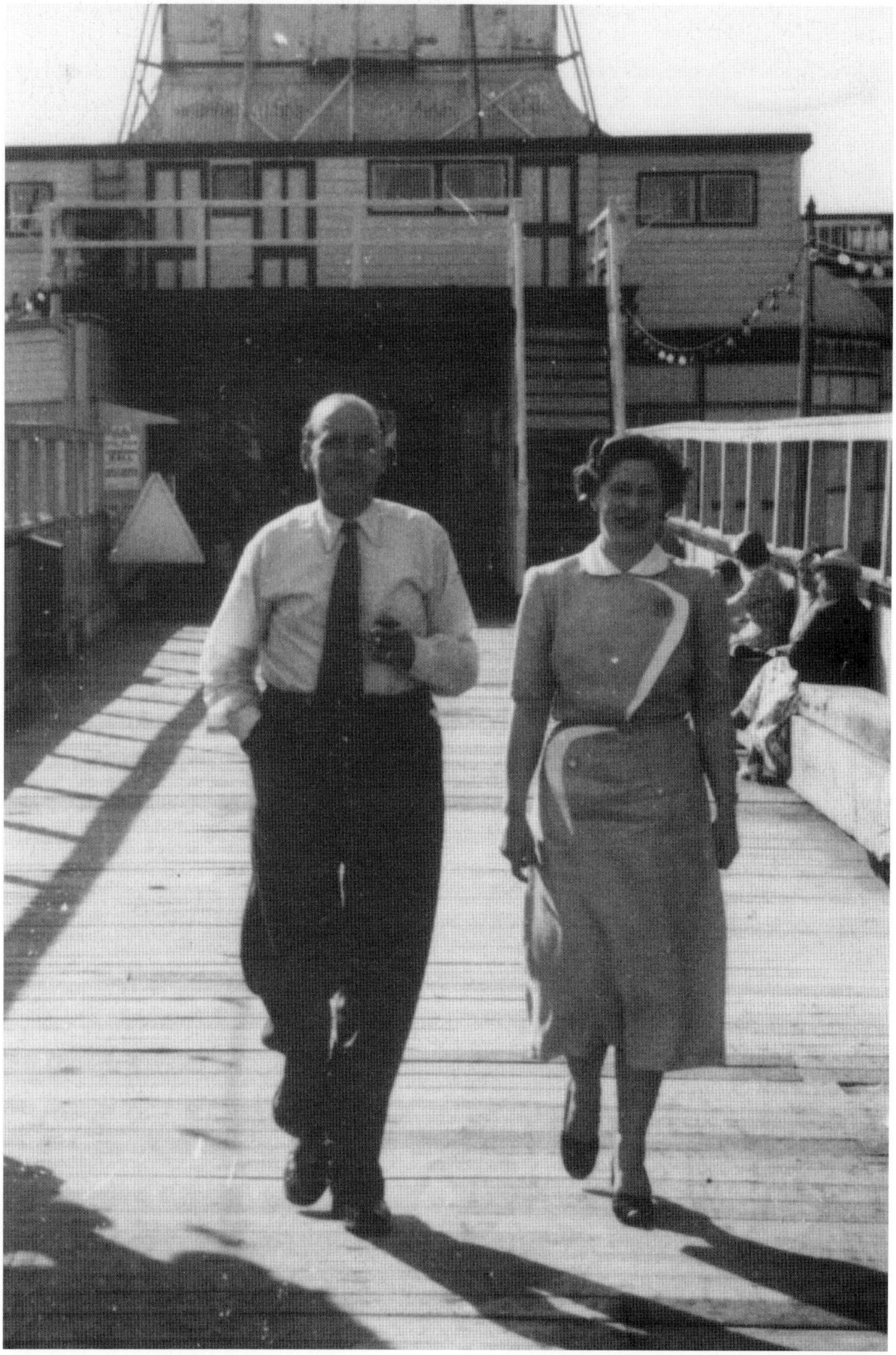

HM Queen Elizabeth II visits Teignmouth in Coronation Year

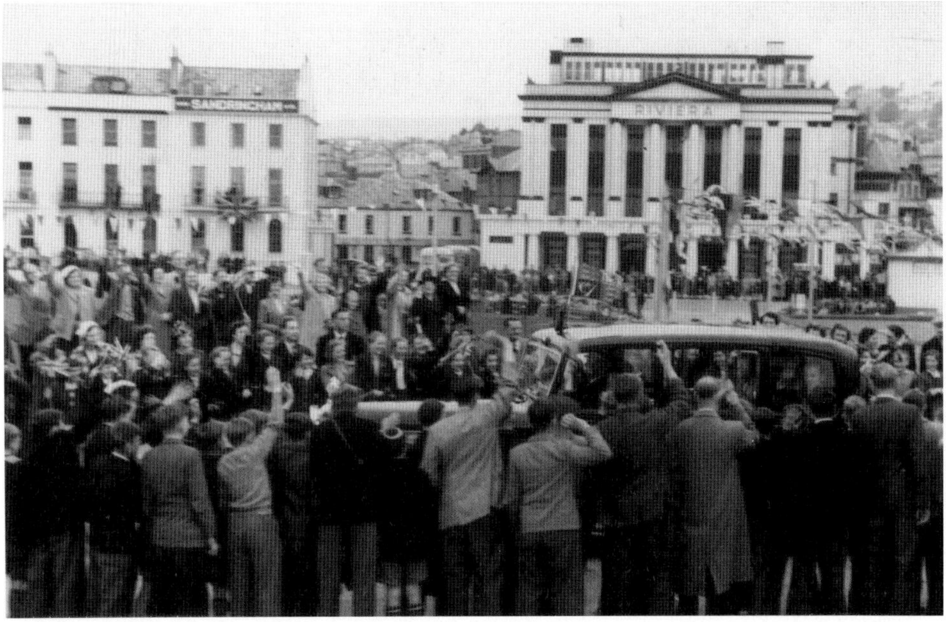

Crowds line the upper Den carriageway to welcome the new Queen

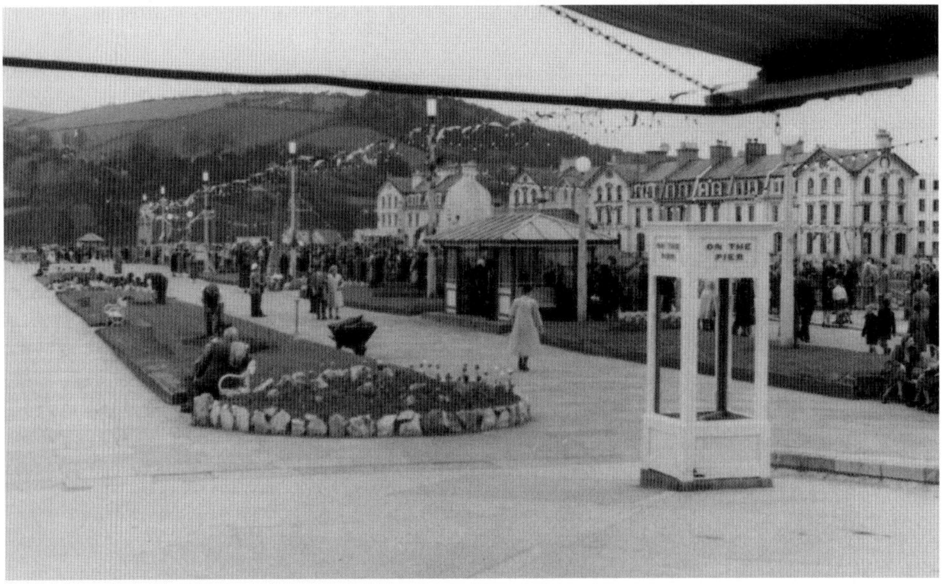

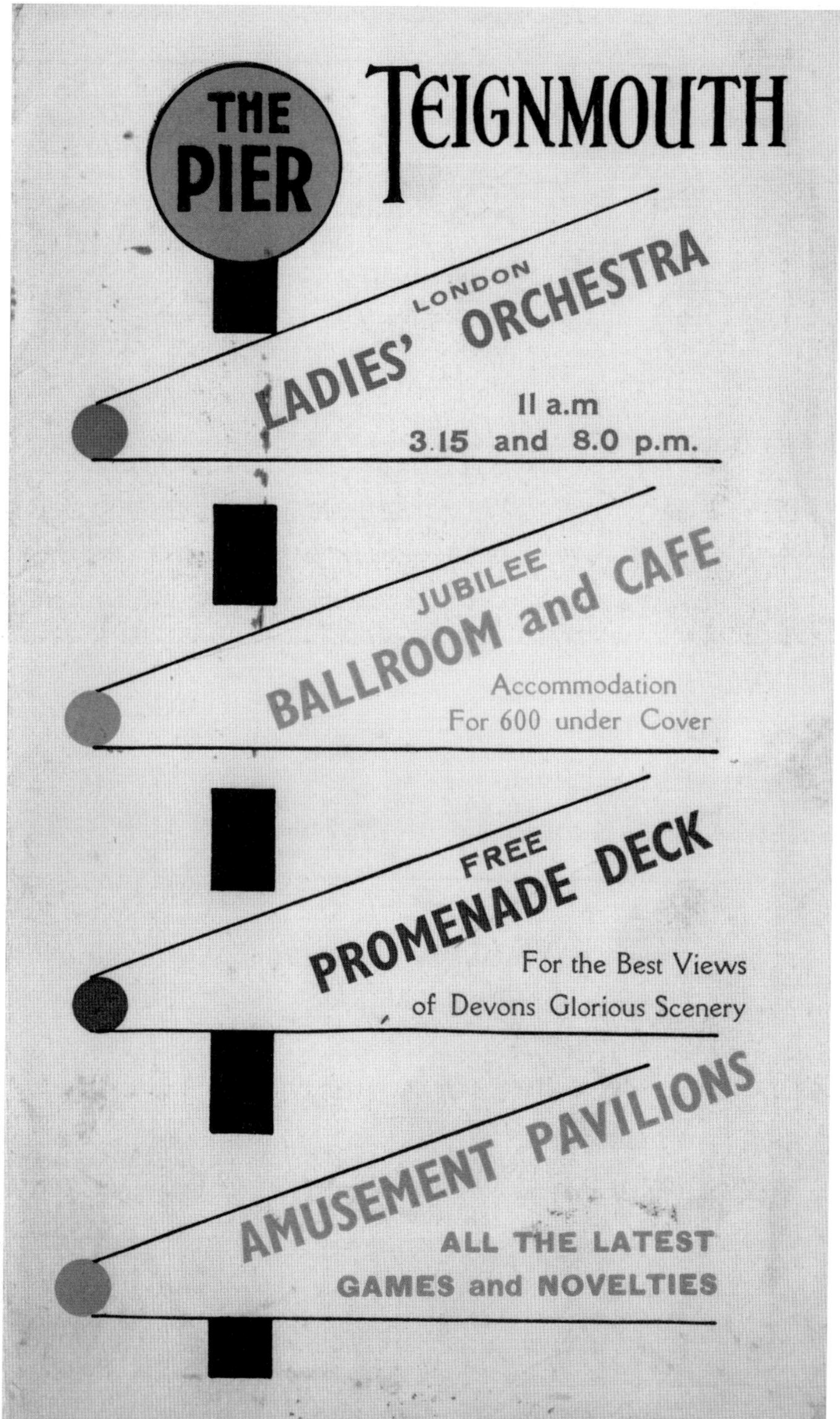
THE PIER
TEIGNMOUTH
LONDON
LADIES' ORCHESTRA
11 a.m
3.15 and 8.0 p.m.
JUBILEE
BALLROOM and CAFE
Accommodation
For 600 under Cover
FREE
PROMENADE DECK
For the Best Views
of Devons Glorious Scenery
AMUSEMENT PAVILIONS
ALL THE LATEST
GAMES and NOVELTIES

THE PIER

TEIGNMOUTH

Proprietors : TEIGNMOUTH PIER LTD. *Manager :* J. J. ANGLISS

DANCING NIGHTLY ~~in the PIER~~ **BALLROOM**
(THE HALL OVER THE SEA)
to EVELYN HARDY AND HER LADIES' BAND
SUNDAY EVENING CONCERTS - 8 p.m. to 10 p.m.
TEA DANCES every Thursday and Saturday at 4.15
(OLD TYME DANCES EVERY FRIDAY)
Morning Coffee, Teas, Ices and Light Refreshments served in the BALLROOM CAFE
Band Plays Daily (except Mondays) at 11 a.m. & 4 p.m.
Free Promenade Decks with Amusement Pavilions
Motor Launches & Speed Boats leave Pier Head daily

THE PIER - Teignmouth's One Bright Spot

THE PIER

Proprietors: Teignmouth Pier Ltd. *Manager:* G. Brenner

The ***CENTRE*** *for all attractions*

DANCING
CONCERTS
AMUSEMENTS
SNACK BARS
GIFT SHOPS
SUN DECKS
MOTOR BOATS
SPEED BOATS
Etc., Etc.

Paddy Brenner (facing) and daughter Sonja, beside the postcard gondola

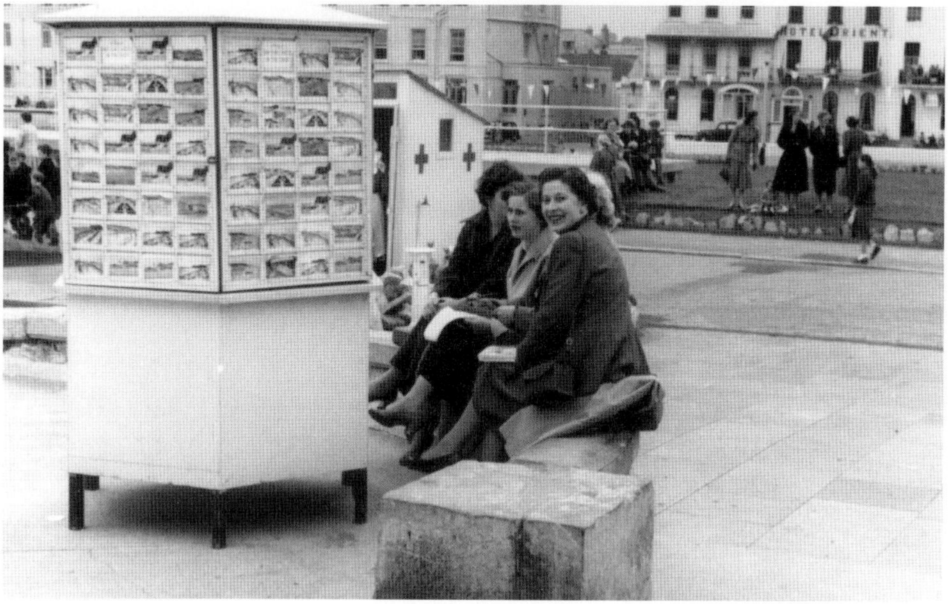

Two huge buoys stored on the deck during the off-season. The Devon Violets range was on sale in one of the kiosks

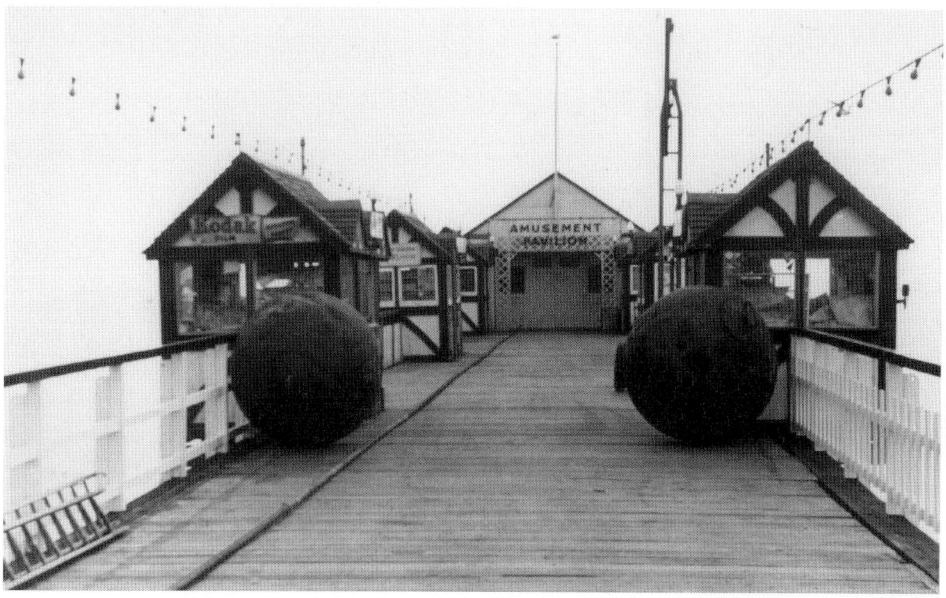

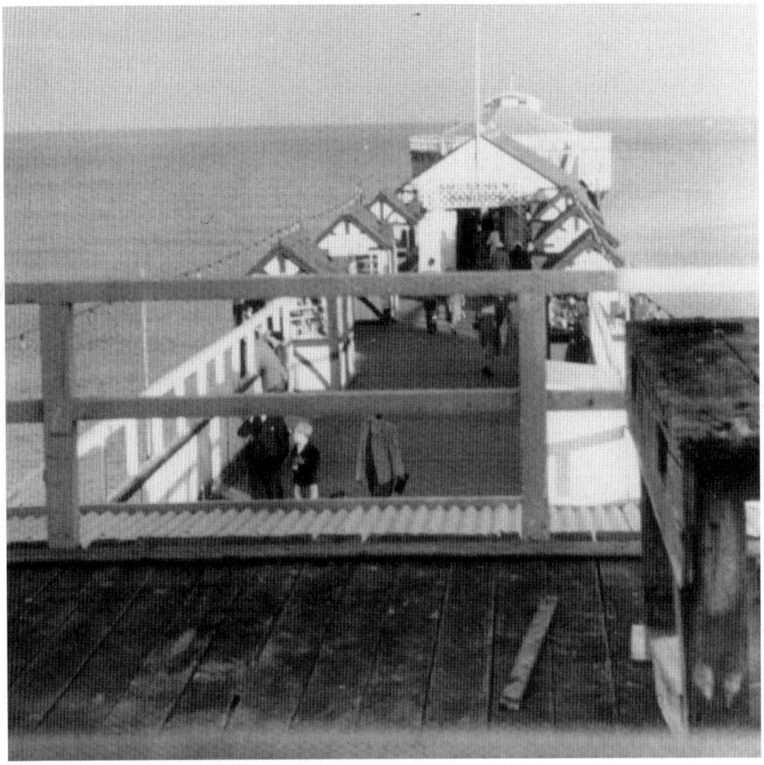

Middle pavilion from the upper deck

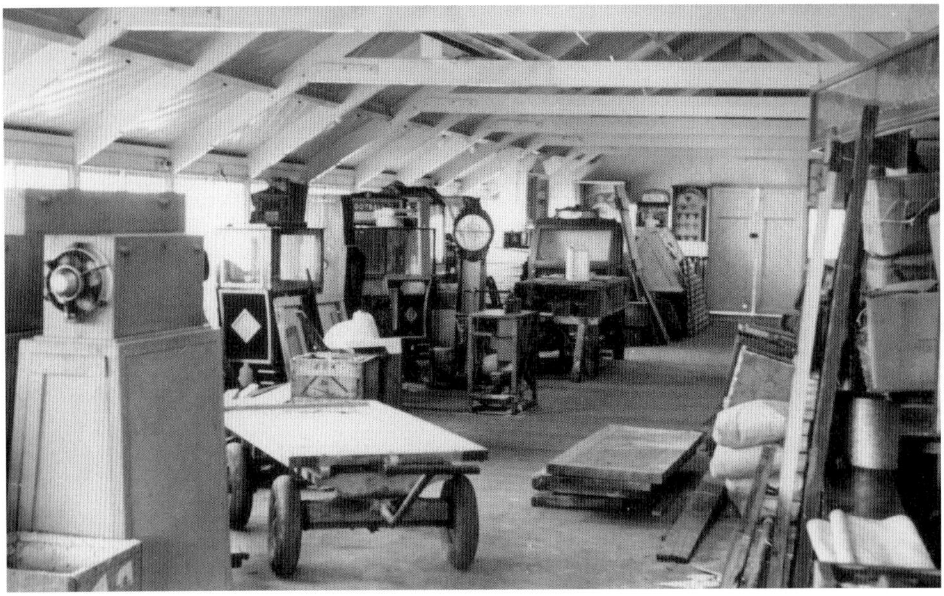

Winter repairs to machines inside middle pavilion

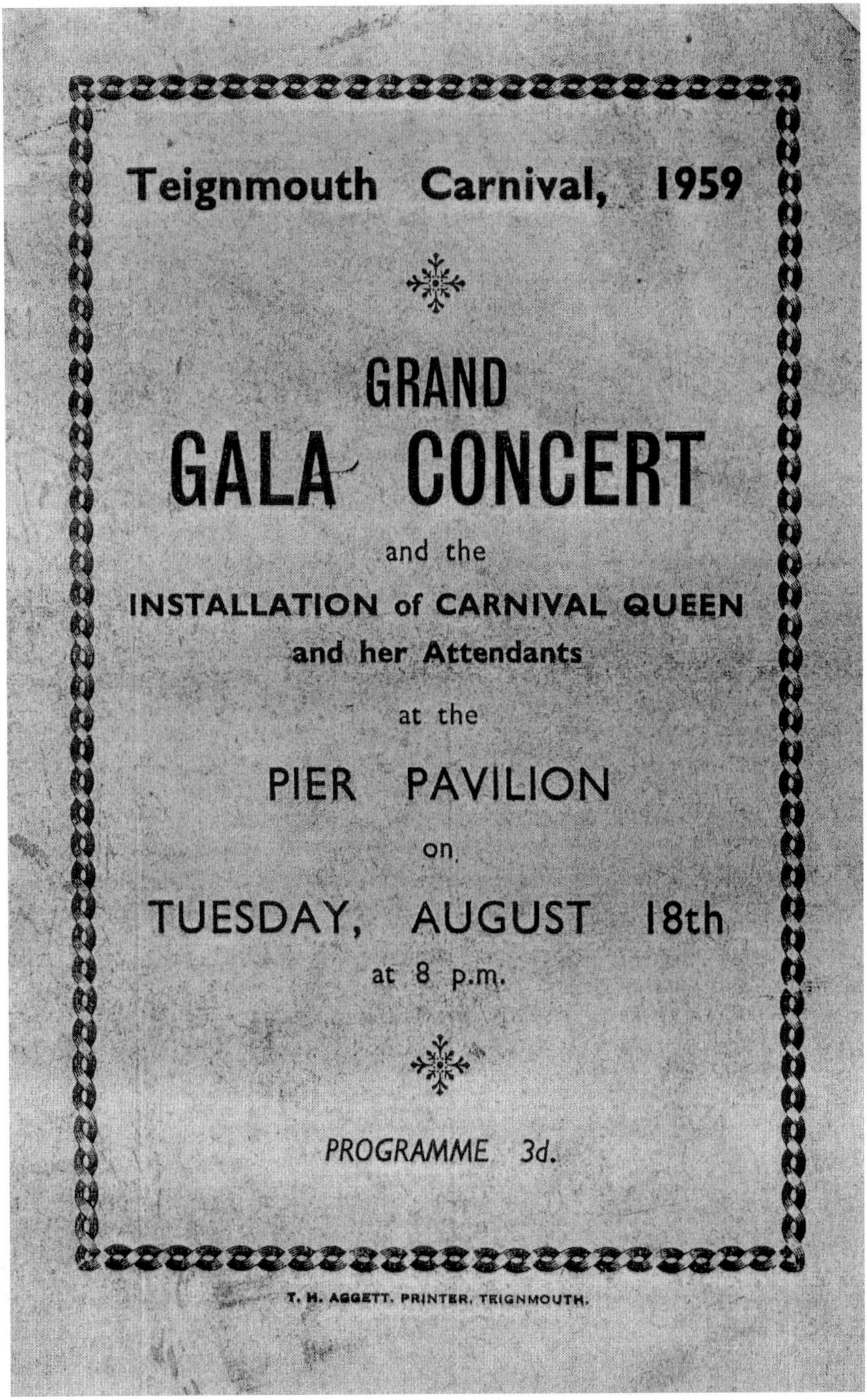

Teignmouth Carnival, 1959

GRAND
GALA CONCERT

and the

INSTALLATION of CARNIVAL QUEEN
and her Attendants

at the

PIER PAVILION

on

TUESDAY, AUGUST 18th
at 8 p.m.

PROGRAMME 3d.

T. H. AGGETT, PRINTER, TEIGNMOUTH.

CHAPTER 4

Headlong into the Swinging '60s when life would change forever

Owners 1961 to the present day - The Brenner Family

Changing values and greater liberty created in the 1960s resulted in young people challenging authority and asserting their right of choice, a situation that was blamed by many on The Beatles. The pier ballroom fell from favour and 1962 marked the last dance. After managing it for 7 years, George Brenner bought the pier in 1961 and was joined by his son Anthony in the business. The pier slipped into a period of ill fortune that escalated after a tragedy in February 1963. George F. Rossiter, optician and meteorologist of Orchard Gardens, went out to check sunshine recording equipment on the ballroom roof. Repair work to the deck was in progress and he slipped from a plank, fell into the sea and was tragically drowned. Before the demise of the jetty, burglars used a boat to get out there one night, broke into the middle pavilion and stole several bags of coins. They attempted to take their haul on a flat topped trolley but the weight of it broke through the planking of the bridge to the landing stage. The wheels became embedded in the deck and the bags of coins slipped off into the sea. Another unplanned slip occurred when maintenance worker, Ted Sessions, fell into the waves from the pier and broke his leg. Seasonal wages in the early '60s averaged two shillings an hour.

Although the landing stage was still popular with anglers, it had become unsafe and in need of extensive repair after withstanding almost 70 years of battering from the waves. Its original purpose of managing passengers on and off large pleasure boats was no longer required so the decision was made to demolish it. Acetylene cutters were used during demolition of its deck and after everyone had gone home one night, some pitch pine burst into flame. A crew went out in Brittania, climbed up a 12 foot rope and successfully fought the fire. Removal of the piles supporting the landing stage was a challenge, requiring the use of dynamite applied by two divers from Torbay Sub Aqua Club.

Music had faded forever within the ballroom now standing without its old jetty companion. The last 12 years of its life were as a store and workroom. Locals were saddened by this regrettable end, and were similarly affected by the closure of the Riviera Cinema nearly 40 years later. Realistically, both venues were victims of changing public demands and represented a classic situation of "Use it or Lose it". As the decade drew to a close, Teignmouth Pier was about to enter the worst decade of its life.

A last look from the Torquay Rd. The ballroom and landing stage face extinction as does Morgan Giles shipyard

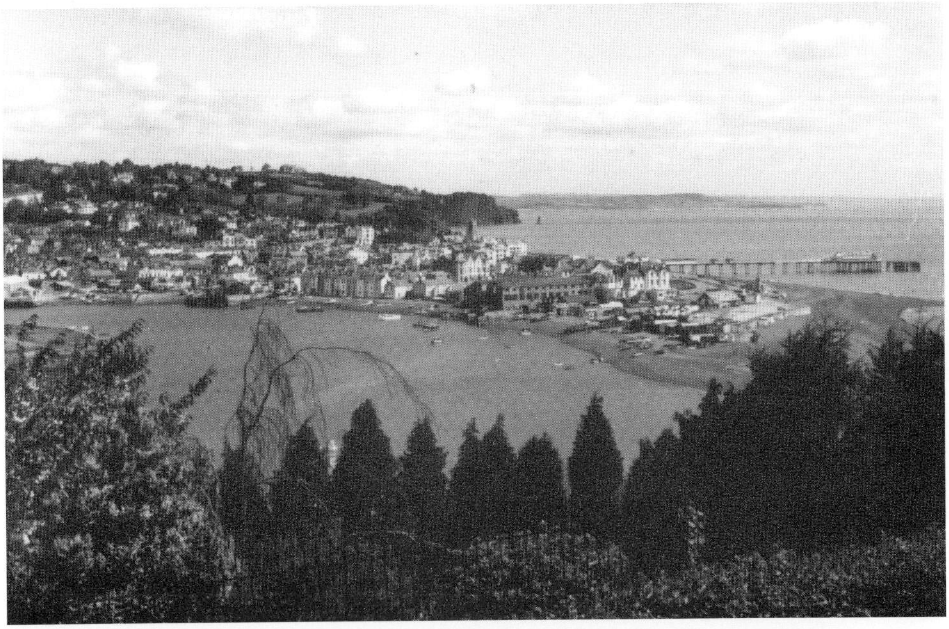

Waves broke through the Amusement Hall floorboards during high seas in 1963

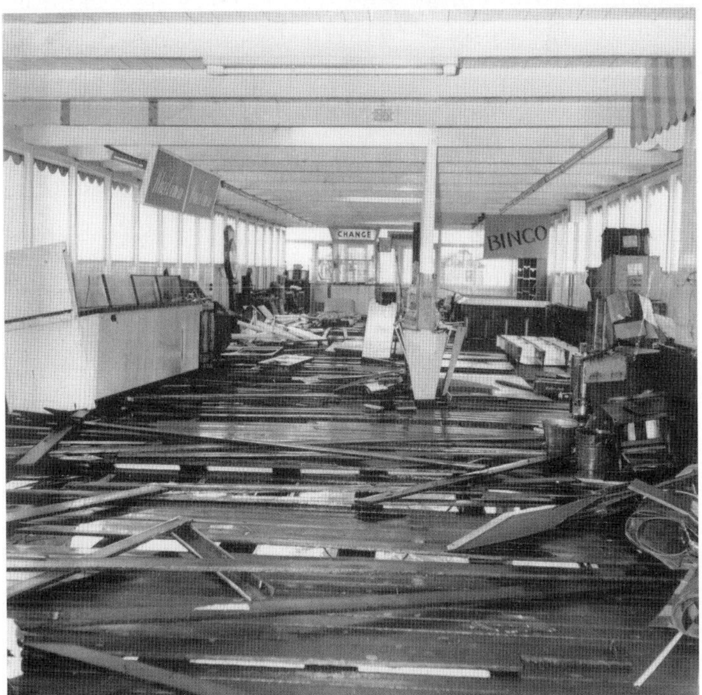

Record-breaking snowfalls in January 1963

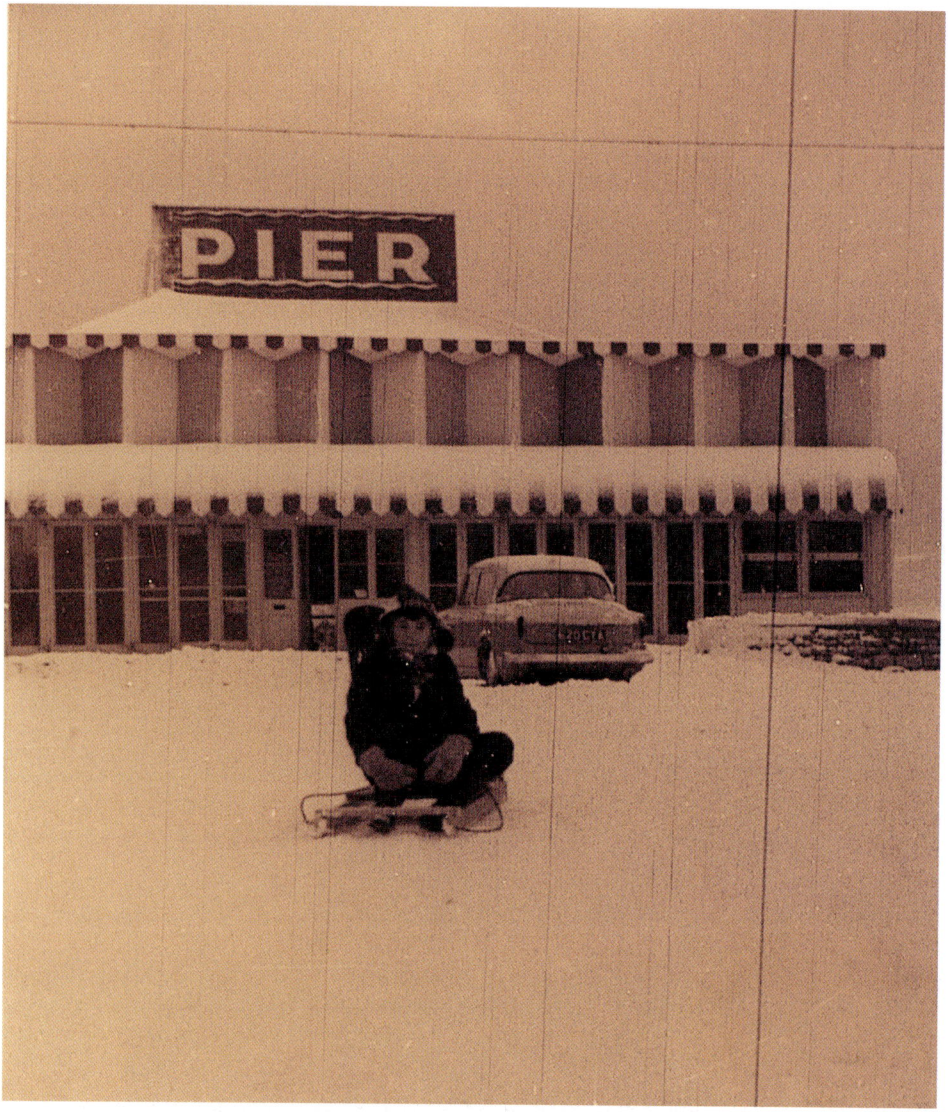

Coin operated Voice Recorder is displaced during a storm

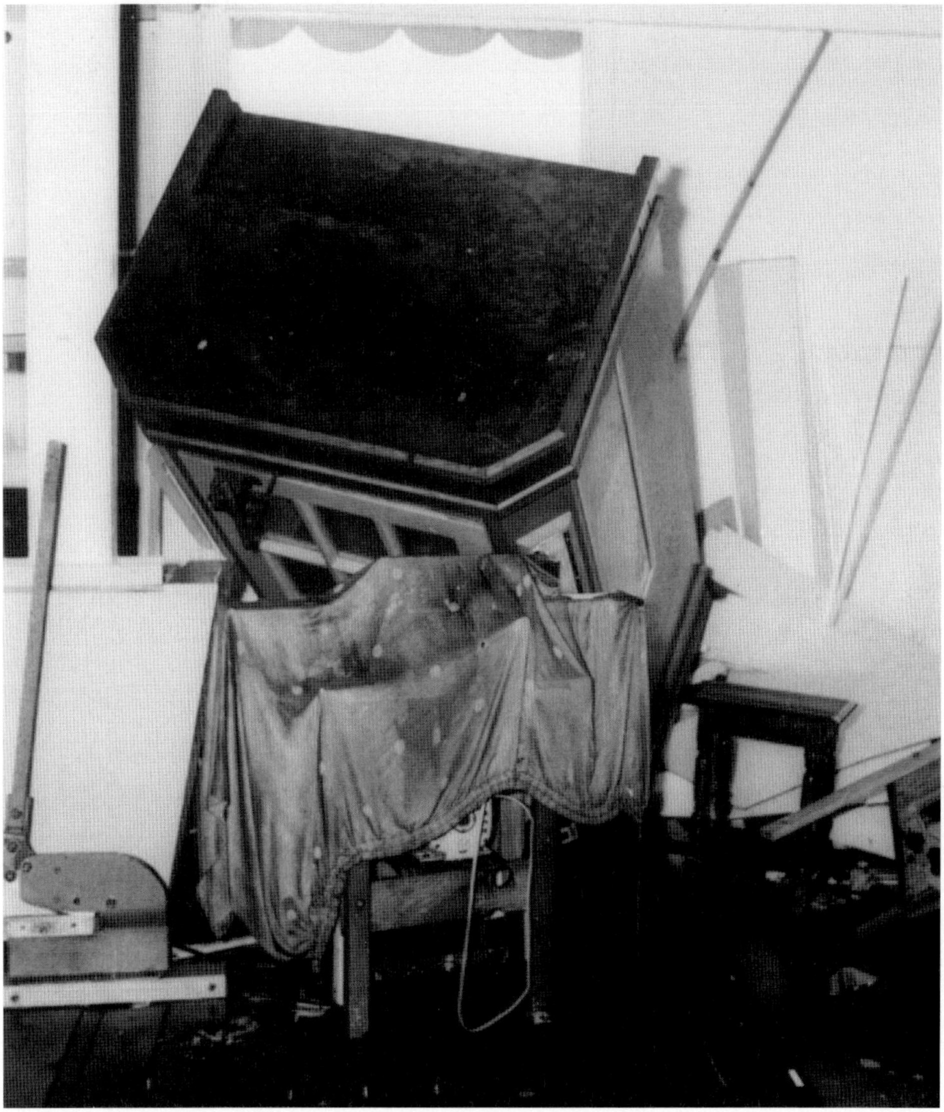

Floor boards have lifted exposing the beach below

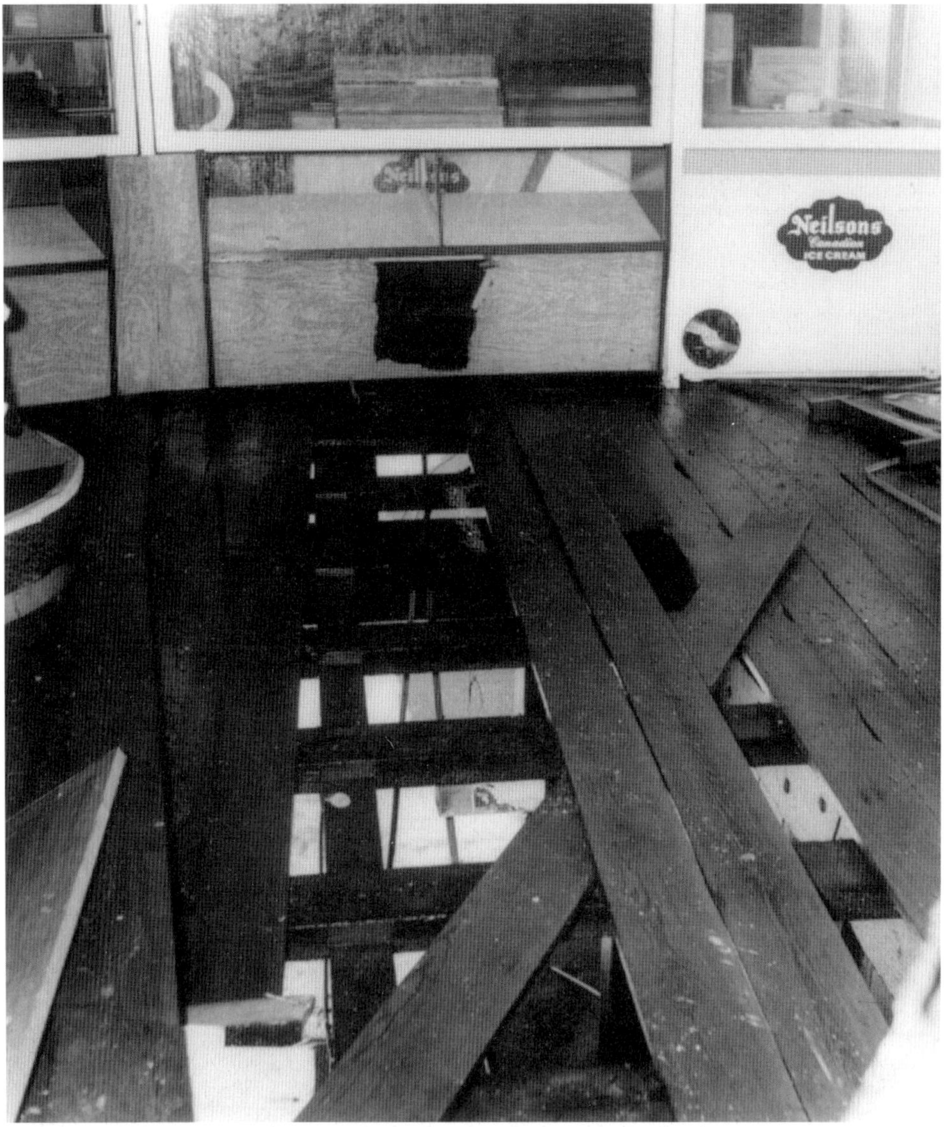

Cllr Sparrow, TUDC Chairman, surveys the damage

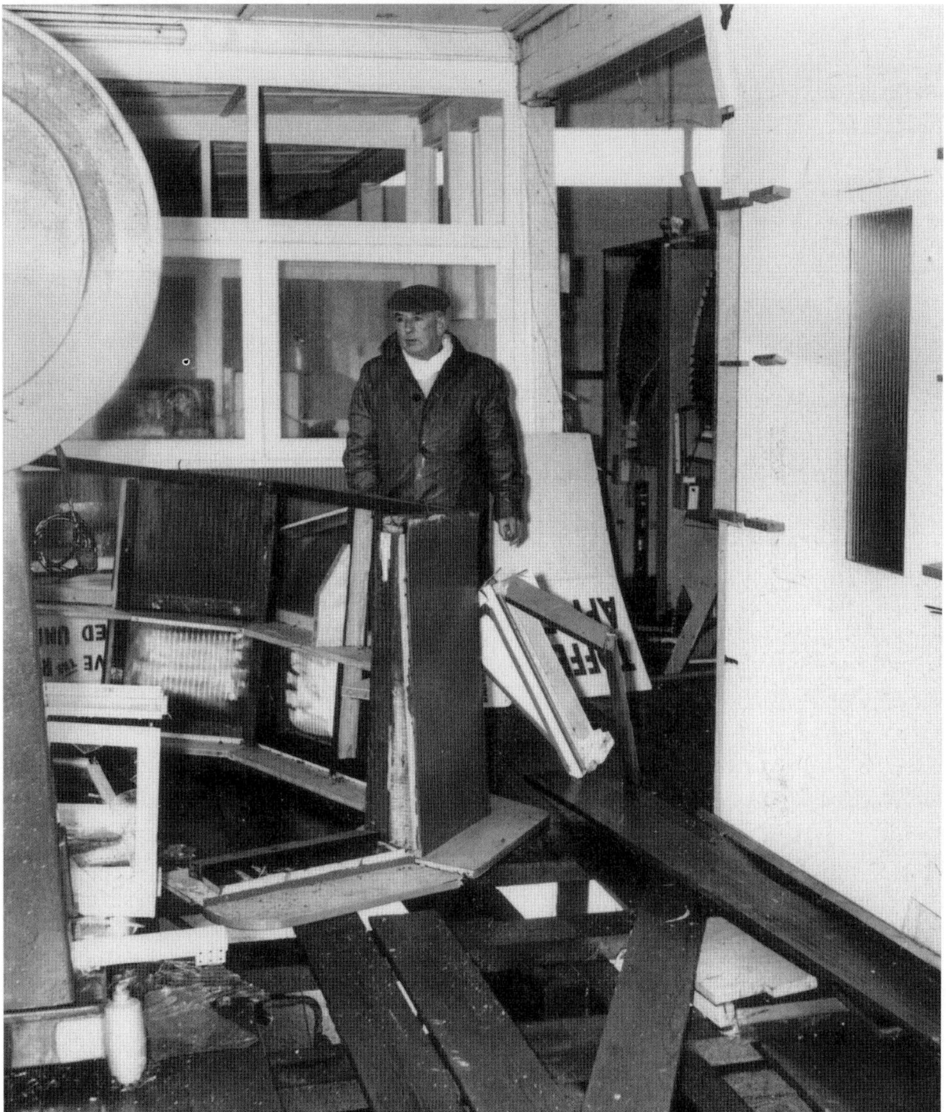

Ballroom minus the landing stage, removed 1963

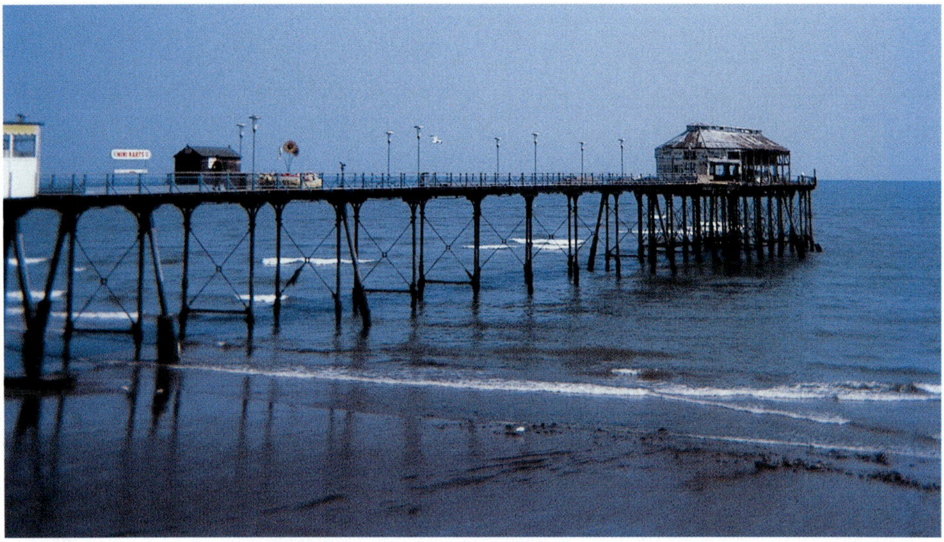

January 1965. Engineers failed to secure the new concrete trestle to the pier deck and it was knocked over by wave pressure. A new one was installed at the engineer's expense

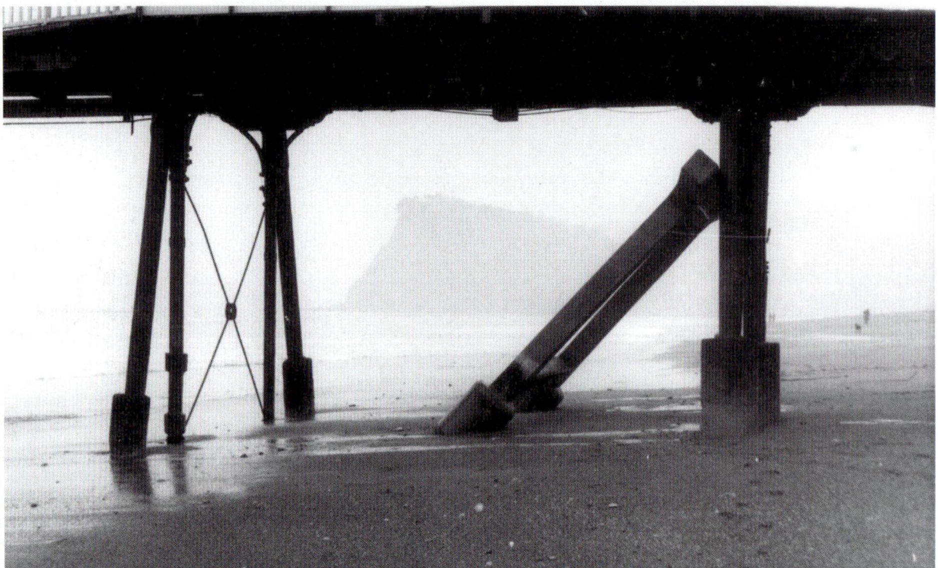

Architect's plan of existing ballroom in 1974, prior to proposed renovation

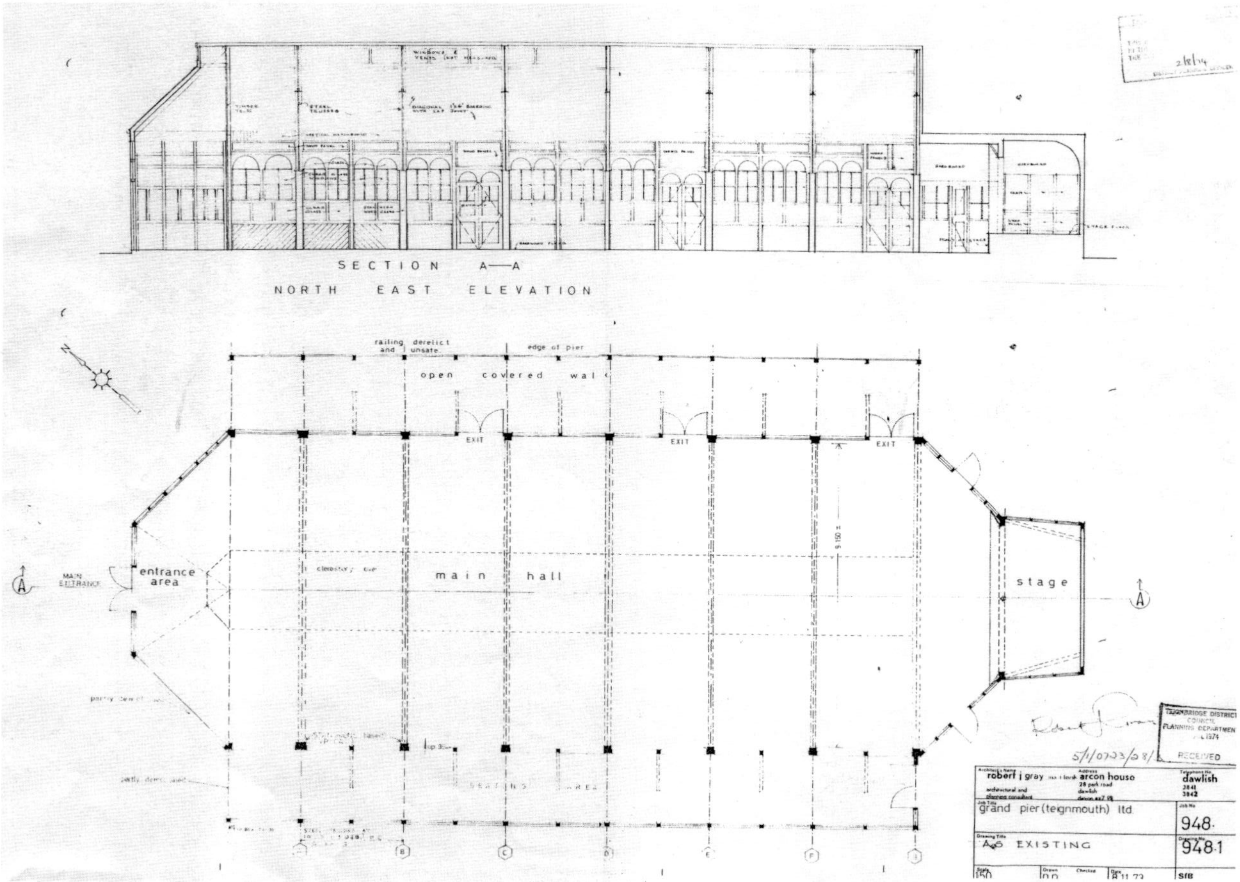

Chapter 5

Pier celebrates its century, survives its worst decade in the '70s and rises again

Did tarot cards and a 300 year-old crystal ball assist Rosina the Clairvoyant foresee what was in store during the worst decade in the pier's history? We shall never know but discourse about the poor condition of the ballroom was seldom out of the local Press. Fears were expressed that the ballroom might even disintegrate and fall into the sea. The change to decimal coinage in 1971 and increased taxes in 1972 caused another down-turn. During the final two years of its life, Teignmouth Urban District Council endeavoured to force the Brenners into upgrading the pavilion ballroom, closed a decade earlier. The Public Health Act of 1961 gave TUDC the power to bring the pier under their control. Cllr Arthur Bladon, pursuing his policy of fair play for the public, was on a Devon County Council committee that prepared a bill to enable them to force the owners to improve or demolish. This "get tough" approach led to the County Council lodging a Bill with Parliament empowering TUDC to serve notice that unless improvements were done, the council themselves would undertake the work and charge the pier owner for it. The ding-dong battle was tedious and drawn-out, the council failing to accept George Brenner's explanation that 60 feet was improved each year and 120 feet were still needing attention. New decking cost £50 per foot at that time. The council rejected plans for a second storey on the landward end to compensate for lost storage if the ballroom was demolished. Proceedings against the pier were not started by TUDC because Teignbridge District Council took over as part of nationwide local government reorganization. It was not long before a deputation from the new District Council arrived to announce that the pier was now under the Public Health Act of 1961 and unless the ballroom was renovated or demolished, the council would do the work and send in the bill. Plans were made for a £10,000 facelift to encase the ballroom in sheets of blue and cream plastic-coated metal and use it for additional attractions. Work got underway with Murphy's of Shaldon ripping off the old panels but the plan foundered on the rocky shore of planning permission. Finally, it was the untimely death of George Brenner that caused the plans to be abandoned because Anthony simply could not fund it alone. A compromise was eventually reached. Permission would be given to extend the front hall along the deck by 50-60 feet if the ballroom was removed. Accordingly, demolition was undertaken in 1975 and a go-kart track laid in its place.

Teignmouth Pier experienced a year that easily qualifies for what our Queen described as Annus Horribilus. A series of groynes were installed as part of sea defence works despite opposition from the Boatmen and Watermen who feared significant sand loss. Their predication was correct and suddenly the pier's foundations lay exposed and undermined. Closure seemed inevitable after the Council Engineer pronounced it dangerous and issued a damaging report warning the public not to go on it. Emergency repairs to encase the foundations in £12,000 worth of concrete made it possible for the pier to stay open all season. Early the following year, part of the sea wall collapsed and a State of Emergency declared by Teignmouth's first mayor, Cllr Edward Card. Thousands of tons of sand were brought in and plans for new sea defences rushed through. County Councillor Wilfred Heggadon pushed the project forward and the firm of E.Thomas undertook the £600,000 scheme, opened in June 1977. A plaque recording the Heggadon Wall is next to the steps to the west of the pier.

Nationally, the future was looking bleak with only 40 of the country's 100 piers still operating. It was believed by some that none of the old piers would survive to the year 2000. Just as things could get no worse there was an unexpected upsurge of interest in Victorian art and architecture. It coincided with an announcement that a National Piers' Society would be formed, involving several organizations and trusts affiliated to the Amusement Industry.

By the end of the decade, major strengthening works and refurbishment was still ongoing, accounting for a further £70,000 worth of investment. A new Malayan hardwood deck, held in place by 30,000 stainless steel screws, was installed, allowing the public to walk to the end of the pier for the first time since 1962. It represented ten years work by pier staff including Jim Williams, Barry Rollason, followed by Malcolm Williams and Kieron Beeks under Anthony's leadership. The 1980s marked an upturn in fortunes and at last, things began to pick up and the business extended to a corner of the Den with the Jolly Roger Play Park and its Tornado radio-controlled boats, discoboats and aquabugs. Pier punters could enjoy some 200 games of skill or hope with the old fashioned Allwin ball types up to the latest electronic machines with about 90% still only costing a penny-a-go! The grab crane and palmist from the 1920s were still in use as well as five other machines that had given a quarter of a century service dishing out rolls of sweets from the bagatelle-based game. New technology from Japan arrived in the form of £5000 laser disc machines offering video views from cock-pit seats.

Thousands of tons of sand were moved from one end of the beach to the other in a beach management programme in 1989. A tipper truck ran into one of the pier's 50-foot lattice steel spans and connected with a 240-volt mains electricity cable. Fortunately the cable was not severed, or the driver would have been killed. The Contractors were ordered off site on the grounds of irresponsible behavior. Improving commerce created sufficient optimism to plan a £300,000 investment for a higher deck to be built above the entrance hall, designed to incorporate a glazed atrium shaped like a huge diamond. Unfortunately the plans did not materialize at that time.

About 10,000 brightly coloured balls were tossed into the waves when the deck was lifted by a significant storm in 1987. A new fun deck was developed with five different rides such as the Hestair Hope Fun House and GoGator. Ambition knew no bounds and a £12,000 pirate ship was purchased. Weighing in at 2 tons, it was too large to be brought in through the entrance so the Royal Navy from 771 Sqdn RNAS Culdrose used a SeaKing helicopter to fly it in. The task became a military exercise involving soldiers from the Royal Engineers and Royal Corps of Transport working with the RAF pilot to collect the pirate ship from Picket Head Hill, near the Ness. Howling gales did not inhibit public interest and hundreds turned out to watch the spectacle that progressed faultlessly.

Anthony Brenner develops his new change-giving machine after the arrival of decimal coinage in 1971

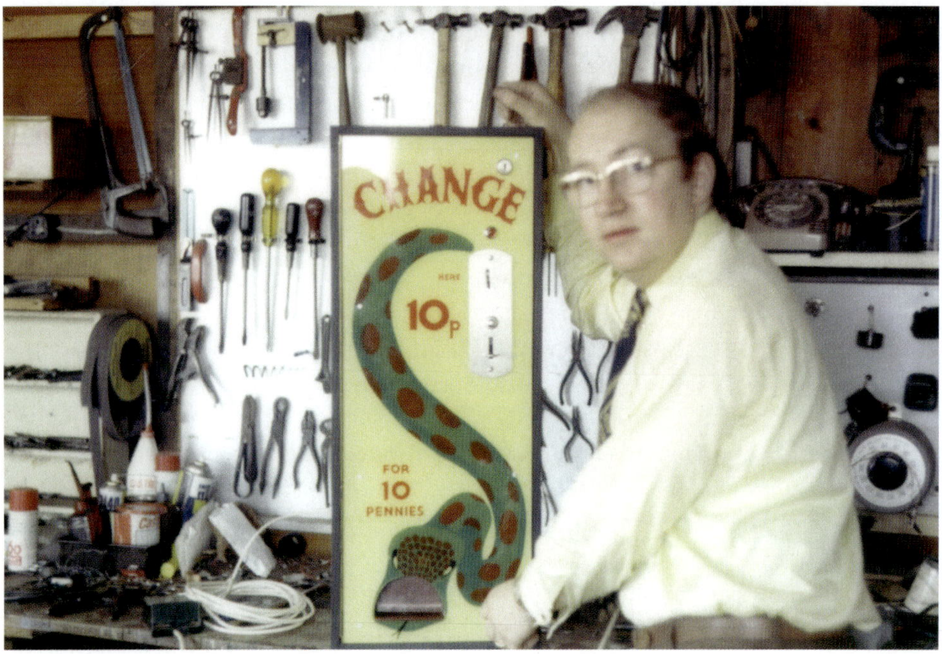

A look of desolation surrounds the ballroom as a fresh breeze stirs everything in its wake

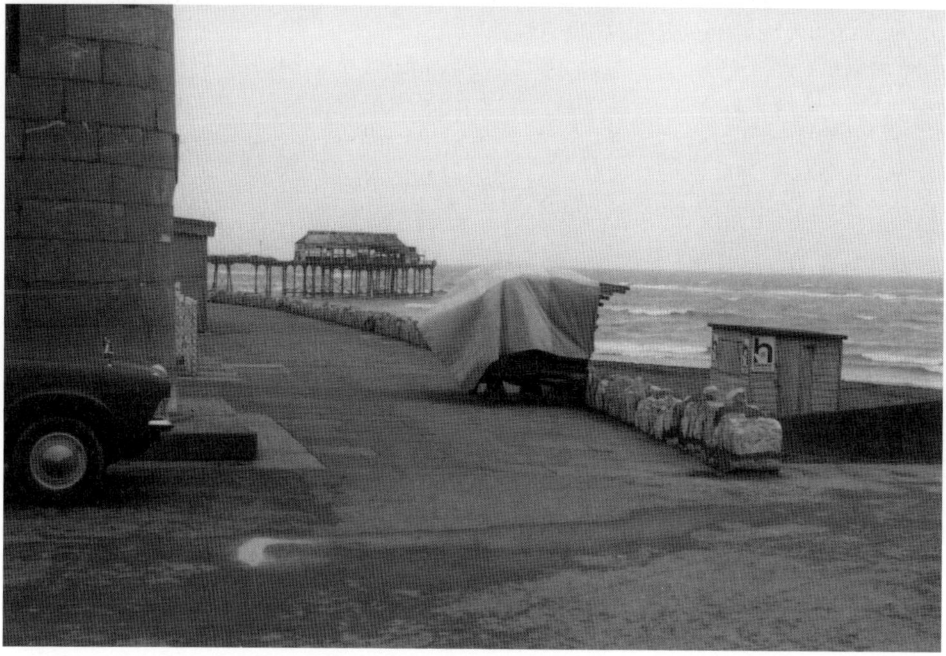

Ballroom cladding stripped away during demolition 1975

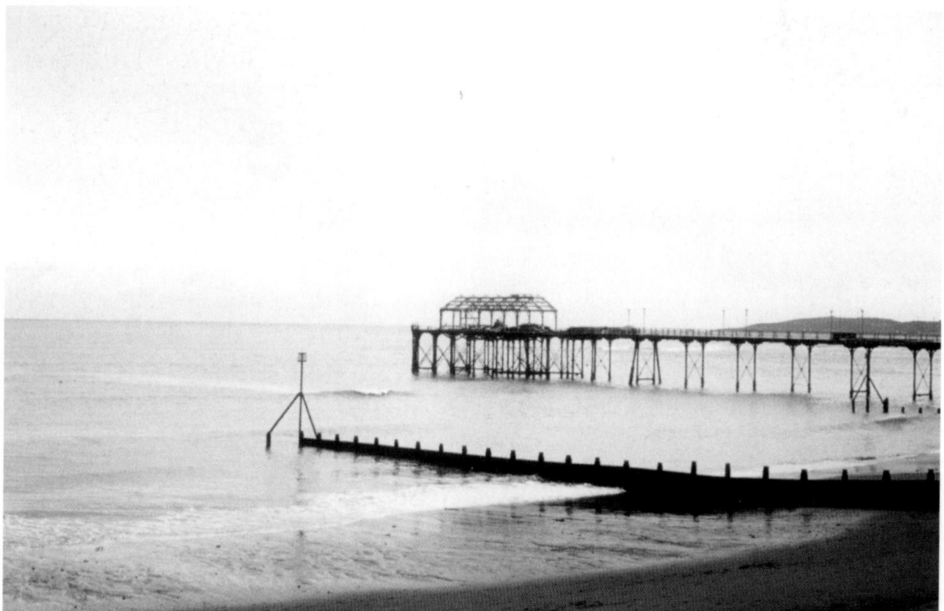

A gaping void appeared on the promenade in February 1975

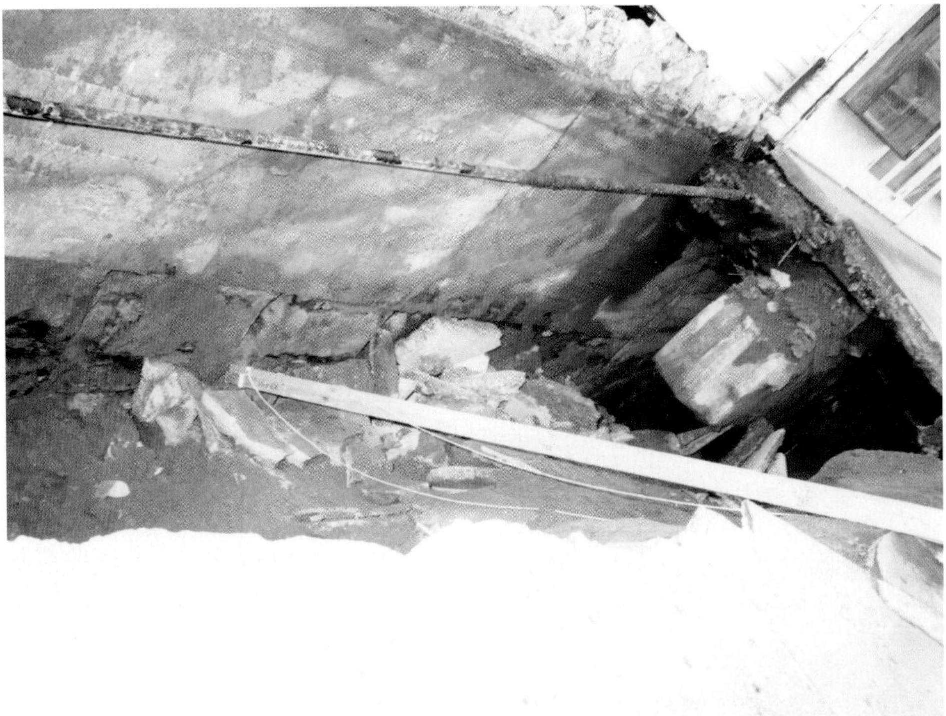

Construction of the Heggadon Wall 1975/6

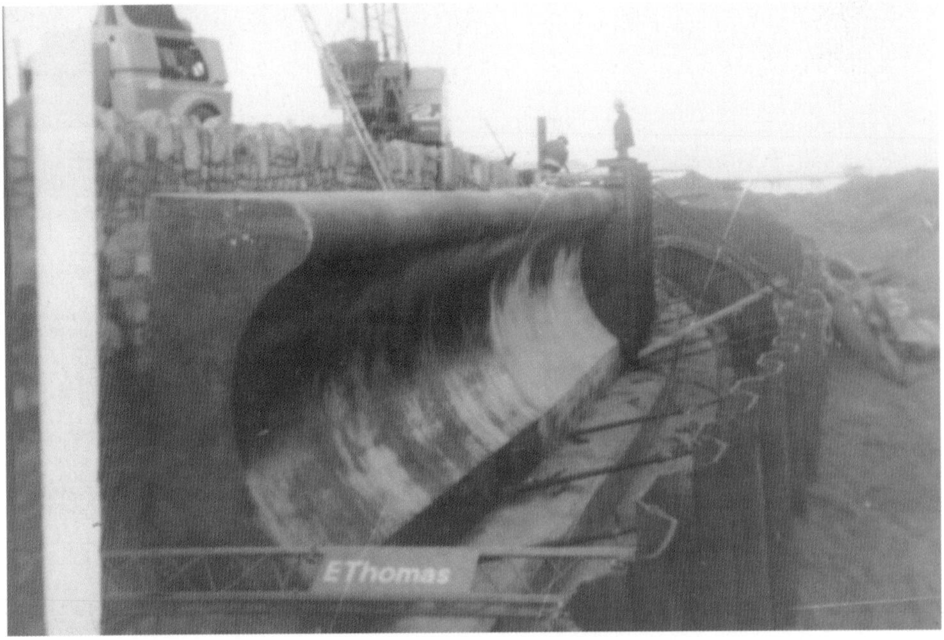

More works in progress during 1979

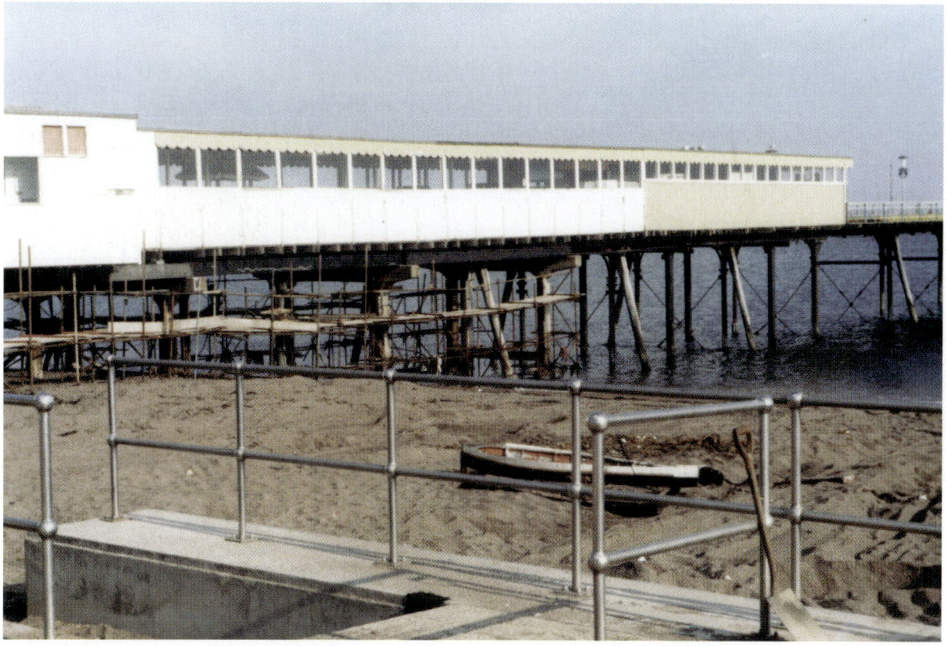

Completion of installation of two new pairs of piles under seaward end of pavilion, 1970s

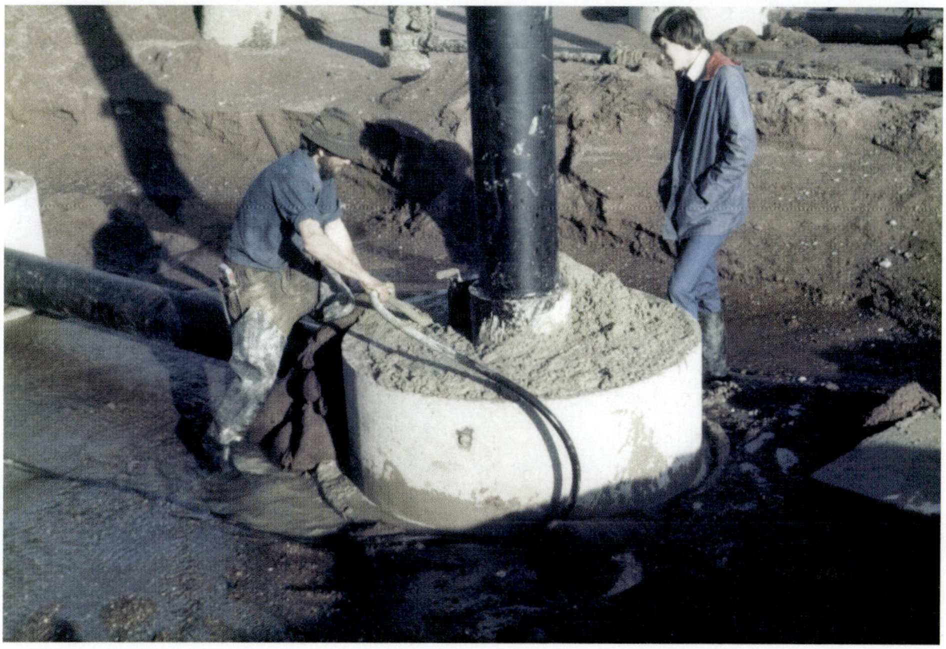

Malcolm Williams (L) and Kieron Beeks preparing GoKarts for the 1979 season

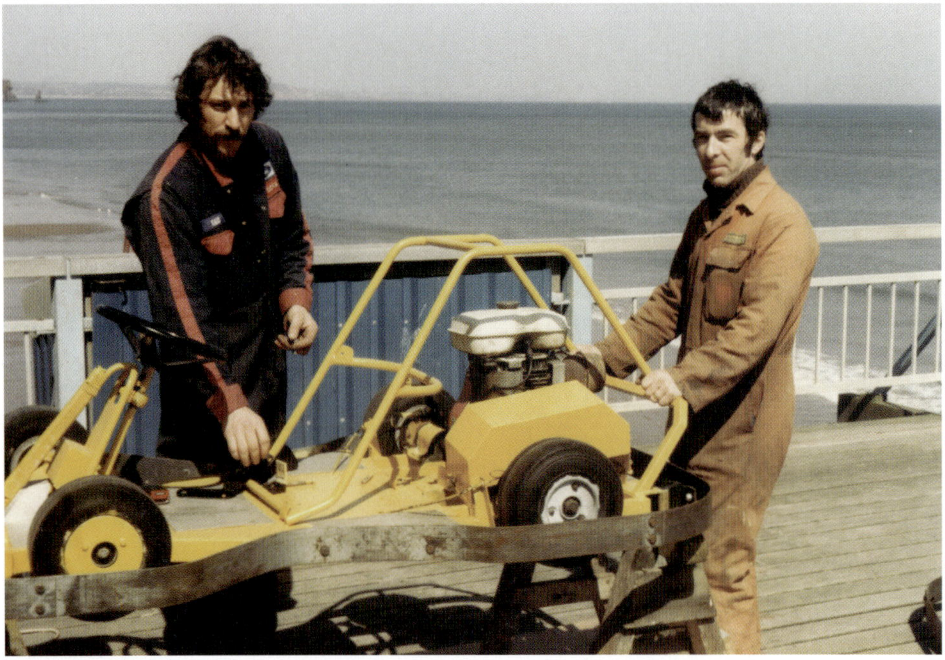

Having fun at the machines 1978

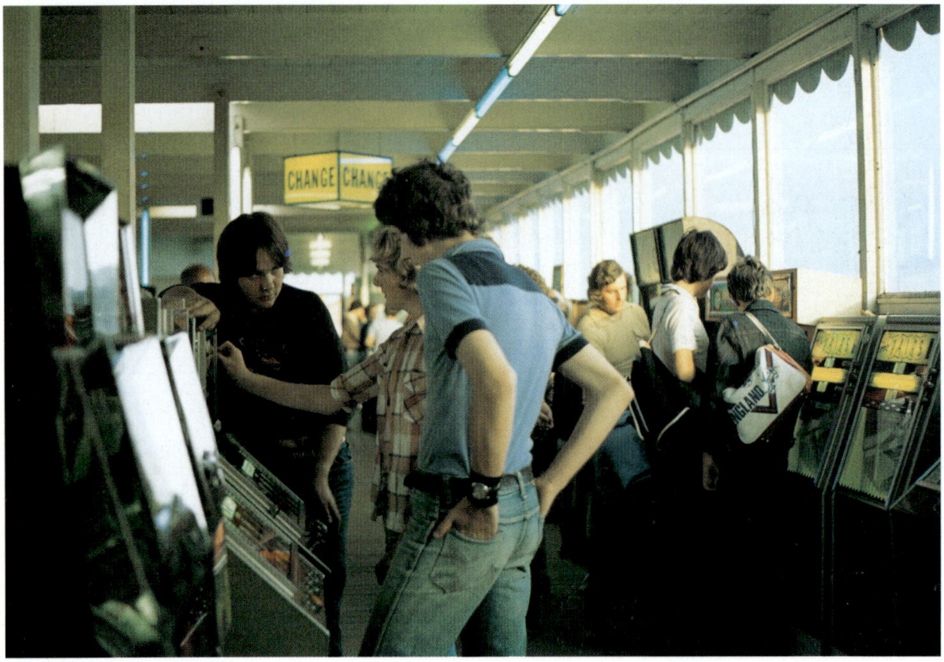

SeaKing Helicopter from RNAS Culdrose flies in with the 2-ton pirate ship, a new ride for the fun deck

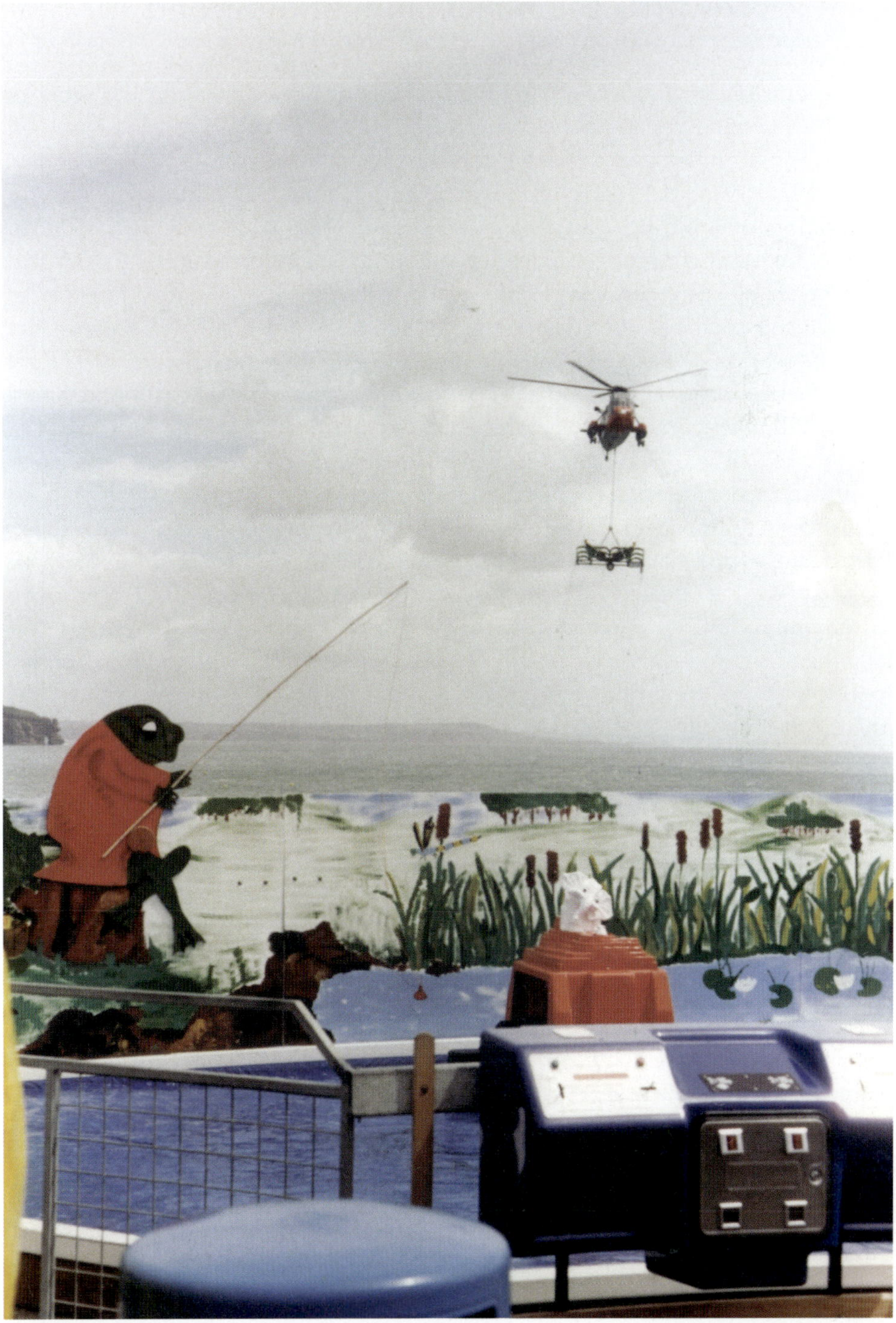

CHAPTER 6

Towards the Millennium and beyond

The decade began with a new frontage to the entrance celebrating 125 years of life. The decision to keep open all year round was made in 1994, at a time when there was discontent over the pier not having been included in a package of new fingerpost signs on the roads into town. A vintage tram was acquired and began a tradition of emitting Christmas carols each year whilst the Rotary Club collects for local charities. Licence fees on amusements shot up to £1375 and each machine was taxed to the tune of £640 a year. The so-called Fun Tax of 20% caused such an outcry that the Government did a U-Turn. Grand Pier Teignmouth, as it was now known, joined the British Association of Leisure Parks, Piers and Attractions. In 1995 it had a summer staff of 20 and attracted over 300,000 visitors. The following year, Virginia Bottomley MP launched the Year of the Pier with Anthony Brenner as Chairman. The scheme was designed to attract more visitors to piers and promote their historical and cultural relevance. Nationwide, 28 took part including Teignmouth, the 13th oldest. Part of the local celebration was the presentation of a play featuring the pier. Halfway to Paradise by Nick Discombe was presented at Teignmouth Community College. Blustery weather prevailed when Patrick Nicholls MP launched Teignmouth's contribution to National Piers' Day on the first Sunday in June with the firing of a cannon. Clouds failed to put a damper on the plans and a large marquee was erected across the entrance where the public enjoyed 14 hours of jazz, theatrical performance and radio roadshow. Crowds were calculated at around 6-7000 people. Great excitement was created through an aerial display by a Yak aircraft that swooped down to 100 feet and within 150 metres of spectators lining the deck and seafront. Enormous attention was drawn to the pier through TV Gladiator Falcon, who signed autographs for two hours. The day ended with a spectacular firework display. Grants were made to piers participating in this great event, but ironically, privately-owned Teignmouth did not qualify. Brighton's West Pier was promised a refurbishment grant of £11.6 million at this time and four other piers restored but grant aid does not keep pace with on-going maintenance. Eleven of Britain's piers changed hands in these years and several were in a state of collapse. The public tends to ignore upkeep costs of amusement palaces, imagining that the owners smile all the way to the bank. A bumper profit in-take often transforms into an equally large out-go. Whilst finding the extra costs to stage the celebration, additional capital of £10,000 was sunk into air-cooling machines and another £6000 spent on security cameras. Another £75,000 worth of timber from Borneo was installed on the deck. Renewing the pier sides in metalwork accounted for a further £8000. A new coffee and ice cream shop was installed at the entrance and the improvements contributed to its vote in 1998 as joint runner-up with Cromer in the Pier of the Year competition, run by the National Piers' Society, that selected Brighton's Palace as overall winner.

After joining the Rotary Club of Teignmouth, Anthony Brenner enabled participation of the annual Kids Out Day, when children with disabilities across the nation are given a thrilling time at a tourist attraction. Each June about 100 children enjoy a free visit to Grand Pier and its additional attractions at Jolly Roger Play Park on the Den. This event is very close to Anthony's heart and the stream of Thank You letters that follow are touching. In1997 the pier was featured in a NatWest Bank TV commercial created by a 45-man film crew. The entrance was boarded up and as the cameras rolled, huge machines created the effect of rain and wind. Several locals were handsomely paid for simply being in shot. When the advertisement finally hit the screens, it created a great deal of interest but some believed that being presented as a wet and windy place did the resort no favours. The pier is frequently featured on local television and Westcountry TV used the deck to make an award to South Devon Seabird Trust for their rescue work. The evening roost by hundreds of starlings is a fascinating side-show in its own right. Approaching in ever-changing formation, they swoop, turn and rise several times before disappearing below decks to chatter and shriek before settling down for the night.

Towards the end of the 1990s, Chancellor Gordon Brown increased licence duty by up to 36% and the National Lottery peeled away 10% of the pier's income. Scratch cards were also a threat, the chance to win a fortune for £1 sent shock waves through amusement arcades all across the country. By the year 2000 another potential outlay was anticipated to meet the cost of conversion for Euro cash on 300 machines. Teignmouth led the way by becoming the first pier in the country to install a bank-type cash machine. The need for a further £250,000 investment arose to comply with the latest fire safety requirements. A new fire escape was needed and local architect Paul Chapple engaged to design the additional elements. The result was a pair of 250-foot long walkways, five feet wide added to the sides of the entrance hall and supported by fourteen steel piles, each weighing 6 tonnes. The piles had to match the depth of the originals, driven 50 feet into bedrock. Work got underway in February 2002, the materials held in compounds placed along the seafront. At the time of writing, work is still progressing.

Public taste long since rejected the old favourites of dancing and informal entertainment in favour of fun and a bit of a flutter and it's a wise businessman who recognizes changing trends and moves with them. Grand Pier Teignmouth remains one of the few piers giving the public chance to walk its length without charge. It entered the 21st century with determination and is on course for a secure future.

New entrance under construction in 1990

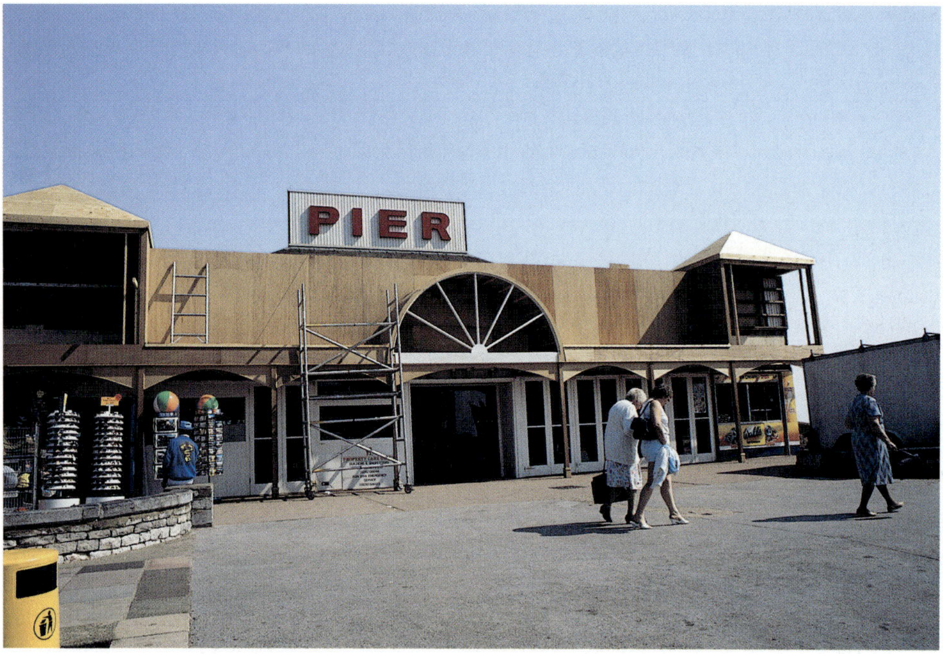

Things are on the up 1993

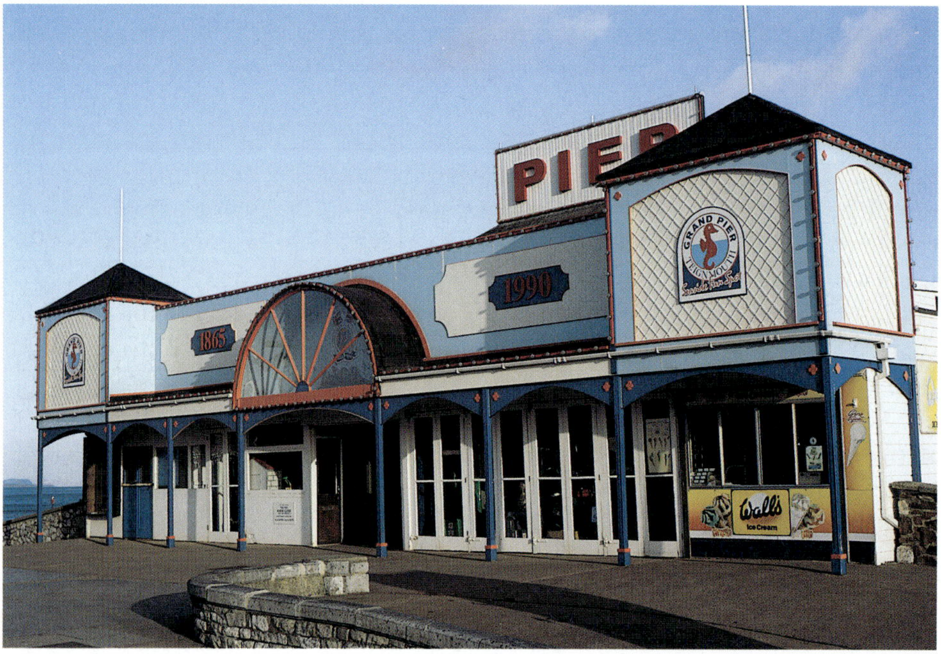

Works Team 1980s L-R: Tony Peers : unknown : Tony Powell : Claire Hammond: Helen Ridler : Malcolm Williams : Kieron Beeks

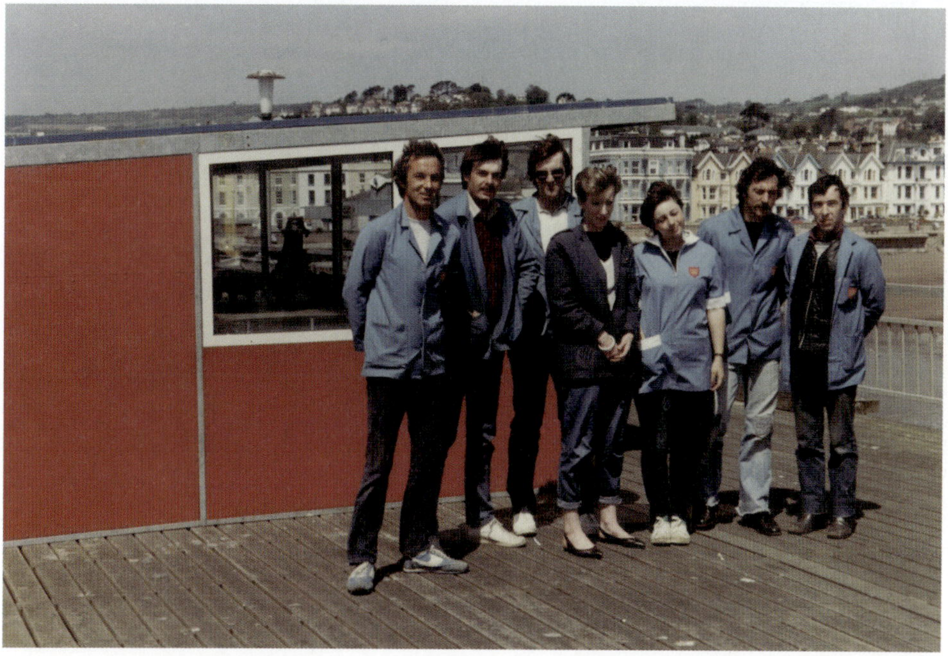

Air Sea Rescue and RNLI combined display 1993

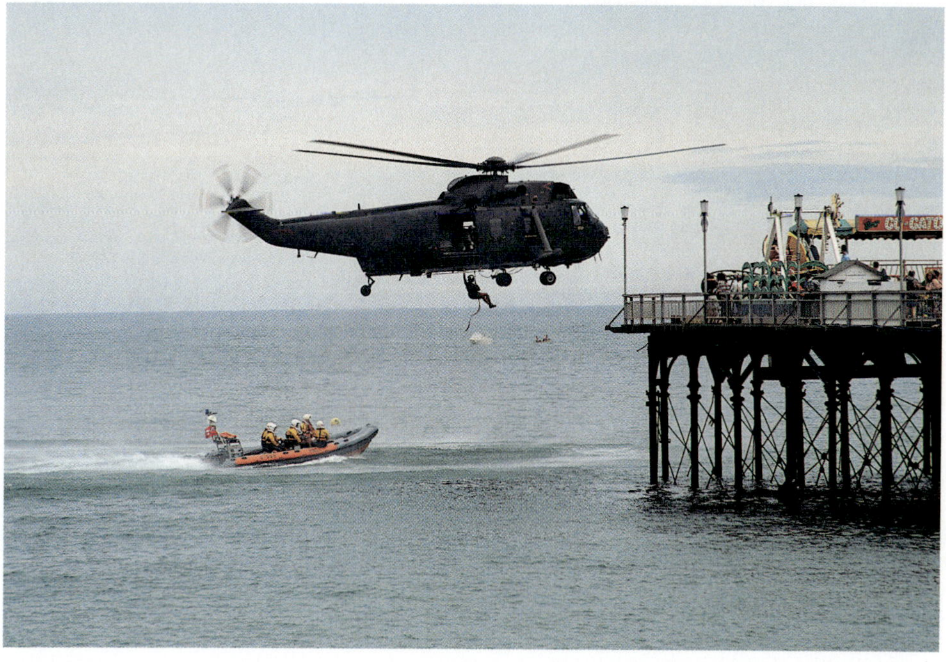

Crowds of onlookers for Lifeboat Day

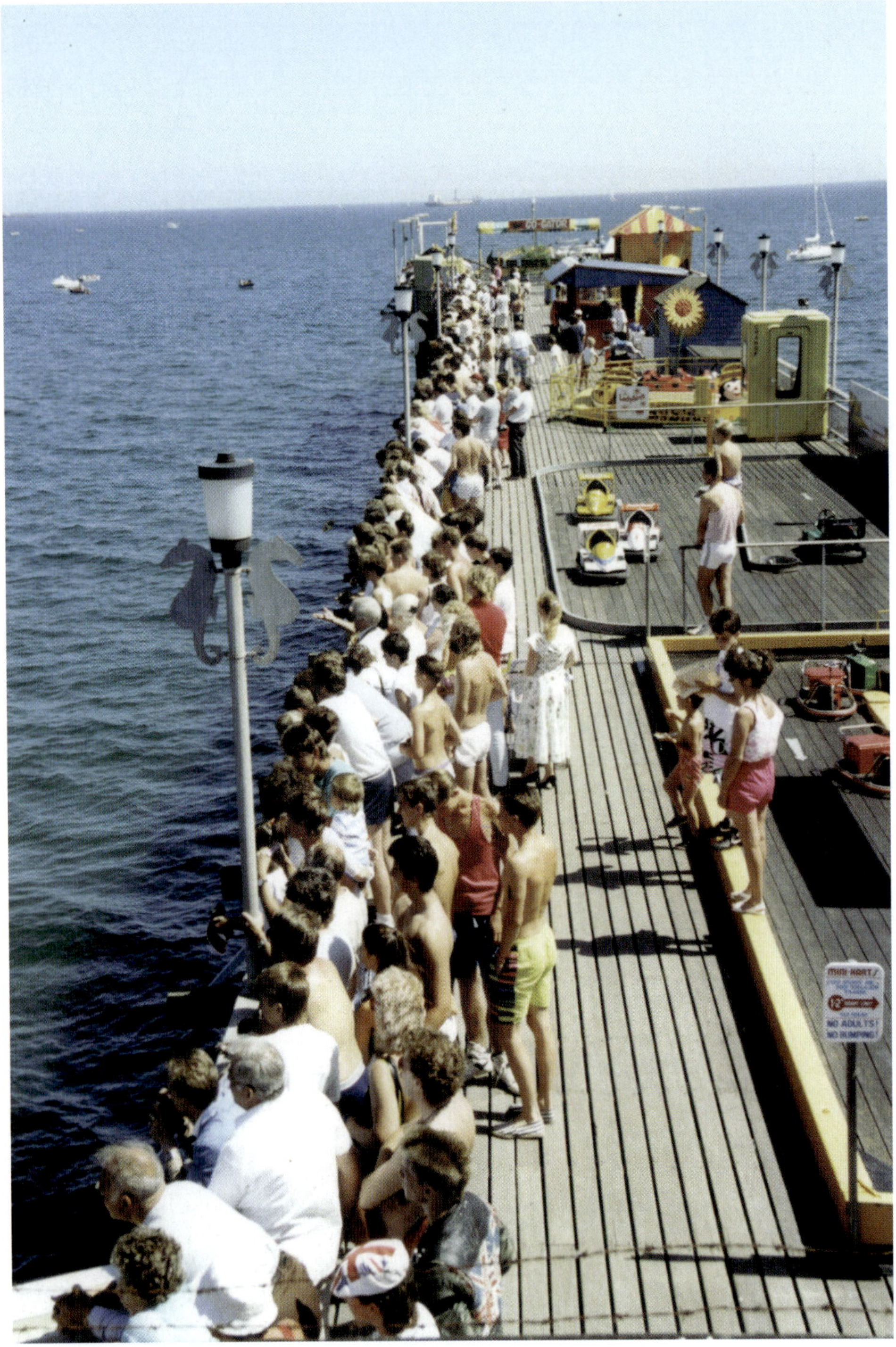

All hands on show for Year of the Pier 1996

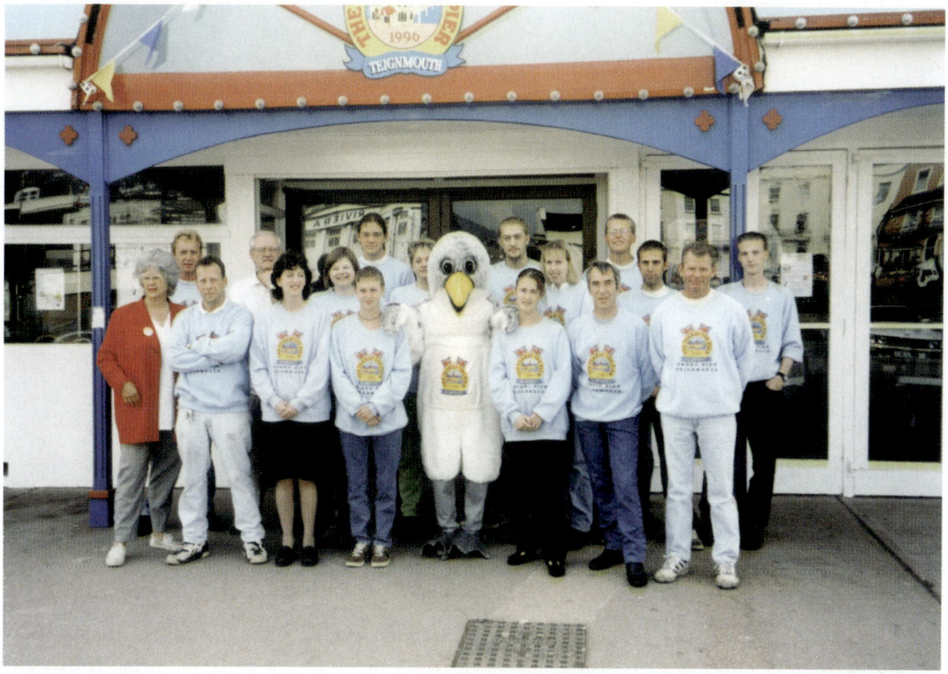

A long marquee erected along the pier's frontage for National Piers' Day, June 1996

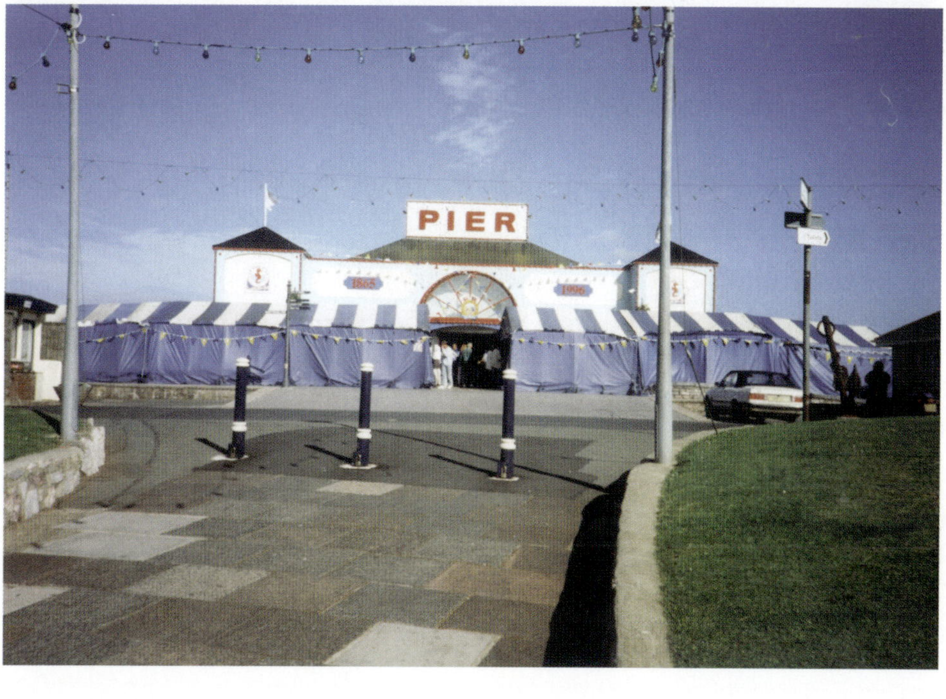

L-R: Kim Cole : TV Gladiator Falcon : Nik Brenner and Kieron Beeks

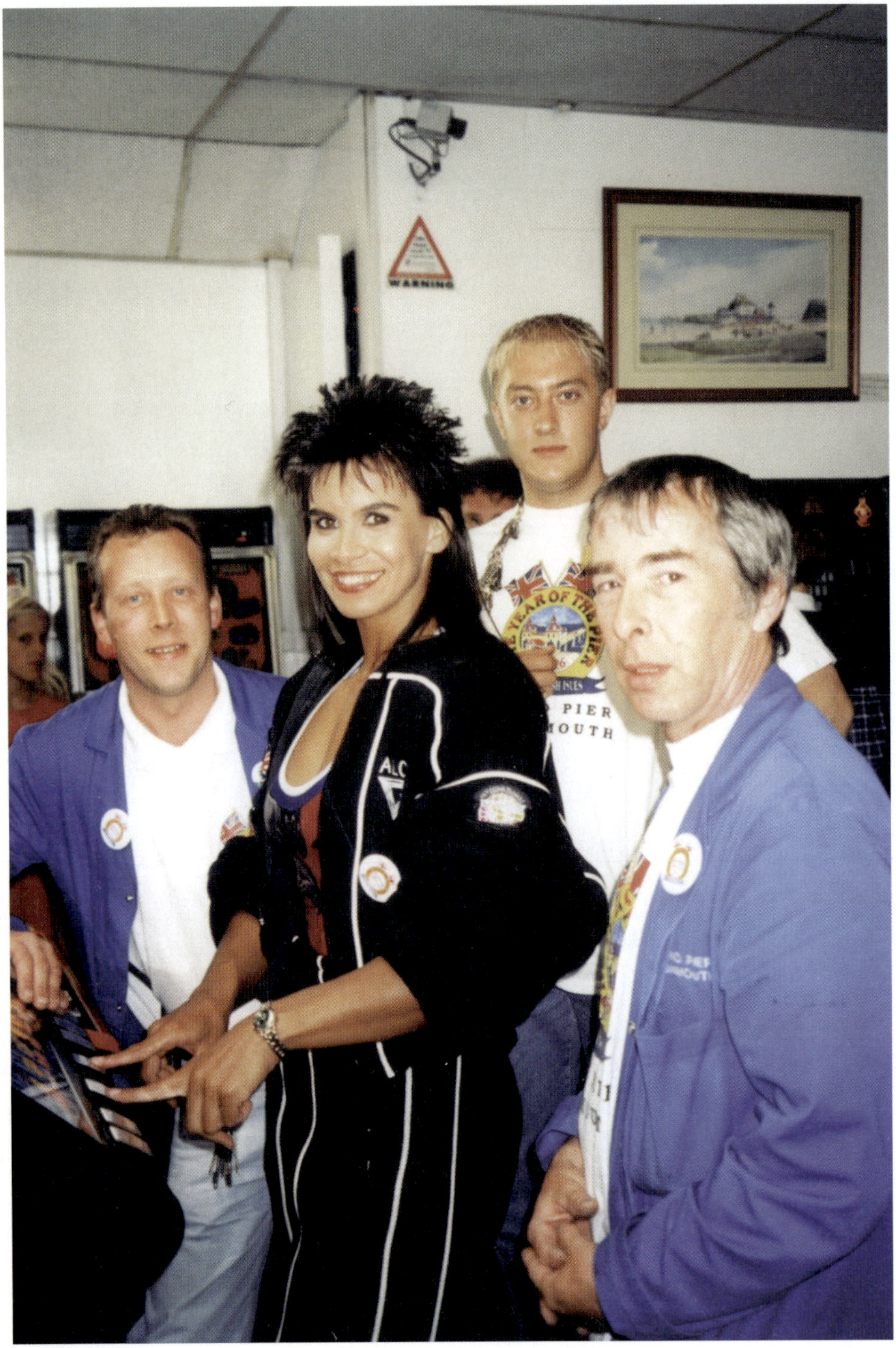

Yak monoplane performs a sensational display above the pier

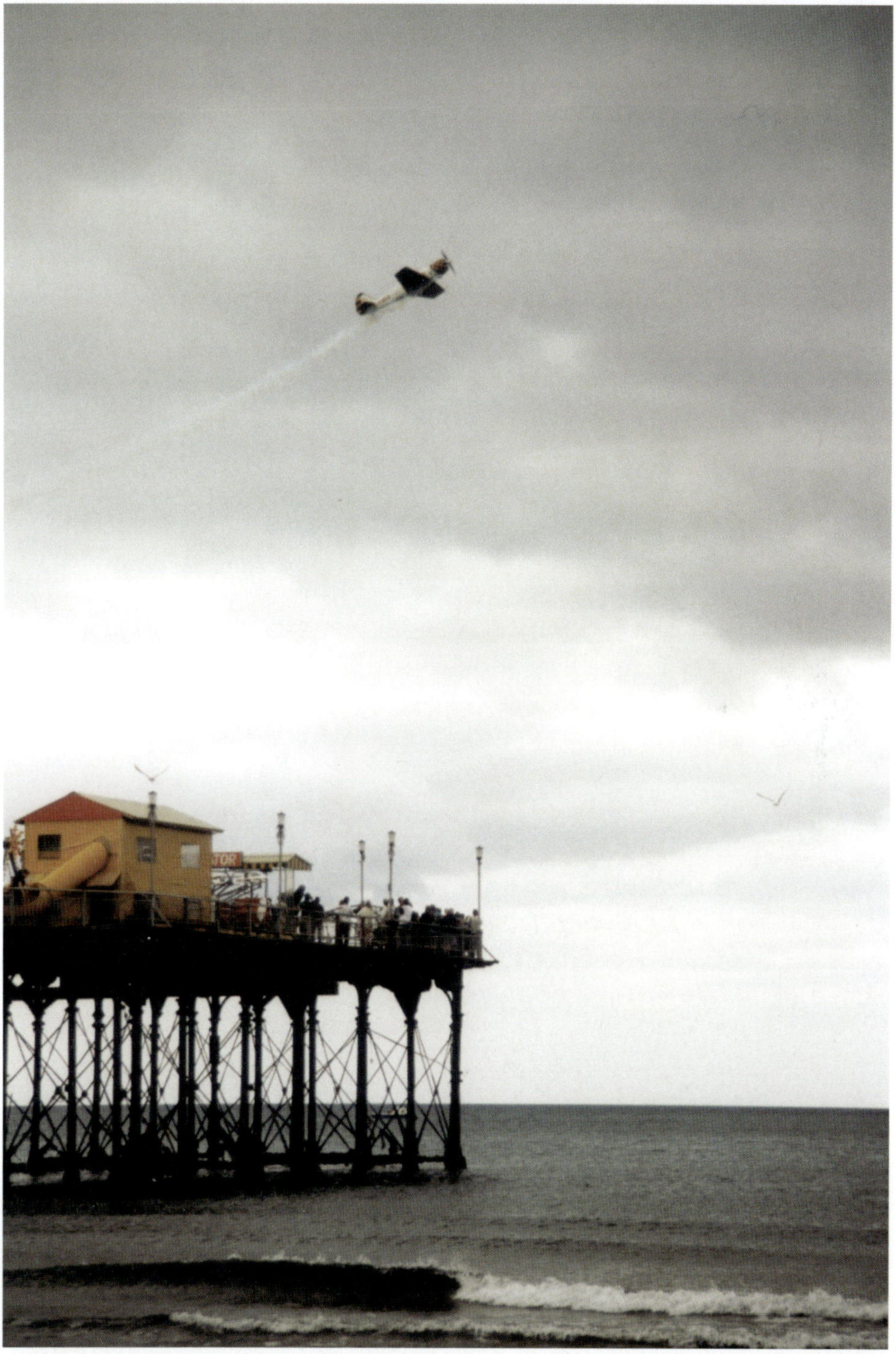

Elizabeth Brenner presents a huge cuddly toy prize to the winner of the children's painting competition 1996

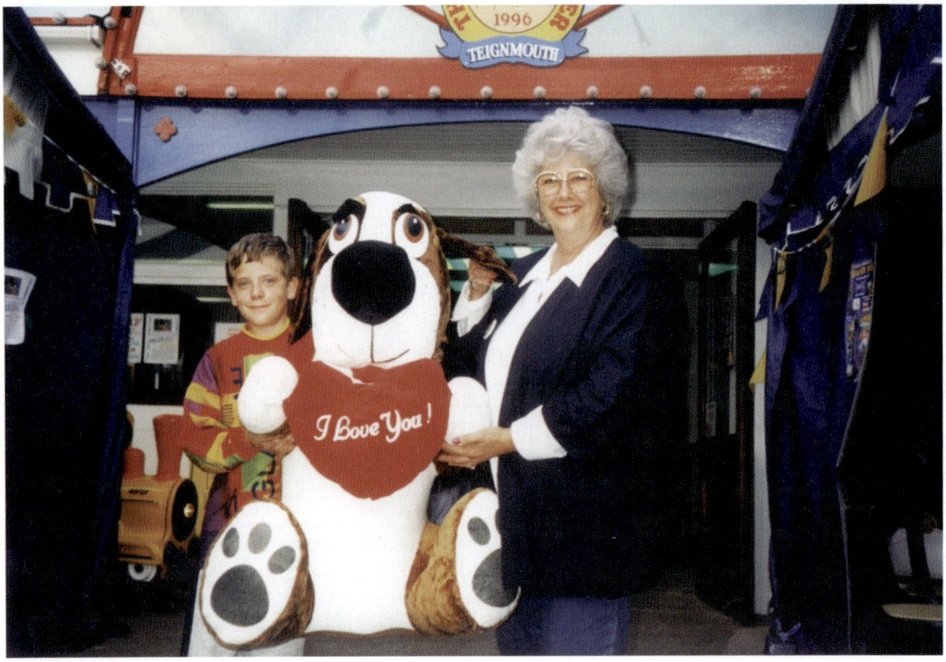

Starring in a TV advert in 1997, the pier was boarded up to fit the storyline

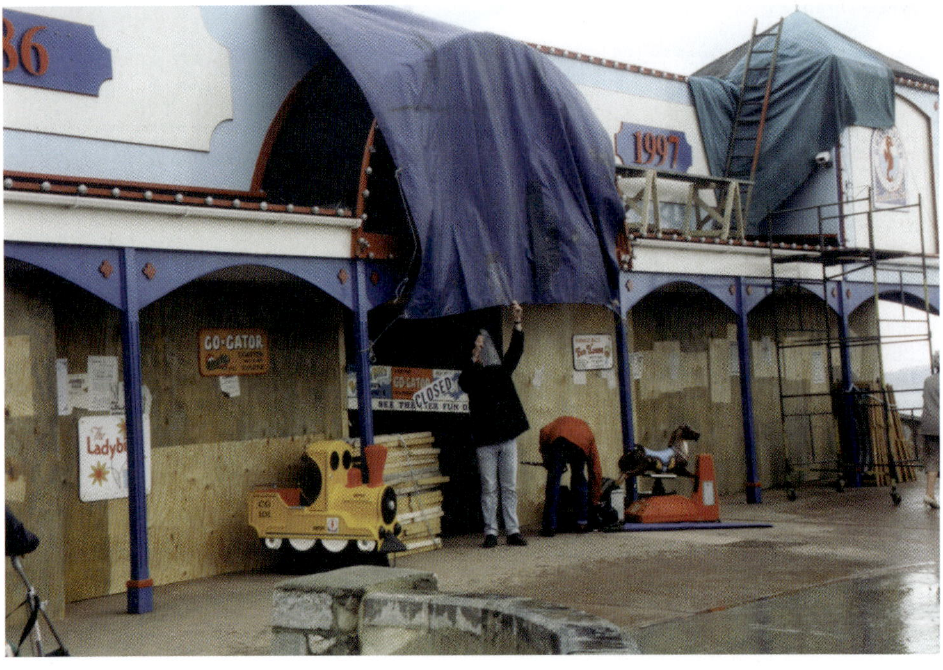

Lights and a wind machine set up outside the pier for the TV advert

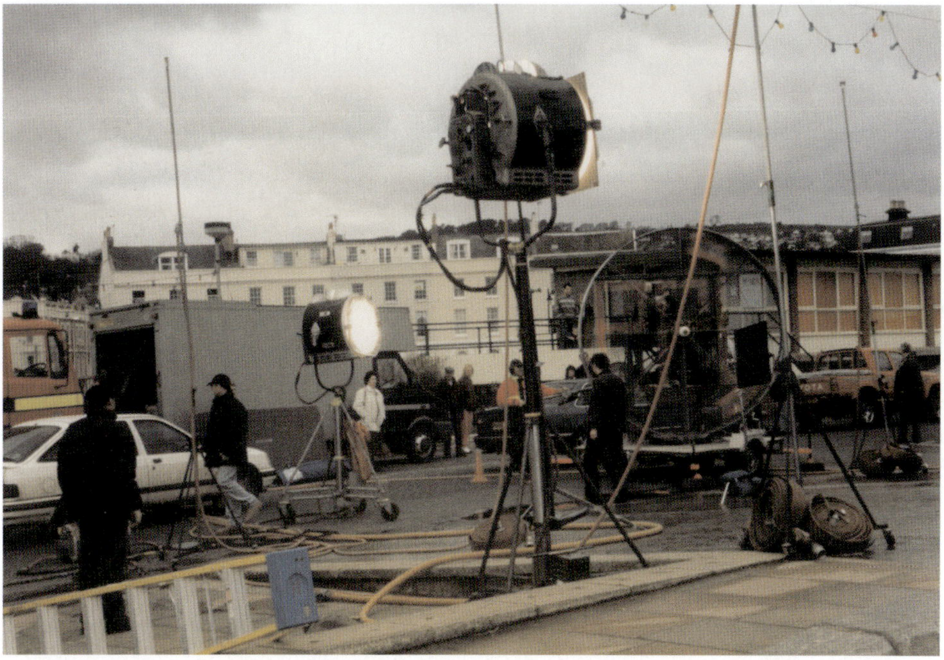

The sea threatens to engulf the promenade

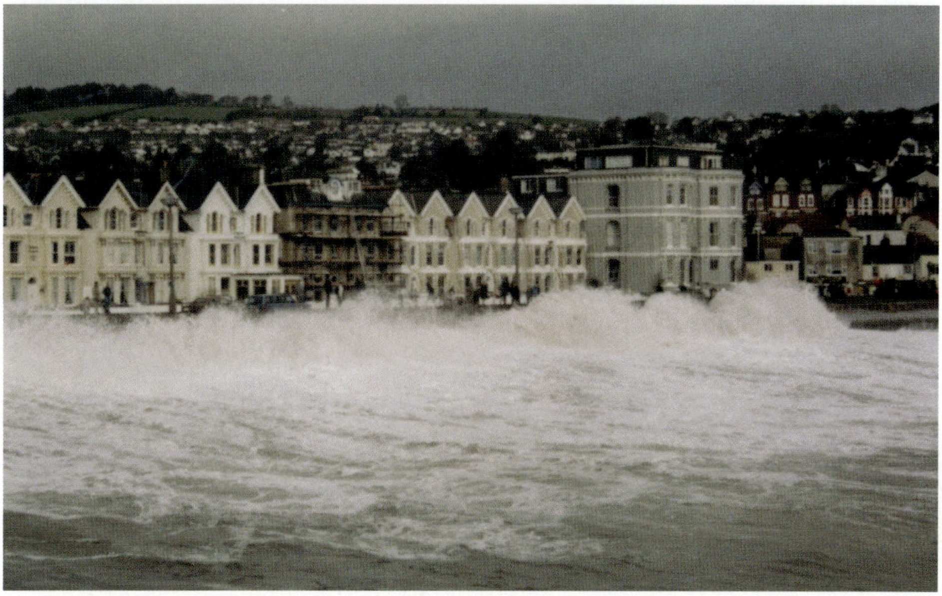

Chapter 7

The Brenner Family

The present owner's grandfather, John George Brenner, was born in Germany in 1883 and emigrated to England early in the 20th century. He became a toy maker and eventually, a noted inventor of slot machines and many other items. Long before anyone had heard of a jukebox, he made a 60 disc record player. It was installed under Blackpool Tower, fed with penny pieces and took an average of £3 a day - that's 720 plays! It was taken to America and if the country had not been in the grip of depression, it could have been a huge success. He also invented a self re-loading mousetrap, an automatic washing machine and a power-greasing system for motor cars but his real love was amusement machines. Among the most successful was a fortune telling machine, the Human Analyst and about 700 were sited outside public buildings all over country.

The next generation of four sons all went into the amusement industry. Bernard, the eldest had interests in Margate's Dreamland and also manufactured machines. Derrick and Arnold ran Weston Super Mare's Pier whilst George Jnr managed, then bought Teignmouth Pier in 1961. He followed in his father's inventive footsteps and created amusement machines. One was the Flying Sorcerer with an old 78 record of a BBC broadcaster saying "Your eyes are like pools...come out of your shell more". George's son Anthony frequently brought his skills as an electro-mechanical engineer to the business and together they built many machines, always with a new one on the stocks each winter. Another of their schemes was a cash conveyor belt system to feed coins into the office and Anthony built a series change-giving machines. He is able to repair any complex slot machine and his hobby of scuba diving enables him to inspect the condition of the pier piles. As Chairman of the British Association of Leisure Parks, Piers and Attractions, he was invited to Buckingham Palace for a Tourism Reception in 2003. After more than 40 years he still loves the industry and his enthusiasm has been nurtured within his own family, all of whom support the business. Anthony now works shoulder to shoulder with his son Nik and daughter Lucie, the third generation of Brenners to be fully committed to the future of Grand Pier Teignmouth.

John George Brenner, Founder of the company

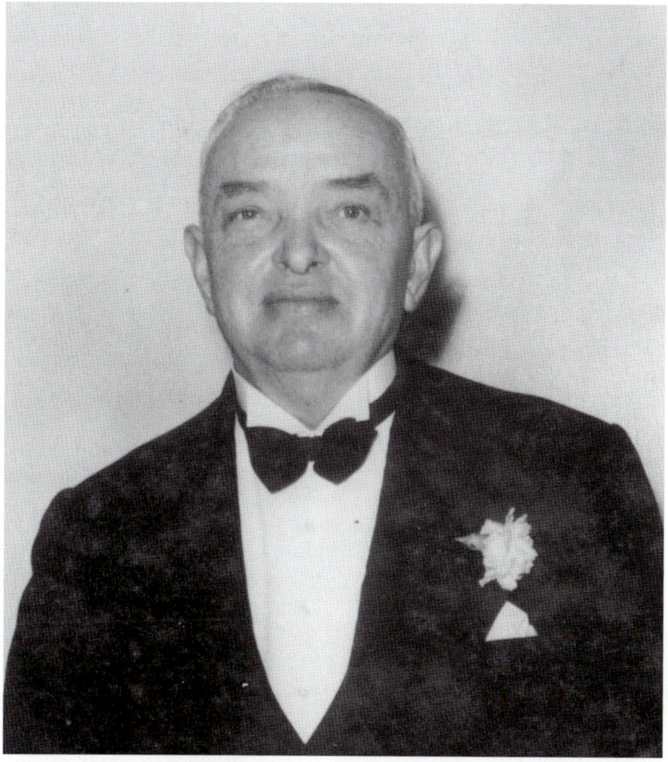

THE READING No. Aq 08393

ON THE OTHER SIDE OF THIS CARD IS BY THE

SCIENTIFIC "WHITE MAGIC" MACHINE

INVENTED AND PATENTED BY PROFESSOR RENERB AFTER YEARS OF RESEARCH INTO ANCIENT AND MODERN MAGIC AND ASTROLOGY, COMBINED WITH UNIQUE ELECTRO-MECHANICAL KNOWLEDGE.

The results achieved by this amazing machine are the opposite to Black Magic which is evil and deceptive, whereas White Magic is attuned to reveal the Good Qualities in human nature, detect shortcomings, encourage Worthy Ambition and especially to Promote Happiness.

ORIGINALS

(see over)

Human Analyst machine invented by J.G. Brenner in the 1930s

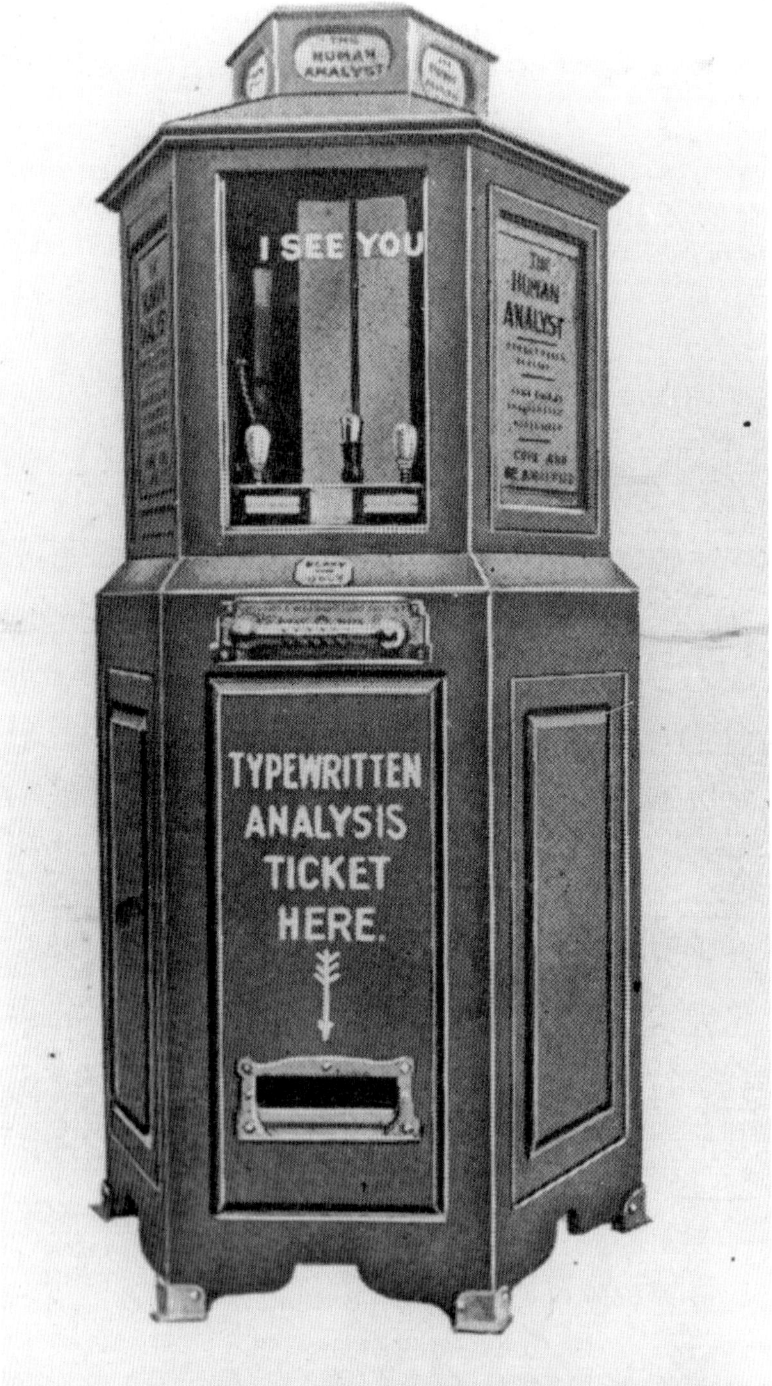

George Brenner who bought Teignmouth Pier in 1961

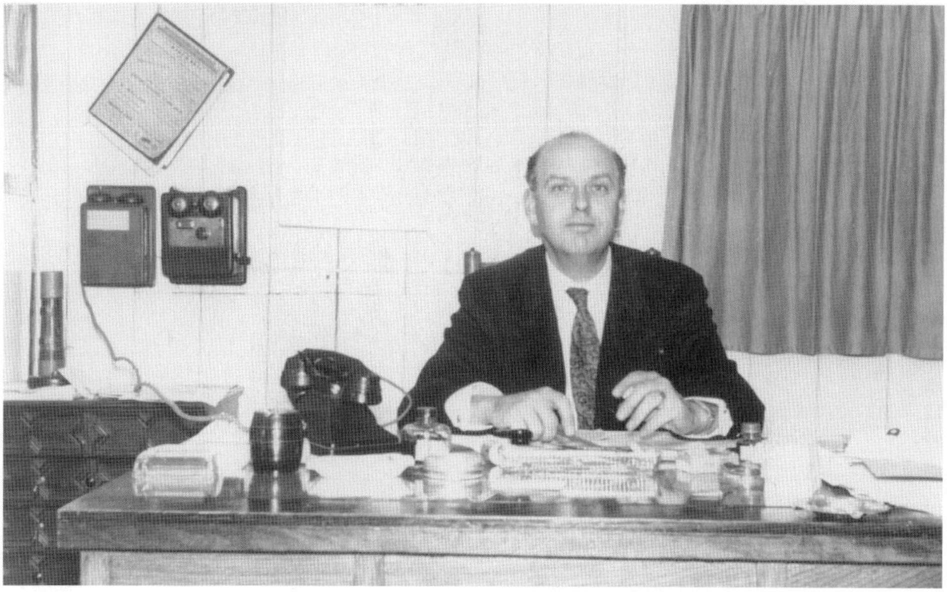

The Midnight Chimes, invented by George Brenner, proved to be popular

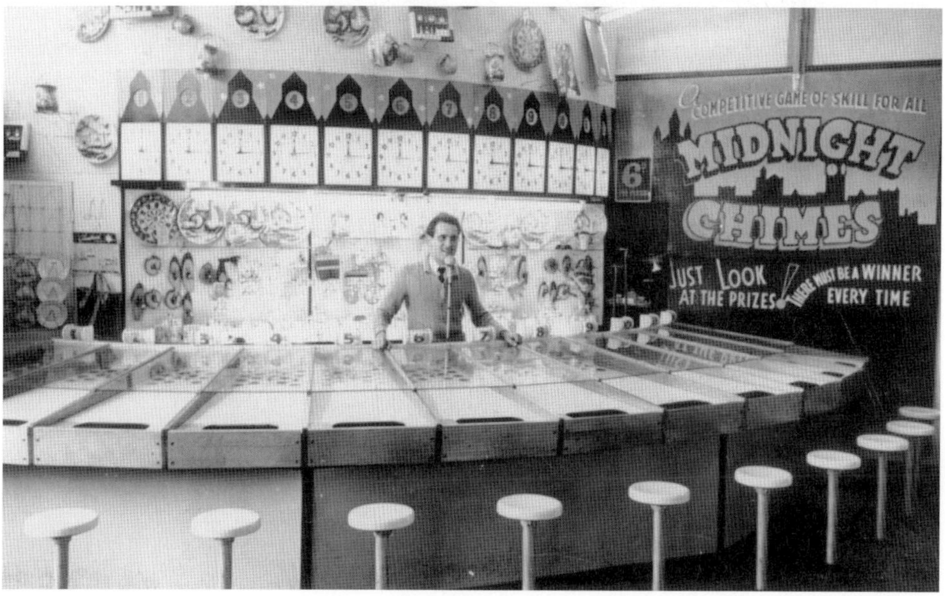

Lucie Brenner at work in the pier office

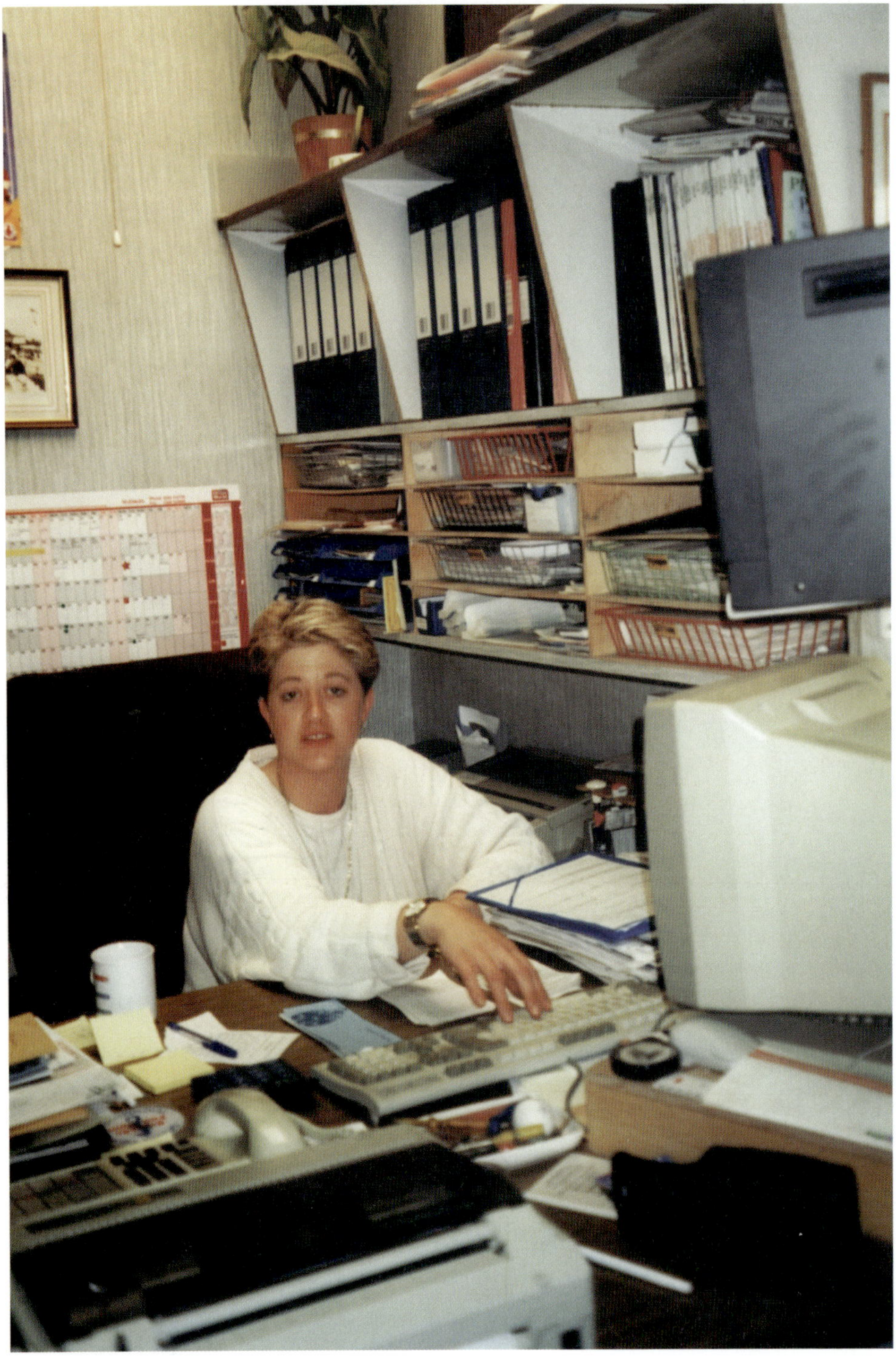

Anthony Brenner captured on the newly opened enlarged deck area during his favourite day of the year, Rotary Club's Kids Out Day 2003

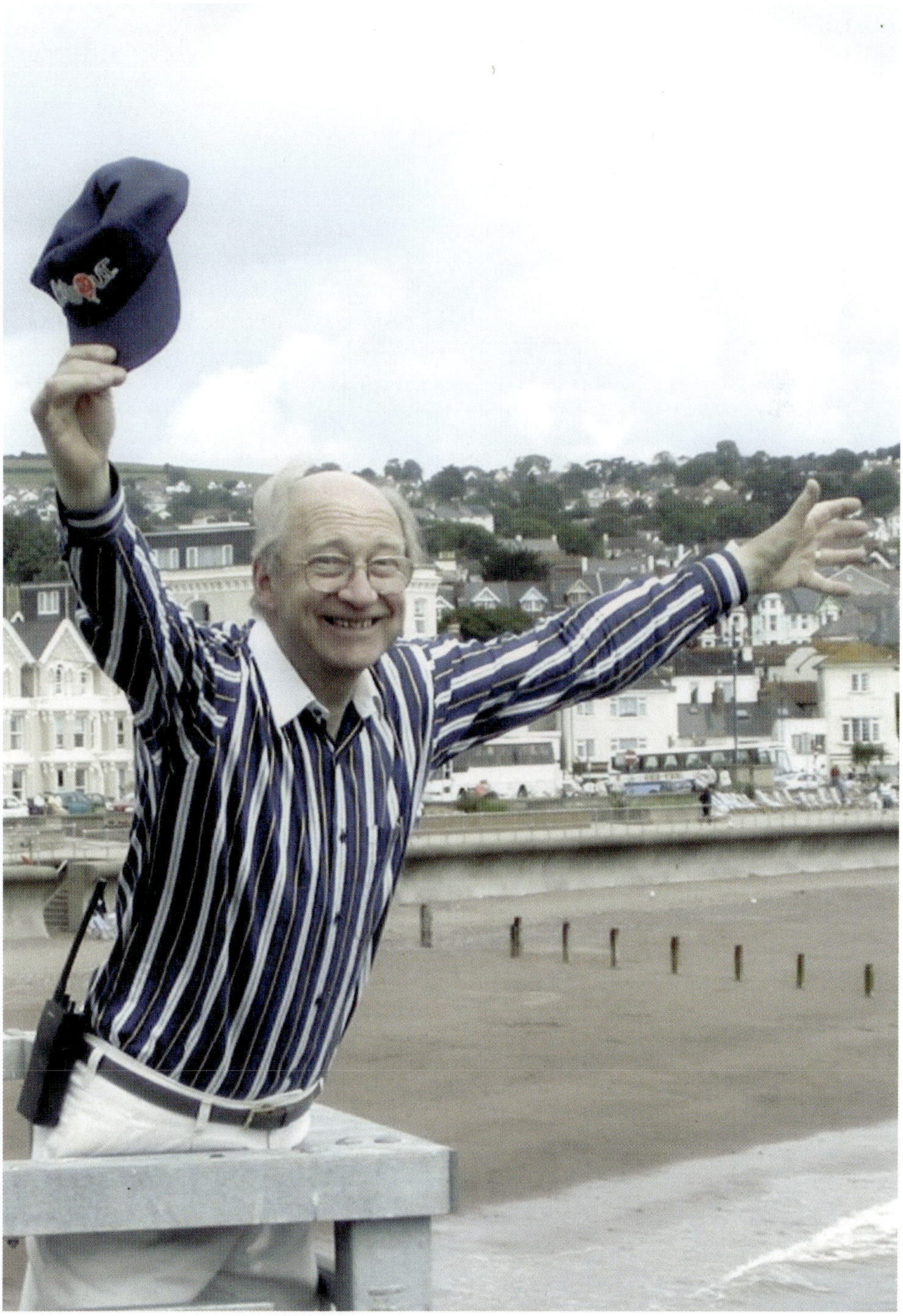

Recorded Owners of Teignmouth Pier

1869 : Samuel Kerkawich Esq

1871 : The Teignmouth Pier Company (Paid £1020)

1887 : A.H. Dendy & I. Woodridge Esqs

1891 : W.C. Jones Esq

1898 : The Devon Steamship Company

1930 : The Devon Dock & Steamship Company

1931 : Auto Rides Ltd

1932 : General Amusements Corporation Ltd with Directorate Mr Herbert Snape (Chairman and Governing Director) Mr Bramwell Collinge FCA (who also owned a pier in Blackpool) & J.A. Matthew. Mr N.A. Marr was Manager in 1933 with J.J. Angliss as Assistant who stepped up as Manager and held the post until his death in 1955

1961 : George Brenner who formed the new company Grand Pier (Teignmouth) Ltd

1986 : Anthony Brenner took over the controlling interest in the company

Summer 1939. Meg Niblett is front, 3rd from left

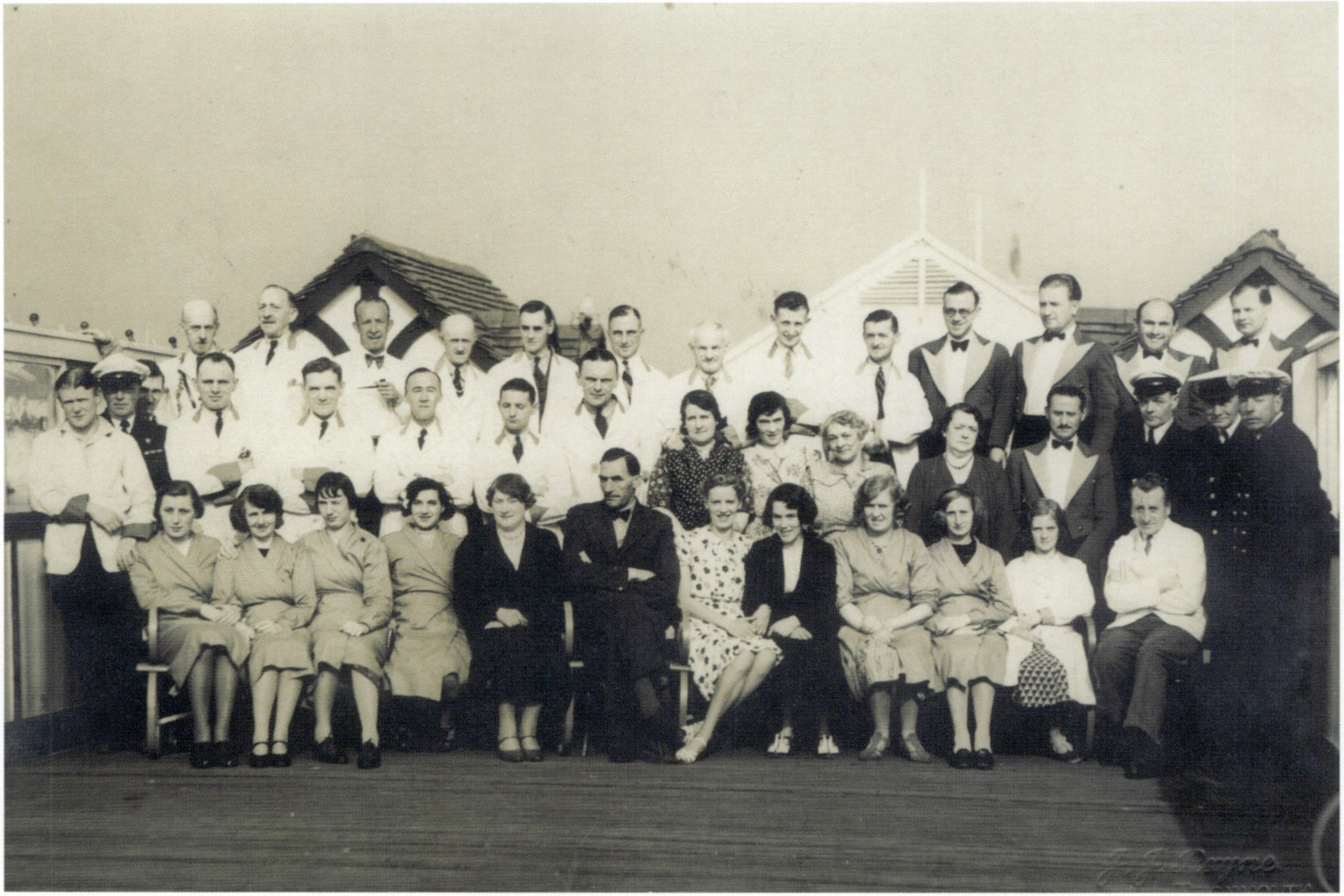

Chapter 8
Memories of the Pier

Meg Niblett nee Wood

I was a waitress in the Ballroom Café in 1938 and '39 seasons. We wore light green overalls and served coffees, lunches and teas. The wages began at seven shillings a week, then it went up to ten shillings. People changed into swimming costumes in huts down on the landing stage where large pleasure boats called daily. Naval ships often anchored in the bay with liberty boats bringing the sailors to the end. About midday on Sunday, September 3rd, 1939, Mr Angliss announced to the staff that war had been declared. We were all very worried and some of us expected planes to come over almost immediately. I was told to go out round the landing stage and tell everyone the news and ask them to leave as soon as possible. They were there at their own risk. We asked if we should leave as well but were told to stay on until the normal closing time. The times I enjoyed most were Wednesday Talent nights when lots of locals got up and had a go at singing - it was fantastic!

Jim Matthews

My memories of before the war include the time when the paddle-steamer, the Duke of Devonshire, landed up on the beach on the higher side of the pier when its engines failed to stop. I can remember Daredevil Curly and Peg Leg jumping off a 75 feet high scaffold in flames and also another stunt man who rode his cycle into the sea from a tower. I was on the pier on the day of Teignmouth's first air raid and was injured in the leg by a piece of shrapnel.

Betty Vickers nee Bace

The pier was always a landmark in my years of growing up. Singing in the Talent Contests in the ballroom made me realize I had a voice, and that was a joy in itself. I loved the dancing and went there as much as possible. The atmosphere was marvellous and we all had some wonderful nights out there. I hold very fond memories of those days back in the late '40s and early '50s.

Peter Prince, baritone, became a leading light in local operatic circles after his early career on the pier

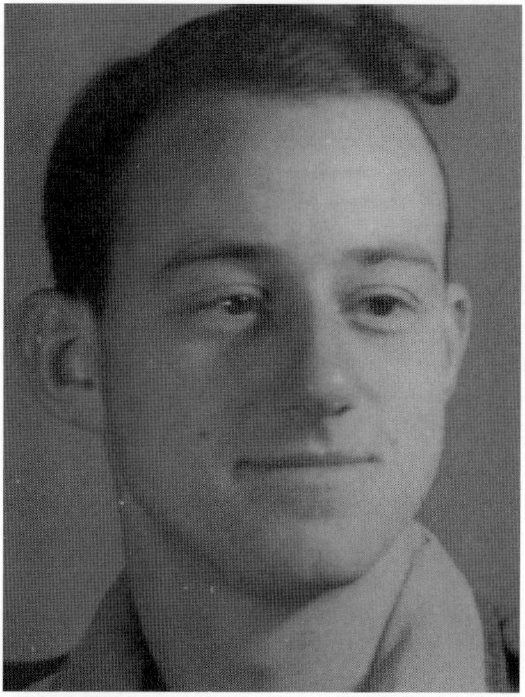

Peter Prince

The pier was for me at the age of 10 a source of small profit. I avoided paying the admission charge by using a home-made paddle and a well-patched inner tube. Seated in the inflated ring, I would row from the beach to the end of the pier and land on the steps of the landing stage on which at one time, paddle-steamers would disgorge passengers. Caution was needed to avoid the pier manager who, despite very short legs could run quite fast. His nickname was optional among my cronies. Some called him 'Bucket-Arse Harris' and others insisted on 'Arse and Pockets Harris'. Mingling with the authorized visitors to the pier I would, by some means I cannot remember, get offers of sixpence to dive into the sea. At low tide that could look perilous but thanks to my inner tube it was clear profit. Many years later I earned a fee for singing at Sunday concerts in the Ballroom. There were fairly good attendances at the Sunday concerts but nothing to compare with those for the Talent Competitions. There were long queues to book for them days ahead. No matter who was accompanying me, I never had the opportunity to rehearse with him, a cause of some anxiety. I remember one pianist who slapped me on the back and said he would follow me - he did - about five bars behind!

Pauline Clark nee Bangs

My favourite memory is of dancing to the music of Evelyn Hardy, who played trumpet with her All Girls' Band in the ballroom with windows overlooking the sea all the way round. I met my husband-to-be, Stan, in that ballroom sometime about 1950. He had just come back from Egypt on National Service and had a lovely suntan. Stan used to walk over from Stoke-in-Teignhead every Saturday for the pier dance and our favourite was the quick step. I was about 20 at the time. In the interval, it was lovely to go outside for a breath of air. Yes - they were very happy times!

Iris Volkner nee Angliss

My father, John Joseph Angliss, managed the pier from 1931 until his death in 1955. He kept 3 monkeys on the pier but feeding was difficult and they were sent to a zoo. War Office instructions to paint the pier white were not followed as it made it an easy target. Instead it was painted grey and some of the decking removed but this did not stop the keen fishermen "walking the plank" to get out to the end. The pier entrance functioned during the summer throughout the war with its penny slot machines. My father's secretary, Mrs Osborne, came down

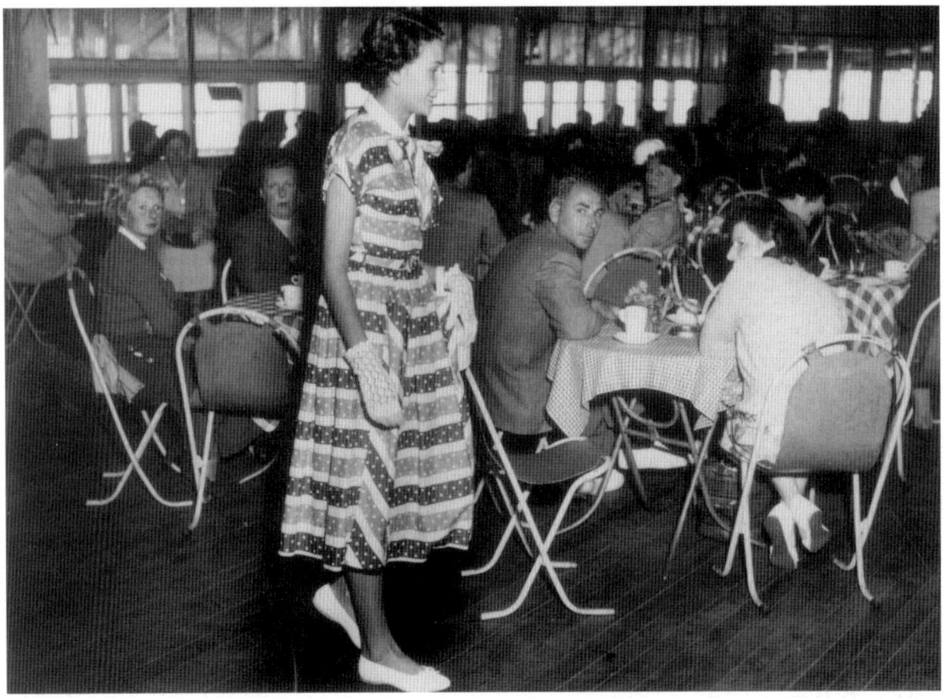

Iris Angliss models the fashions of the early 50s

from Blackpool each season to keep things rolling along. The windows of the ballroom were blacked out, allowing American and Canadian servicemen to hold a dance, providing their own musicians and refreshments. After the war when the ballroom floor was being refurbished, workmen tipped sawdust into the sea. From a distance it looked like smoke and people thought the pier was on fire! During Carnival Week, RN ships usually visited for 3 days and the crew always attended a dance and the Constabulary always made a special visit during the evening. Dumbo, a paddle-steamer, still called with passengers into the late '40s and if it bumped the pier, Dad got really annoyed. One stormy winter the piles were badly damaged and it was feared the pier would collapse into the sea. Barrels of concrete were sunk to prevent further damage.

Harold Lusher
I formed a band and we played on the pier for two seasons - 1950 and '51. I met Min Steer, my wife-to-be, who was a waitress in the ballroom café. We made our home in Mill Lane and I later formed a duo with local drummer Cecil Kelly, the two of us playing all over the south west. The days on the pier were good ones, I enjoyed myself!

Pianist Harold Lusher centre and his band, resident in the pier ballroom for 1950 and '51

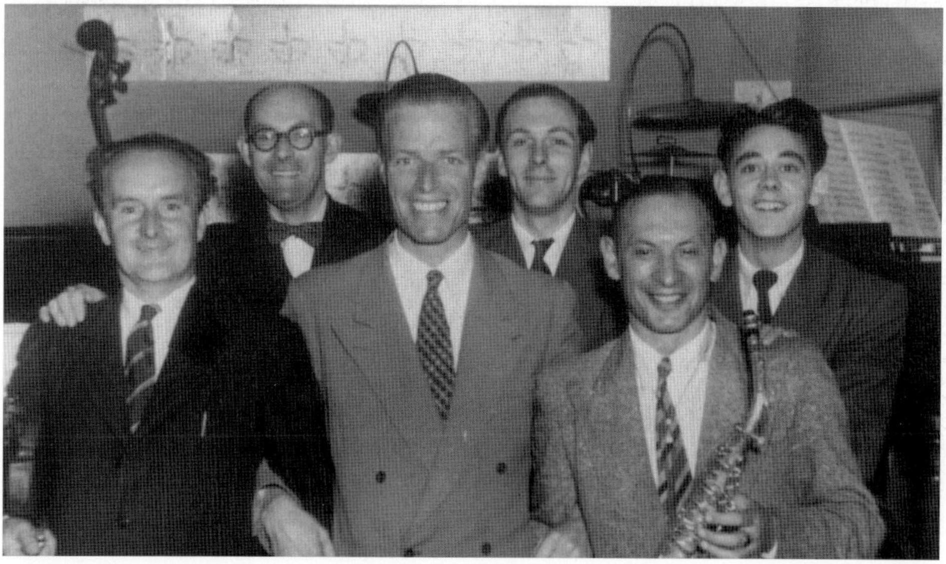

Ron Warne
Dedicates this poem with gratitude to the boys and girls who touched his life during this time.

The Pier at Teignmouth

During my carefree youthful years
T'was the meeting place of all my peers,
In fact it was the centre of the known universe
With worldy talk of things diverse.

The war had finished, the Yanks had gone
The days were happy and the sun shone
The pleasure boats had returned to the beach
A trip to the Parson and Clerk cost a shilling each.

The view from the pier was all a young man could wish
If you wanted, you could always fish
Or take a trip in a boat from the end of the pier -
Pity it was shut for most of the year.

There was Leo and Wally, Ferdie and Ken
We really were the lords of the Den
Then along came Roy, his dad was a cop'
He lived in Station Road over the shop.

While Evelyn Hardy and her All Girls' Band played
We listened and watched and were sometimes amazed
At the skill of the dancers who took to the floor
There was no way you could get us through the door.

We were quite innocent then and girls were mostly a bore
But time moved on at the pier by the shore
We became distracted
By girls so attractive.

Our carefree years came sadly to an end
For wives and children we had to fend
I often wonder as I try to recall
If those days were as idyllic after all.

Ken Bennett

Happy times were spent at the pier in those early post-war years. It was a focal point for our activities and I remember Mr. Aggett wearing his black top hat as MC for Olde Tyme Dancing on Fridays. We used the deck between the front and the long-gone middle arcade as a vantage point to watch water polo matches that drew crowds to the pier and the prom. We watched the feats of the high divers further along, between the ballroom and landing stage. Ron's poem certainly rolls back the years....oh happy days!

Easter 1949 and the gang's all here! Back L-R: Hubert Fursdon : David Copeland : Peter Waldron : Ken Young
Front L-R: Bernard Leaman : Ken Bennett : Ron Warne

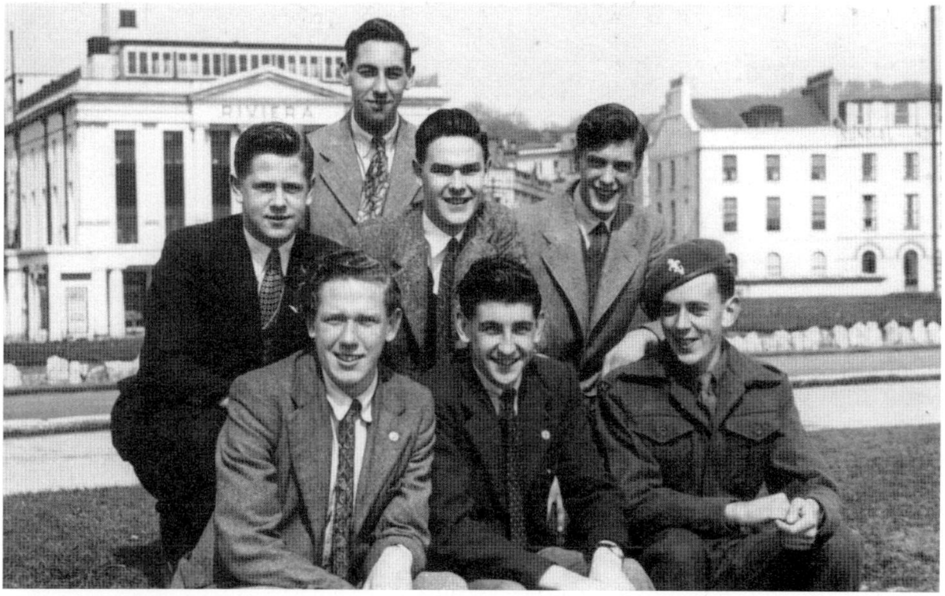

Joan Matthews

I was a Shaldon girl and returned from London soon after the end of the war, working as a waitress on the pier. Within a year, I was made Manageress in charge of a large seasonal staff of girls in the ballroom café. Morning coffee, light lunches and teas were served at tables for four, with red gingham cloths. Ice cream orders were phoned through to London and despatched by rail the same day, arriving at the station in the early hours for railway staff to deliver to the pier. Gervis Café supplied all the bread and cakes. Mrs Boyne and Mrs Tozer were wonderful kitchen staff. Mr Boyne ran a pleasure boat named Gorgeous Gussie after a Wimbledon star who set a fashion by wearing frilly pants on court. A similar pair was used for the boat's ensign! Wally Moss did the Bar and after a busy night, we cleared up then adjourned to the kitchen to talk over events of the night with a quiet drink. We left for home in the small hours and Peter Mole always ran ahead, slipped a coin in the slot and set off the Laughing Sailor.

L-R: Minnie Steer : Joan Wharton, Manageress : Pauline Roberts : Phyllis Steer and Mrs Tozer seated

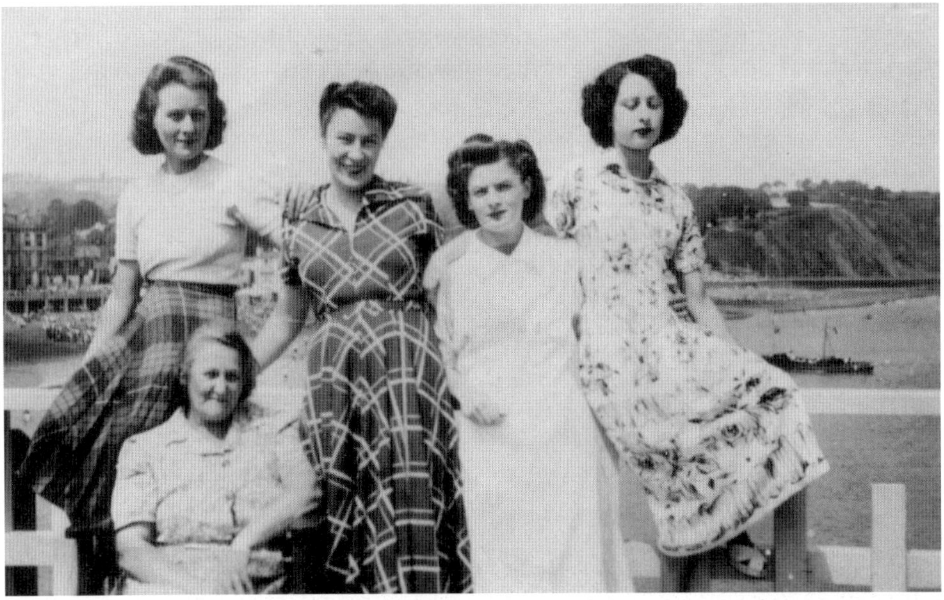

Margaret "Tiny" Knight
Teignmouth Pier was part of my growing up. I have very early memories of being lifted up by my father to put little balls into the mouths of clowns whose heads rolled from side to side. When I had learned to swim, a few of us would try running the length of the pier without being caught to jump off the end and swim back to the beach - only at high water! My lasting memories are of the talent competitions, a good way of earning five shillings if you were lucky enough to win. The thrill of singing with Evelyn Hardy's Band is something I'll never forget.

Stan Causley
A man called Bertram Green, who owned the speedboat, lived away but when he visited, he always booked in at 20 Bitton Crescent for "Room and Attendance" for two guineas a week. This meant that guests bought their own food in and it was cooked to their liking by their hosts and in this case, it was the parents of my wife, Gladys.

Frank Jones

In 1946, the Royal Navy sent me to Marina Hotel, Powderham Terrace on Survivors' Leave. During my stay, I went out on the pier for a dance and met a local girl who was to become my wife. I went to work with Sleeman & Hawken, stripping down engines on the local pleasure boats. In the summers of 1951, 2 and 3, it was my job to drive a speedboat for trips from the landing stage at the end of the pier. It belonged to a Bertram Green, who worked for the Admiralty and didn't have time to run it himself. It carried 10 passengers - two rows of four then two more seats in the stern cockpit. It cost half a crown (12.5p) for adults and one shilling for children for the trip lasting about 4 minutes. Sometimes I did a 20 minute evening trip to Torquay. Jack Stewart worked the ropes for me and I had to make a big circle to come in at the landing stage on the port side, facing out to sea. It was a 7-day week starting at 10am and on until the crowds thinned out. I was being paid on a bonus and the money was good. Ted Sessions and Harold Rodwell went to Southampton to select maple for a new floor in the ballroom and Charlie Bartlett and I helped them lay it in the evenings. It was all done with secret screws. It was a great time - I really loved it!

Little Audrey speedboat trips with Frank Jones at the wheel 1951

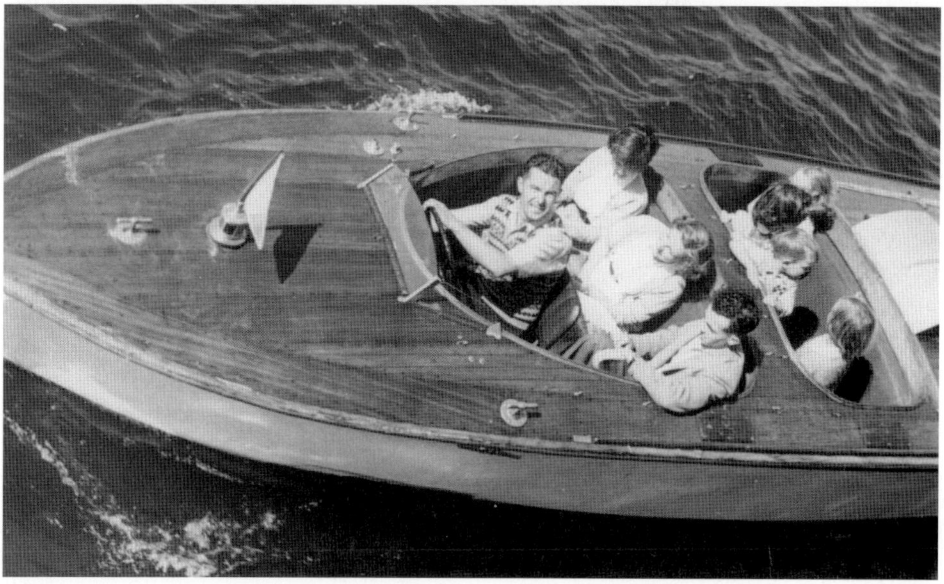

Neta Drew

My favourite memory is of winning a free pass to all pier events as runner-up in the contest for Miss Teignmouth in 1948. I went to everything! The dances were lovely and my Mum used to buy a ticket to sit in a basketweave chair and watch the dancing through the windows. Even in those days, fights sometimes broke out by the Bar at the end of the evening. I staged charity dancing displays there and also modelled clothes for Paynes of Bank St. in fashion parades in the ballroom. My husband, Ken, winked if he liked a certain outfit then I whispered to Mrs Payne, whilst she was doing her commentary, to reserve it for me. Happy Days!

Neta Drew, a popular mannequin for Payne's Fashions

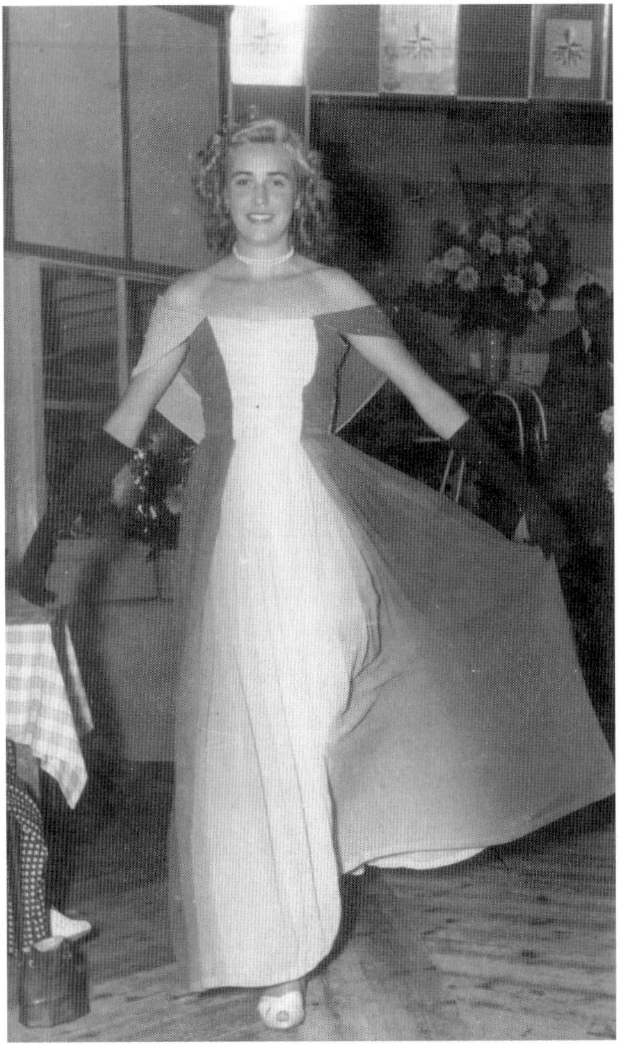

Eric Searle

My connection starts on the day of my birth, 1st July 1932 when the Ark Royal was anchored off the pier. My father was serving on the ship and came ashore to see me. I have fond memories of playing with Don Cavalo's Band for morning coffee and afternoon tea in 'The Hall over the Sea' in the 1950s. I also put on Sunday concerts with my own small light orchestra with Josephine Came (Piano), Tony Richards (Drums), Miss Herbert, Mr. R. Miles and Mr. S. Osgood (Violins), Miss Horsefield (Cello), Miss V. Sessions and Miss P. Holmes (Vocalists) and Brian Winstanley as Vocalist/Compere. Each Sunday there was a guest artist and one of the most popular was Joan Haywood, who sang and played the piano for a brilliant rendition of Granada. Another favourite was Peter Prince, whose fine baritone voice was a joy to listen to. Our signature tune was "La Mer" and I recall standing and playing on the stage and through the floor I could see the waves rolling in! We were the last band to play in the pier ballroom before it was closed and became a workshop and storeroom - such a shame as it had a superb Maple sprung dance floor. I don't play alto sax, clarinet or violin these days, but enjoy playing keyboard for shows at the Carlton Theatre. People still tell me they remember dancing to my band on the pier back in the good old days!

Eric, at the beginning of his musical career that is still going strong after more than half a century

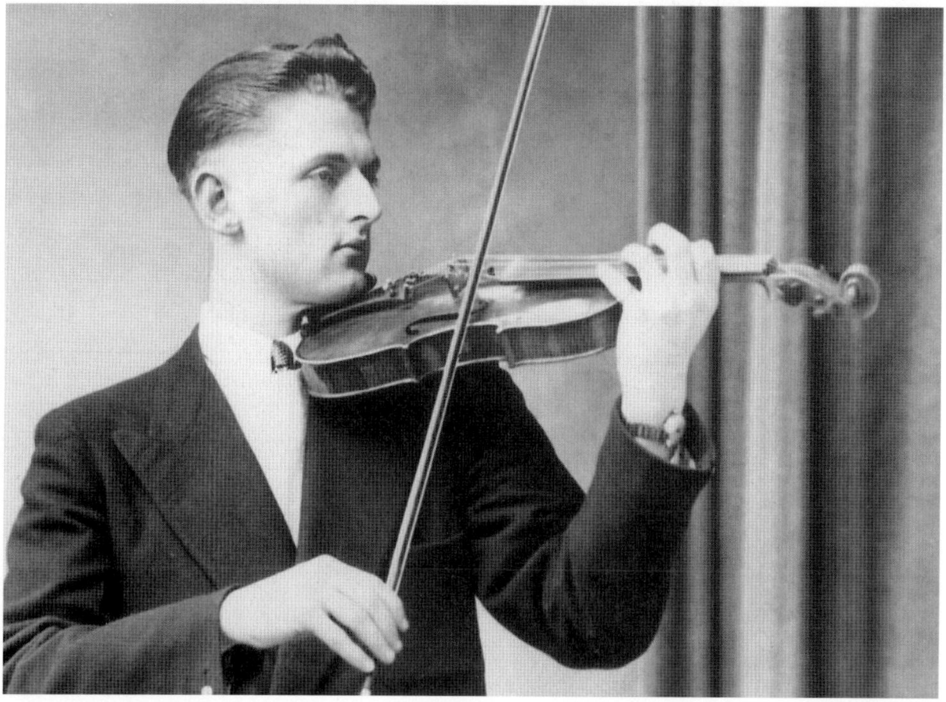

Barbara Skinner nee Stocker

My brother and his friend, both RAF Air Cadets, took me to a dance one night. They bought some soft drinks, all we were allowed then, and we sat by the open sliding window, enjoying the sea breezes. The friend decided to have a bit of fun with the tray. "I wonder how far this will travel?" he said and skimmed the tray out through the window towards the sea below. It was dark so we didn't see what happened to it. It's not just today's youngsters that get into a bit of mischief! In later years, my daughter, Linda, was one of six finalists for the Carnival Princess. Very happy memories indeed!

Pat Penwill nee Brown

We used to play on the ha'penny slot machine and found that if we fed it with thin coins, we got our money back at the end of the game. The lady that ran the roll-a-penny stall would not pay out unless the penny was dead centre of the square. Sometimes we just sat watching the world go by and we always loved to go dancing to the Evelyn Hardy Band.

Teenagers Pat Brown (L) and Daphne Osborne

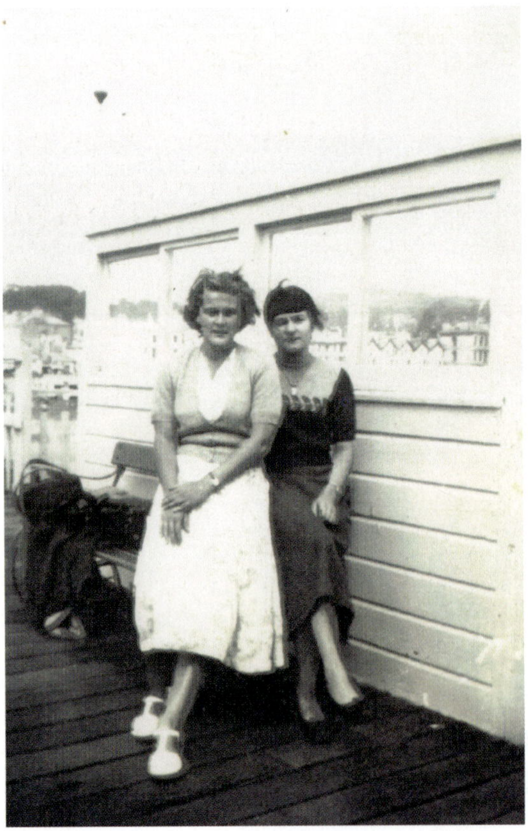

Len Matthews

As a child of 10 in 1931, I paid 2d to go rollerskating in the ballroom in the winter. I also remember watching a toffee-making display out there and the Met station where Mr. Rossiter took readings. Mr. Hoy, the Piermaster, always looked official in his white cap. After the war, my father, Pixie, rented the jetty to use for trips in his pleasure boat, Brittania. I was great friends with Joe Angliss, who lived in Ivy Lane. I was given the job of demolishing the jetty in 1963 and used Brittania for this work. We began by removing all the iron using acetylene torches to cut through the iron bolts connecting the jetty to the piles. I informed the local Police and Fire Brigade of our activities but one night, Greybird Matthews phoned me and said the pier was on fire! We went out in Brittania and dealt with it successfully. We turned our attention to getting rid of the piles and stuffed diesel-soaked rags into the tops. They were greenheart and pitch pine, about 18 inches thick and would not burn. Divers were brought in and we carried a crate of dynamite out in Britannia. Divers had to tie four sticks of explosive to each pile before they would blow up. We went about 50 yards off to detonate them. The piles towed away by my nephew Reg and Syd Hook can still be seen on the back beach to this day.

Len Matthews (L) who organized removal of the landing stage, pictured with George Brenner. Parrot and monkey were the photographer's props

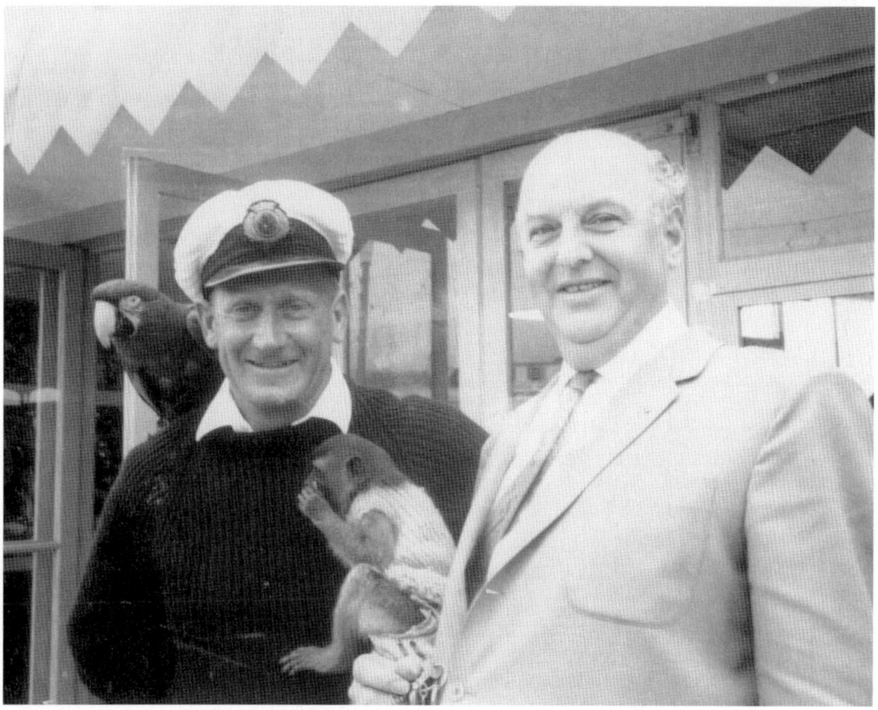

Audrey Matthews nee Ford

When Beryl Adams and I won Teignmouth Grammar School's Eisteddfod with a piano duet called Capricante, we entered the Talent Contest on the pier and won again.....a pound between us! Alfie Dodd was in the audience and on his way out he met Reg Matthews and told him we had won. It was a surprise for Reg as we had only just begun courting and he didn't even know I played the piano! I also went in for the Miss Teignmouth contest - we ALL did!

Veronica Stothard

My father was a cashier in the early '50s working in a cabin halfway down the deck. He often did watercolour views from the pier during his lunchtime. One summer, an RAF Air Sea Rescue vessel was giving trips from the jetty and it was too rough for the public. Dad and I were offered a trip providing I wasn't seasick. Being a Sea Ranger, I made sure not to let the side down!

Watercolour by cashier Joseph E. Stothard in the 1950s

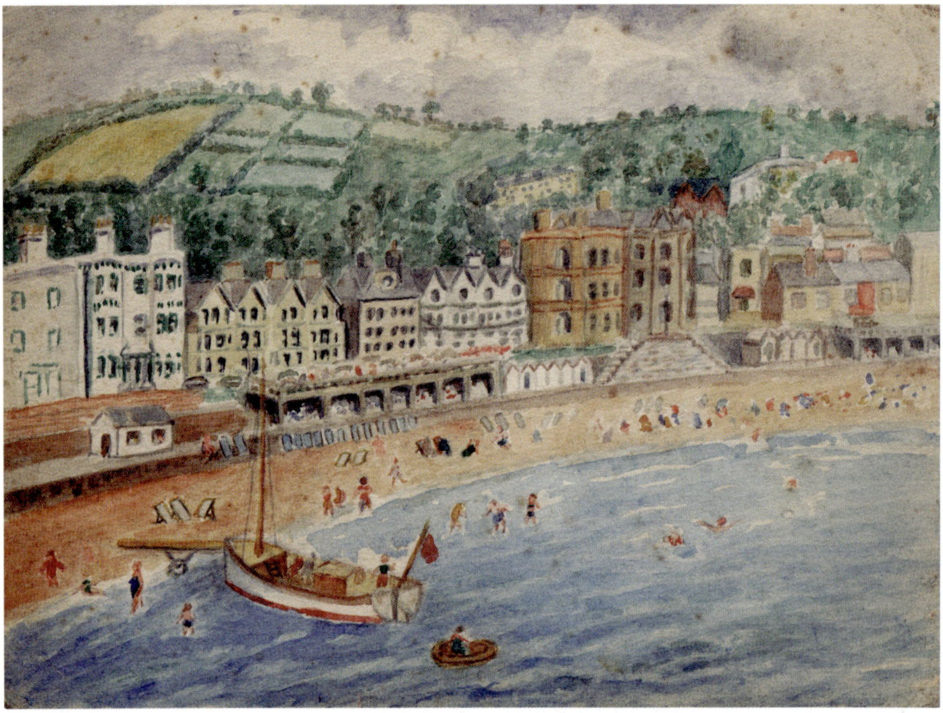

David Quantick

My earliest memory is of the war years when the pier was closed and the seafront fortified with concrete blocks and barbed wire. Later, I remember playing on the penny slot machines and trying to grab a prize with the model crane. I watched water polo matches and air sea rescue displays from the deck and our challenge at high tide was to swim out to the end of the pier and back. I remember the old landing stage where people used to fish and have rides in a speedboat and you heard the voices of the boatmen shouting "Trips round the bay". As a teenager, I often went to dances, the music usually provided by Evelyn Hardy, who had a music shop in Somerset Place. The old ballroom is gone and the pier modernized but we still have our memories.

Presentation to R.W. Aggett (L), Chairman of the Gay '90s Dance club, who taught Olde Tyme dances in the pier ballroom

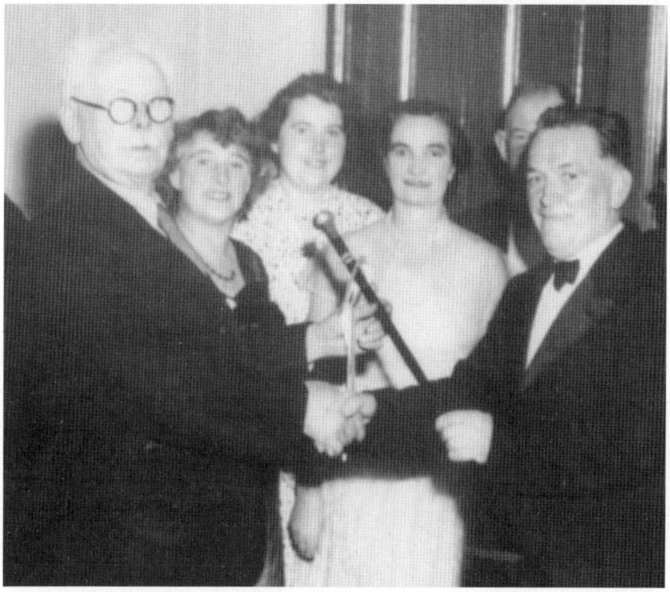

Evelyn Hardy

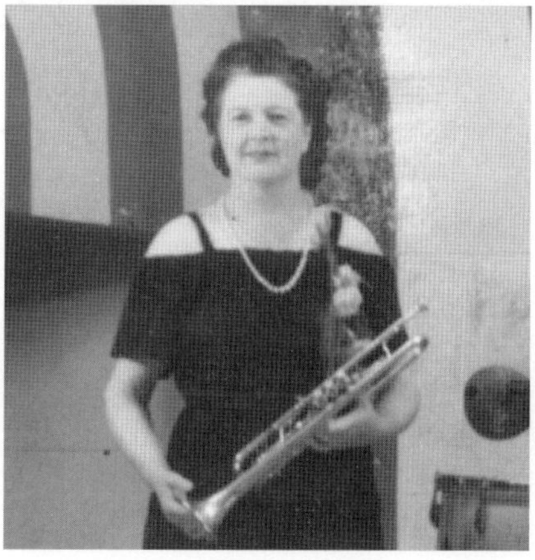

Ted Collins

An enthusiastic postcard collector, Ted has loaned the following six pictures from his collection.

Steamboat beside the newly-built landing stage

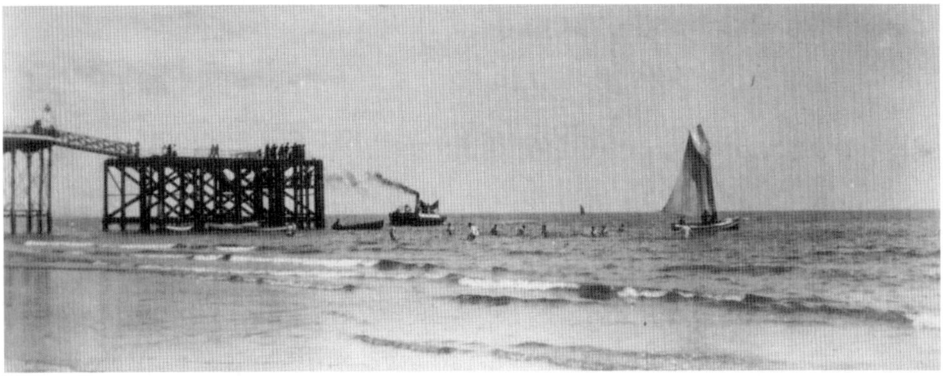

Lane's fruit shop at pier entrance c.1900

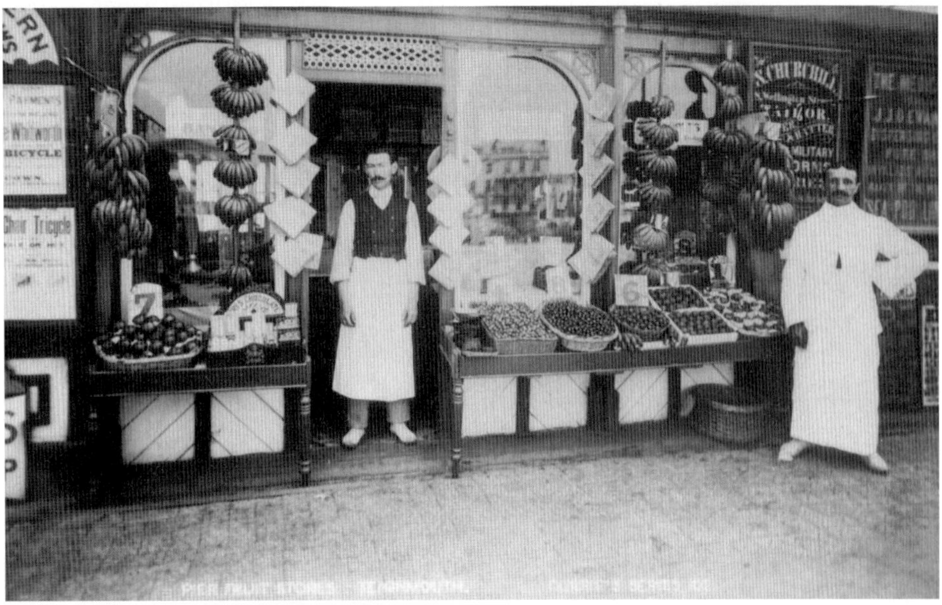

Crowds in the Roaring Twenties

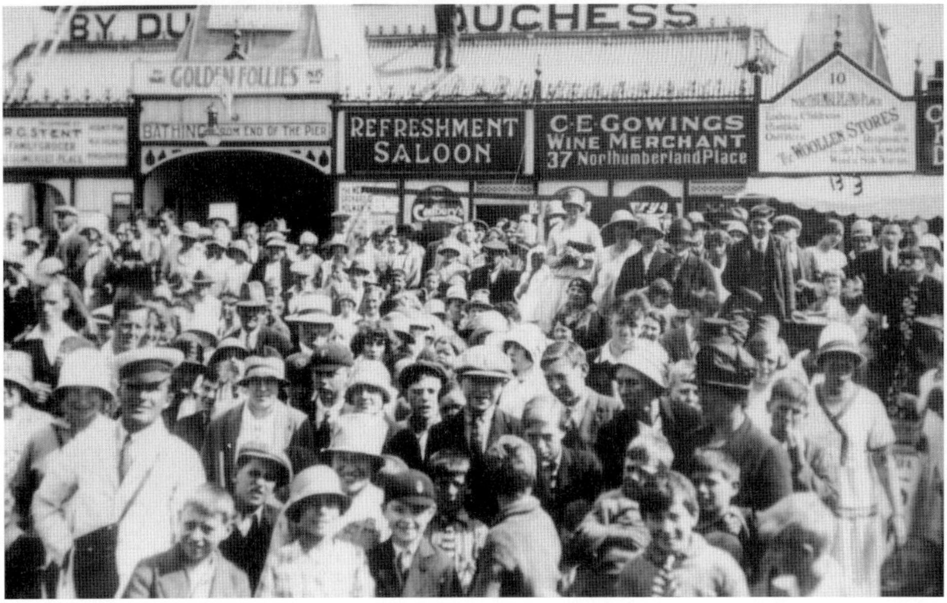

End of the pier show with the Bohemian Concert Party, 1921

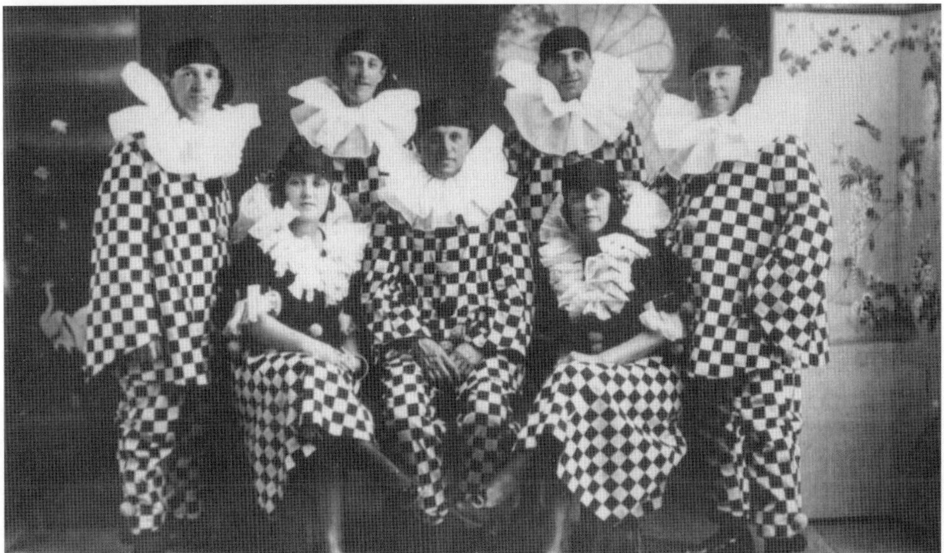

Suave performers on the ballroom stage

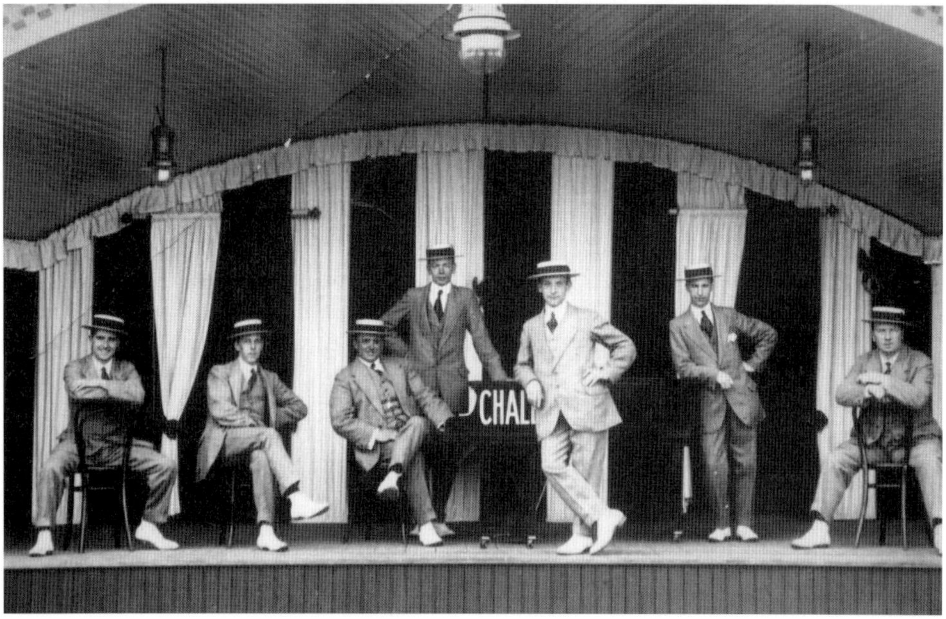

Illuminations of the '30s

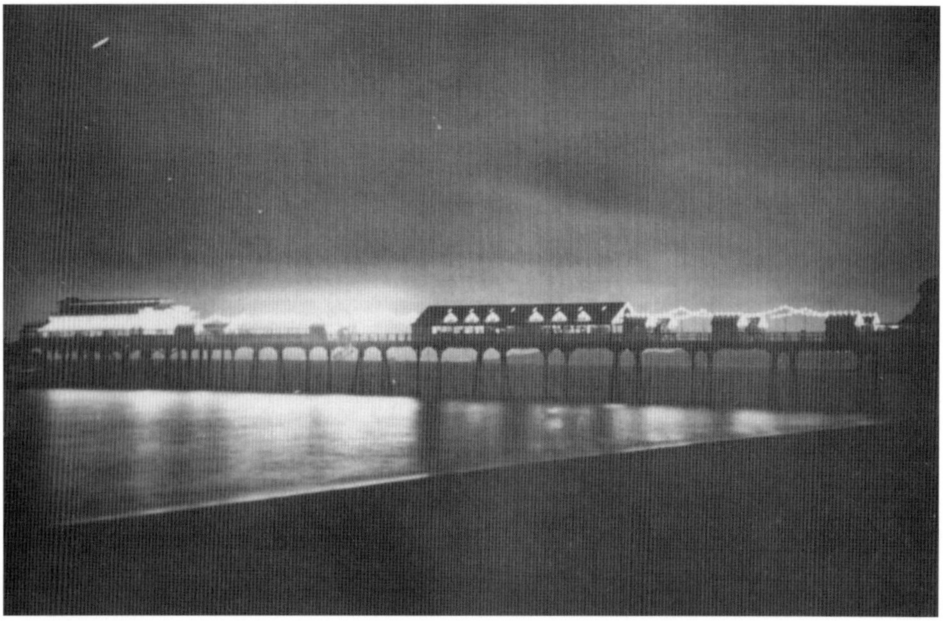

Viv Wilson

In the '50s, I often stayed with relatives who lived near Teignmouth and discovered the delights of the pier amusements. Particular favourites, probably because winning a small prize was almost guaranteed, were the Tuck Shop bagatelle machines that dispensed rolls of sweets as well as the crane where persistence was rewarded with aniseed balls. My eldest sister sometimes rode her bicycle on the tough route from Exeter to have a slice of the pier's joys and our middle sister sometimes took the train down for an evening of jive in the ballroom. It was certainly the "IN" place for youngsters.

Viv Wilson and cousin Richard Arscott with their Aunty Amy next to the pier in 1954

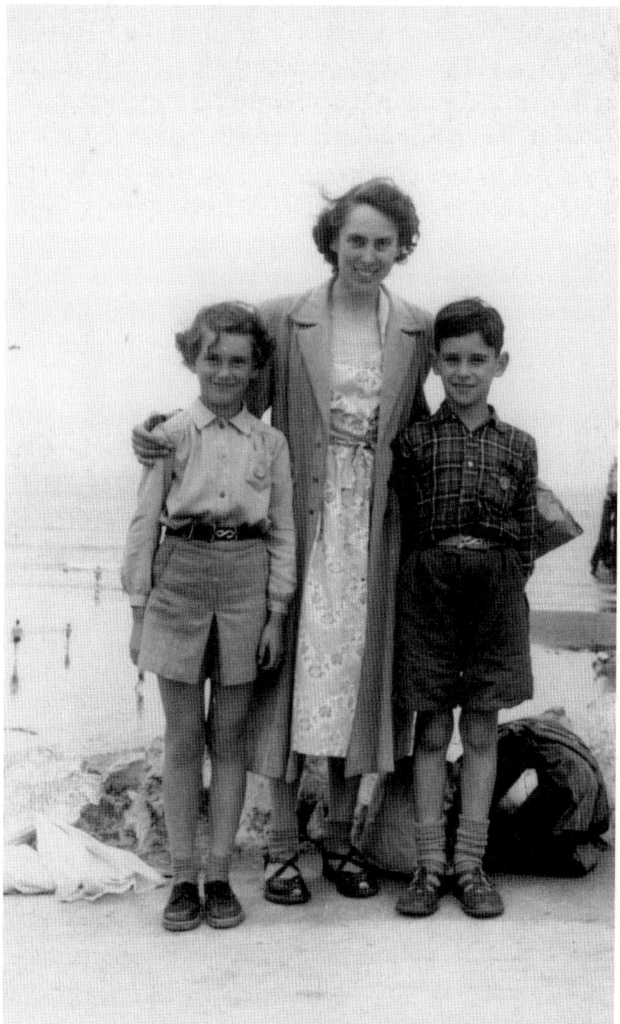

Wilson's Last Word

Dear Diary,

The heatwave continues and I wonder how much longer these temperatures will last. It's not at all conducive to work and I am concerned about meeting the deadline for getting the pier book to the Printer. The only way to cope with it is to start very early in the morning, forget it during the highest heat of the day and do other things including a swim in the sea, then get another hour or two in before bedtime in the small hours of the morning. It was low tide when I went in today, so I decided to swim right underneath the far end of the pier for the first time ever. The lurid green GoGator squirmed through its predestined course and the pirate ship swung north and south as I entered the shadowy oasis. Gulls pecked greedily at the miniature mussels encrusting the old iron piles as I counted them - seven rows of four - that supported the old ballroom. I gazed up at the stretched hexagon and marvelled that 600 tickets were sold for the annual Carnival dance there one year. The thought of limitless pleasure created during dances, shows and other entertainments filled my thoughts along with those of midnight swimming. I wondered how many babies had been conceived on the sands below the very spot where I was swimming. All at once the sound of the romantic melodies of the '40s and '50s seemed to waft faintly down through the deck. It seemed as if time had gone into reverse and that, perhaps, after all, I was a child of the '30s rather than the '50s. In that moment, the brine-filled wavelets breaking gently on my cheek mingled with salty tears as I wept for the friendliness of those post-war years. The craving to return to yesterday suddenly overwhelmed me as I gazed up once more at the underside of pier and came to the conclusion that more happiness was forged in these few hundred square feet than anywhere else in Teignmouth.

Bridge View
12 August 2003

Bibliography of Teignmouth References

History of Teignmouth - Grace Griffiths
Visitors' Guide to Teignmouth - Ann Pearson
Cuttings from Teignmouth News and Post
Cuttings from Western Morning News
Grand Pier's archive of photos, cuttings, letters
Ward Lock Guide c.1905.
Seaside Piers - Simon H. Adamson

Sally Anderson, local artist, features the pier in many paintings

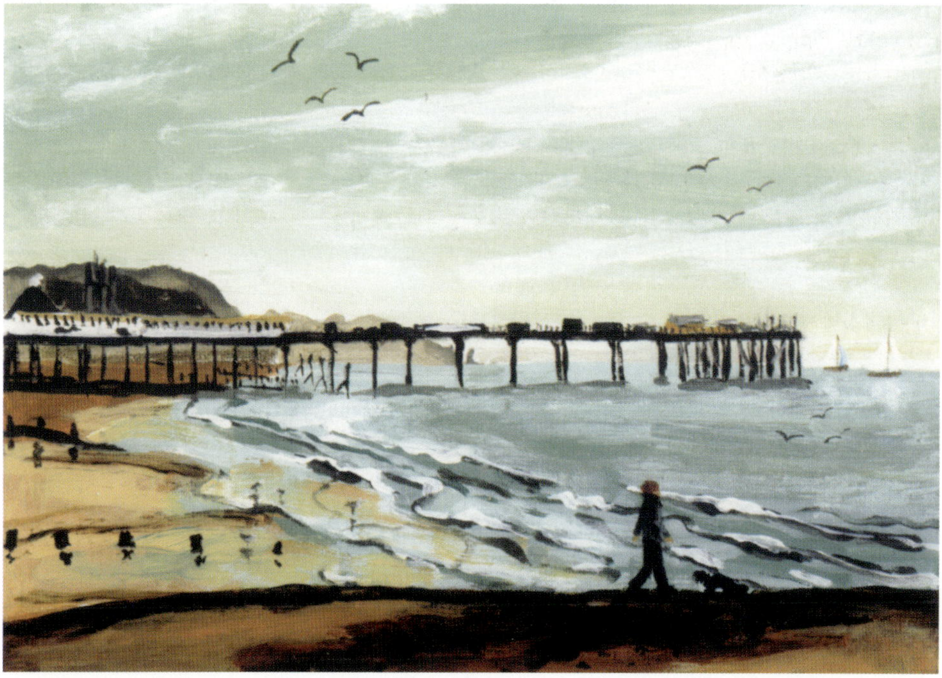

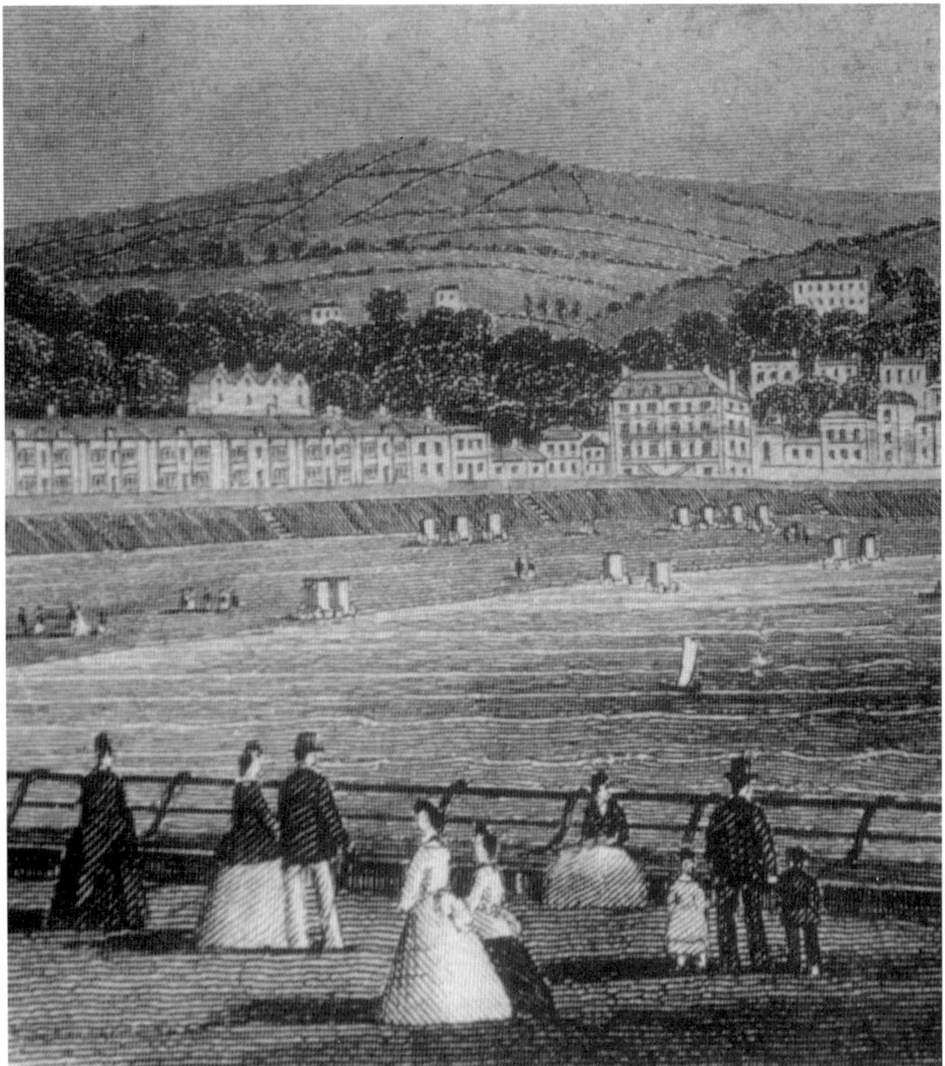